METAPHYSICS OF AQUINAS

A Summary of Aquinas's Exposition of Aristotle's Metaphysics

Pierre Conway, O.P.

Edited by Mary Michael Spangler, O.P.

University Press of America, Inc.
Lanham • New York • London

B
434
.C65
1996

Copyright © 1996 by
University Press of America,® Inc.
4720 Boston Way
Lanham, Maryland 20706

3 Henrietta Street
London, WC2E 8LU England

Library of Congress Cataloging-in-Publication Data

Conway, Pierre.
Metaphysics of Aquinas : a summary of Aquinas's exposition of
Aristotle's Metaphysics / Pierre Conway ; edited by Mary Michael
Spangler.
p.   cm.
Includes bibliographical references and index.
1. Thomas, Aquinas, Saint, 1225?-1274. In Metaphysicam Aristotelis
commentaria. 2. Aristotle. Metaphysics. 3. Metaphysics--Early
works to 1800. I. Spangler, Mary Michael. II. Title.
B434.C65   1996   110--dc20   96-10253 CIP

ISBN 0-7618-0292-4 (cloth: alk. ppr.)
ISBN 0-7618-0293-2 (pbk: alk. ppr.)

Contents

Preface

Thomas Aquinas's exposition of the *Metaphysics* of Aristotle may be divided into two sections:

1. introduction to philosophy (books 1-6);
2. first philosophy or metaphysics (books 7-12).

The present enterprise has followed this general division, with chapters 1-9 covering Aquinas's exposition of books 1-6 (book 3 omitted), and chapters 10-13 covering that of books 7-12.

The procedure here followed has been to set out clearly the order that Aquinas himself sees in this undertaking, and to present the key points and main developments in Aquinas's own words. It is felt that the reader will thus have the opportunity to judge for himself what Aquinas understands by metaphysics.

The numbers following the textual citations of Aquinas refer to the numbers in the Latin edition of his exposition, *In Metaphysicam Aristotelis Commentaria*, ed. M.R. Cathala (Marietti: Turin, 1935), which numbers have been retained in succeeding editions. These same numbers are also those of the English translation of this exposition: St. Thomas Aquinas, *Commentary on the Metaphysics*, trans. J.P. Rowan (Henry Regnery Company: Chicago, 1961).

Each chapter of the present text indicates the books of the *Metaphysics* being treated. A translation of Aristotle's *Metaphysics* is available in *The Works of Aristotle*, vol. VIII (Oxford University Press), reprinted in the readily available *The Basic Works of Aristotle* (Random House).

Aquinas's own text, however, dispenses to a certain extent with the simultaneous reading of that of Aristotle, since he does not simply presuppose the latter, but regularly restates its contents in his own exposition.

This work appears subsequent to the enlightened and unrelenting efforts of Mary Michael Spangler, O.P., of Ohio Dominican College. Gratitude is also owed to Laura Landen, O.P., of Providence College for class utilization and continuing collaboration, to Gale Morris, T.O.P., and Romanus Cessario, O.P., for provisional word processing, to Professor P.R. Masani of the University of Pittsburgh for ample documentation of science's firm act of faith in an objectively ordered universe.

Prologue of Aquinas

Aquinas begins his exposition of Aristotle's *Metaphysics* with a prologue in which he establishes the need for, and the nature of, a single ruling science. This science, because of its diverse functions, will be variously called wisdom, divine science or (natural) theology, metaphysics, first philosophy.

In treating of this science, which enjoys the name of first philosophy, Aristotle and Aquinas begin by treating the notions of philosophy in general, its genesis and development. It is for this reason that *Metaphysics* I-VI and the exposition thereof constitute an admirable and precious introduction to all of philosophy.

A. Need for a Single Ruling Science

The need for such a ruling science is based upon the fact that whenever many things are ordered to one end or goal, as, for example, the soldiers composing an army are ordered to victory, then one of them must be the ordering element, for example, the commanding general, while the others, i.e., the remaining soldiers, must be ordered.

Consequently, since all the actions of the human being, all the sciences and arts, are ordained to one end or goal which is human perfection, wherein lies happiness, there will necessarily be an overall ordering art or science, directing all the others to their end.

"As the Philosopher [Aristotle] teaches in his *Politics,* whenever several things are ordered to one, it is necessary that one of them be ruling, and the others ruled or directed. This is indeed evident in the union of the soul and body, for the soul naturally commands and the body obeys. It is also likewise among the powers of the soul, for the irascible and the concupiscible [powers] are ruled by reason by a natural order.

"Now all the sciences and arts are ordered to one thing, namely, to the perfection of man, wherein lies his happiness. Whence it was necessary that one of them should be the ruler of the others, which science rightly claims the name of *wisdom.* For it is the part of the wise man to order others" (Prologue).

Since to order is the characteristic of the wise man, the science which orders all the others will rightfully be called wisdom. This and other characteristics of the wise human being, casting light on what one expects in the science of the wise, or wisdom, will be examined below.

B. The Nature of This Science

To order and to rule is a function of the intellect. Consequently the science which is fitted to rule and to order will be the most intellectual science. The senses, indeed, know individual things, but only reason or intellect knows the order of one thing to another. Thus the problem becomes one of discerning the most intellectual science.

C. What Is the Most Intellectual Science?

Sciences are determined by their objects. Consequently the most intellectual science, the one most fitted to order and direct, will be that about the most intellectual things. What are they?

1. The Highest Causes

Certitude is a mark of intellect. That is because a person of intellect is able to arrive at the reason why, at that which explains things. This is nothing other than to know the causes of the thing or the matter in question. Consequently the most intellectual science will be that which reaches out towards the highest causes.

2. Universal Concepts

Since it is the property of sense to know particular, individual things, and that of intellect to know universals, it follows that the science which deals with the most universal principles will be the most intellectual. What are they? They are being and the things which follow on being, such as one and many, potency and act. Since every science of some specific realm of being necessarily presupposes a knowledge of being itself, the science which treats of being and the things which follow being will necessarily be the most universal and the most intellectual.

3. Separated Substances

Since intelligibility depends upon separation from matter (i.e., the mind knows the forms of things, and to the extent that something is formless, with the indeterminacy of matter, to that extent it is unknowable), the science which deals with those things totally separate from matter, i.e., God and the spiritual substances or angels, will necessarily be the most intellectual. In this scope are included not only those things which are actually separated from matter, as is God, but those things in whose concept matter is not necessarily included, for example, the concept of being in common. Thus it is clear that the thought of being does not necessarily imply matter, as does the thought of man.

D. All Three Properties Belong to One Science

In effect, it belongs to every science to search for and consider the causes of its subject, since scientific knowledge is precisely knowledge of the causes of something. Consequently, since the causes of being in common, of universal being, must necessarily be the highest and first causes, both will belong to the same science. Finally, since the highest causes are none other than God and the other separated substances, they too will belong to this science.

E. Yet Only Being in Common Is the Subject

This is caused by the fact that in a science the aim is to prove something about a subject, namely, its properties. Such proof is accomplished by discovering and invoking the causes of the subject. Thus in geometry, treating a particular aspect of its subject which is continuous quantity, such as triangle, one invokes certain basic truths already learned about lines and angles to prove, for example, that property of a triangle which is to have the sum of its angles equal to two right angles. The basic truths invoked to prove this are the actual reasons, or causes, why such a property is true.

Hence, in the science of being in common the aim will be, through a knowledge of its causes, necessarily the first and highest causes of all being, to know the properties of being. Thus, while being in common is the subject of metaphysics, to know the first causes of being as the means of knowing being is the end of that science. These first and highest causes which are the end of metaphysics have already been identified, as has been noted, with God and the spiritual substances.

F. Names of This Ruling Science or Wisdom

This science is generically called wisdom since its function is to order and rule all the others in the movement of the human being toward that perfection of himself wherein lies his happiness. Since it is the part of the wise person to order, the supreme ordering science is rightly called wisdom par excellence, while the ordering element in any particular realm may be called wisdom in a particular sense, as one may speak of a wise architect, a wise statesman, and their corresponding wisdoms.

With relation to the specific characteristics, however, which are proper to this science as the most intellectual of all and the one occupying the ordering position, there are three names:

1. first philosophy, as dealing with the first causes of things;
2. metaphysics, as dealing with universal concepts which extend beyond the physical (Aquinas's meaning for *metaphysical*);
3. divine science or (natural) theology, as considering God and the spiritual substances.

1. First Philosophy

Why should there be a single ruling science or first philosophy? It would derive from the fact that all the arts and sciences are ordained to one thing: the human being's perfection, culminating in happiness, the latter, as a goal, seen as the total and simultaneous possession of all good. The ruling science will place that goal, perfection leading to happiness, uppermost. What is the nature of these arts and sciences in general? They are seen to be constituted by certain universal principles derived inductively, such as the guidelines on a seed packet for planting tomatoes.

In proportion as the human being was able to discover the arts and sciences conducive to living and leisure, time became available for speculation concerning the highest and ultimate cause of reality. The pursuers became known as wise men and ultimately, more modestly, as philosophers, i.e., friends of wisdom.

There was also a shift of motivation in the search for causal first principles, from something to be produced (the arts) to something to be contemplated (the sciences). Thus, whereas the tomato grower's attention in utilizing the general principles or instructions on the seed packet, is directed to the product, the philosopher, in endeavoring to grasp the general principles of the order of the universe, and the first cause of that order, does not do so to utilize that first cause for his own purposes, since he perceives that first cause as the cause of himself and himself as existing for the first cause's purposes.

Traditionally the pursuit of the knowledge of causes for their own sake, and not for production, has been known as philosophy. Understandably the pursuit of the knowledge of the first cause responsible for all reality, will be first philosophy.

Thanks to Aristotle in the *Analytics*, a fundamental distinction is perceptible in the pursuit of causes, whether for productive purposes or contemplation—the distinction between the demonstrative and the dialectical. By the former is meant something proved as necessarily existing, perceived as deriving from principles of a similar nature. Thus in Euclid's *Elements* there is proved of the triangle that the sum of its angles is equal to two right angles, deriving from the taking of the parallel postulate as necessarily true.

By the latter, the dialectical, is meant the procedure whereby conclusions are drawn from principles whose certainty has not been established but which explain the appearances and may even be a source of reliable predictions. Thus while one no longer believes that the sun, moon, stars, and planets rotate daily around the earth and move yearly (except for the stars) through the zodiacal circle or ecliptic; nevertheless this supposition, now considered imaginary, produces, in celestial navigation, reliable surety today of latitude and longitude.

Consequently, one perceives that objectively proved premises are not a prerequisite for successful prediction, the latter being the criterion of the acceptance of an hypothesis into the body of modern science.

It is plain that for practical purposes or production (today's technology) proven principles are not a requisite. Such would be the case in the production, in a modern cyclotron, of hitherto unseen subatomic particles. Insofar as the hypotheses which are the premises of such productions are concerned, objective status is not claimed. Yet it is a temptation to adopt such a viewpoint when such predictions work.

This is the fate of the Aristotelian causes for the constant terrestrial appearances of days, seasons, and eclipses. While predictions are confirmed, the causes, geocentric circular motions, leading to an immobile immaterial first mover, are not demonstrated as necessarily true, the same appearances being better explained by the heliocentric concept.

Such causes (although like those for the heliocentric concept, they must be somehow in line with the ultimate order in the universe because of their ability to predict) cannot themselves be contemplated as existing universal causes requiring the existence of an immobile first mover and first cause, the pure act of Aristotle's metaphysics.

Nor for the same reason (unproveness in themselves) can the hypotheses of relativity and quantum theory be so considered. There remains the universally and necessarily believed-in-as-objective order of the universe, aligned with both Aristotelian and modern physics.

Both of these are necessarily dialectical because their premises are seen to be dialectical, not demonstrative or objectively proved. Both operate in the physical world dealing with the same realities. The domain of Aristotelian physics, starting point of Aristotelian metaphysics, is identical with that of contemporary physics. Both are compatible with each other from the dialectical viewpoint where reliable prediction, not proved premises, is the sole criterion. Here Aristotelian physics and metaphysics have a special role to play in demonstrating the universally dialectical nature of modern physics.

There remains the agreed-upon-as-objective order of the universe which today's science, while holding it as necessarily believed, maintains as unprovable—along with all physical universal principles. But is it? The Catholic faith, maintaining God's existence as provable from the physical universe, would certainly consider the divinely ordained order of the universe as inseparable from such a proof. Conversely, a proved order of the universe opens the way to a proved orderer as the unavoidable explanation. One should ask science: "Starting with the necessary acceptance of the order of the universe as objective, what proof can you give that it is unprovable? The word of Hume and Kant?"

As may be derived, the term *science* as used by Aristotle and Aquinas designates, not a certain area of knowledge as when one speaks today of the world of science, but rather a certain aspect of knowledge, namely, certain knowledge through causes. This is what Aquinas means as he states in his prologue the need for a single ruling science, ordering all the others. He sets forth the subject of this science, being in common, meaning not a universal abstraction, but rather all existing beings considered under the aspect of being. What is sought here are the causes of the subject, by which the subject is known and under-stood. In the case of first philosophy, by knowledge of the first causes of being, God and the separated substances, one is able to understand the subject, i.e., the meaning of all existing beings. In the same vein, to the extent that one knows the ultimate causes of material being (material, formal, efficient, final), one understands the nature of mate-rial being. In the science of pathology, or science of sickness, the sub-ject is sicknesses and the goal is to understand them by ascertaining their causes, e.g., what is the sickness made up of (material and formal causes), what causes it (efficient cause).

This assemblage of knowledge of the causes of a given subject is called science by Aristotle and Aquinas to the extent that it is certain knowledge. This means that it must be such that it cannot be other-wise. Thus the Ptolemaic theory is intended by its positing, as causes, of an immobile earth and daily rotating sun, moon, planets, and stars, to explain the appearance of the universe as a subject. The elaborated body of knowledge, prediction of seasons and the like, was considered as resting on certain knowledge of causes: an immobile earth, daily rotating heavens. This would be the science of astronomy.

However, when it had to be admitted that these premises were not certain with the advent of the greater plausibility of the Copernican theory, the Ptolemaic astronomy could not be called a science in Aris-totelian terms. What then of the metaphysics erected on this astron-omy? The same would have to be said. To whatever extent, however, metaphysics can be conceived of independently of physics, e.g., in the demonstrative defense of first principles, it would be called a science. In this connection, the causal principles of sciences as thus understood must be self-evident, i.e., seen to be necessarily true immediately and directly. Should proof be required, that proof would require proof in an infinite regress.

Meanwhile the Aristotelian pursuit of causal knowledge is open to fruitfully productive, and even tentatively explanatory, knowledge, on the dialectical level even should the strict requirements of Aristotelian science not be fulfilled (as they are fulfilled nowhere on a purely ra-tional level). The whole realm of contemporary science is thus ger-mane to Aristotelian thought since the former is explicitly based on the dialectical approach which makes premises acceptable, not on the basis of their being perceived as necessarily true, but on the basis of their being able to make reliable predictions (see appendix).

2. Metaphysics

The word *metaphysics* as applied to this science of the first causes of universal being or being in common is taken by Aquinas in the sense of transphysical or beyond the physical, not only in the sense that it extends to realities beyond the physical, i.e., to God and the spiritual substances, but also in the sense that these are attained through, or across, the physical. That is, it is the discovery in the science of physics that there is a nonphysical first cause which is the ultimate reason of the physical, which indicates the need for an overall science extending both to the physical and to those things which are discovered to be beyond the physical. Consequently this science will extend to the matters treated in the physical sciences, and in the mathematical sciences derived therefrom, insofar as such matters have being, but it will likewise extend to the purely spiritual beings such as God and the angels which are not treated in any of the physical sciences, since it embraces everything which has being, whether in matter or separated from matter.

3. Divine Science or (Natural) Theology

Since the treatment of God as the first and universal cause of all being, whether physical or nonphysical, is the special prerogative of this science, constituting it the highest of all, it is properly called divine science or, in the Greek-derived word, theology (from *theos*, "God," and *logos,* "science"). To distinguish it from that knowledge of God which is derived through divine revelation rather than the unaided use of reason it is called, however, natural theology, i.e., derived from the natures of things, in contrast to sacred theology, originating from knowledge revealed by God himself. Because of this twofold mode of theology, dealing with a single God, it is possible for one to be a substitute for the other. Thus an uneducated man who possesses the knowledge of God in revealed faith which constitutes the principles of sacred theology actually has an infinitely higher knowledge of God than that acquired by the purely human efforts of even the greatest thinker in natural theology. Consequently, too, should a man master something of the sciences of the physical world but never attain by reason to the highest overall ruling science, nevertheless there is supplied to him in the revealed knowledge of God a complete and guiding view both in the speculative and in the practical order.

Chapter 1

The Human Being Naturally Desires to Know

(*Metaphysics*, I, c.1)

A. Why the human being desires to know
   1. Aquinas's reasons
   2. Aristotle's sign
B. The superiority of sight
C. The sequence in knowing: toward causes
   1. Knowledge in the brute animals
     a. Wherein they all agree
     b. Wherein they differ
       1) Those with local motion also have memory
       2) Those with memory and hearing are teachable
   2. Knowledge in the human being
     a. From memory to experience
     b. From experience to art
       1) As particular reason produces experience, so universal reason, art
       2) Experience compared to art
         a) Experience resembles art
         b) Experience is the foundation of art
         c) Superiority of art over experience
           (1) Not in the realm of action
           (2) Rather in the realm of knowledge
             (a) Art knows the cause and the reason why
             (b) Art has the ability to teach
         d) Superiority of speculative art over practical

The Human Being Naturally Desires to Know

(*Metaphysics*, I, c.1)

A. Why the human being desires to know
B. The superiority of sight
C. The sequence in knowing: toward causes
D. Conclusion

"All men by nature desire to know. An indication of this is the delight we take in our senses; for even apart from their usefulness they are loved for themselves; and above all others the sense of sight. For not only with a view to action, but even when we are not going to do anything, we prefer seeing (one might say) to everything else. The reason is that this, most of all the senses, makes us know and brings to light many differences between things" (opening paragraph of Aristotle's *Metaphysics*, Oxford translation).

A. Why the Human Being Desires to Know
1. Aquinas's Reasons

Aquinas, before elaborating on the sign which Aristotle gives of our natural desire to know, namely, our preference for sight—the most knowledgeable sense—over all the other senses, first sets down three reasons showing the truth of Aristotle's opening words, "All men by nature desire to know."

1. Everything seeks its proper perfection, and the perfection of the human being is the intellect. In effect it is the intellect, and nothing else, by which the human being is human. Now the intel-

lect is not brought from potency to act except by knowledge.
Therefore the human being naturally desires to know.

2. Everything has a natural inclination to its proper activity, and the
   proper activity of the human being is intellectual activity. Therefore the human being is naturally inclined to knowing.

3. Everything desires to be conjoined to its principle or source,
   which in the case of the human being is done only through the
   intellect in act. In effect, the source of the human person's being,
   God, is immaterial, and may be reached only by immaterial powers, i.e., by the intellect in act, by knowing. Therefore the human
   being naturally desires to know. It is in this conjunction with the
   ultimate immaterial reality, through the human being's immaterial powers, that the ultimate happiness of the human being consists.

Although human beings are distracted from knowledge by worldly
cares, by laziness, by a love of sensible pleasures, by the difficulties
involved and by intellectual deficiency, none of this militates against
there being a natural desire for knowledge, whether always perfectly
fulfilled or not.

Why is Aristotle intent upon establishing that the human being naturally desires to know? Aquinas states that this is to offset those who
would object that the pursuit of the knowledge of the highest causes
has no practical usefulness. If it is a naturally implanted desire, it cannot be in vain—since no such naturally implanted desire or inclination
can be in vain or purposeless.

"Now Aristotle proposes this [namely, that all human beings by
nature desire to know] in order to show that to seek causal knowledge
which does not have any ulterior usefulness, as is the case with this
science [*Metaphysics*], is not in vain since a natural desire cannot be in
vain" (no. 4).

2. Aristotle's Sign

Aristotle's sign of our natural desire to know is our predilection for
sight over all the other senses, even when there is not the slightest
practical utility involved. This is observable in our natural delight in
picture magazines, movies, television, simply for their own sake without any practical gain in view.

B. The Superiority of Sight

Sight, "most of all the senses, makes us know and brings to light many differences between things." As to the range of its knowledge, one should note that while the other senses, such as touch, taste, hearing, are limited to terrestrial things, sight is not: one cannot touch a star, but one can see one. In relation to knowing the differences in things, while both sight and touch come into direct contact with the thing itself—in contrast to smell and hearing, for example, which receive something emanating from the object and do not terminate in the object itself—sight still enjoys the advantage over touch. This may be seen in the fact that while both are able to appraise the shape and size of the thing itself, sight, nevertheless, has the greater extension in this respect. This is true in general with respect to all the common sensibles, i.e., those characteristics perceivable by more than one sense, namely, movement, rest, number, shape, size. This is because of the fact that every body, by virtue of having quantity and extension, falls within the domain of sight, yet not necessarily that of touch: one can see the outline of a planet, but one cannot touch it.

C. The Sequence in Knowing: toward Causes
1. Knowledge in the Brute Animals
a. Wherein They All Agree

Every animal has sense, because it is by virtue of having a sensory soul that animal is animal. Yet all do not have all the senses. But all have at least one sense: touch. For touch is of the things necessary for life—things hot and cold, things dry and humid. Touch is thus the most necessary and indispensable sense, while sight is the most perfect.

b. Wherein They Differ

1)**Those with local motion also have memory.** Animals which do not move about to live, for example, oysters, clams, do not require memory but simply have the immediate sensation of that required for life. Their food comes to them; they do not have to look for it. But animals which move about to live, for example, mammals, birds, need memory to continue their motion toward what they have preconceived as the term of motion—not to mention their return to the starting-point, the nest or lair.

2) Those with memory and hearing are teachable. This may seem a somewhat surprising statement, yet reflection sustains it. In effect, to begin with the human animal, one will note that the greater part of our education in the classroom is through hearing rather than sight. It has been ever thus, which corroborates the naturalness of this characteristic. If hearing is indeed naturally the sense of learning, then no efforts to give visual education an equal role will be successful.

2. Knowledge in the Human Being
a. From Memory to Experience

In the human being there is, over and above the memory of isolated events, a coalescing of the many memories of some one thing into something called experience. Animals have something of this sort but not to the same degree as the human being. Where the other animals, in harmony with their estimative power (instinct), learn from sensation and memory to pursue or avoid certain things, the human being, by something called the cogitative power or particular reason, which he has in lieu of instinct, collates individual sense perceptions. This collecting of individual sense perceptions into the unity of experience on the sense level corresponds to the collating of sense perceptions into universal concepts on the intellectual level. Hence the name of particular reason given to this internal sense faculty as against the universal reason of the intellect.

"Now over and above memory in men...there next comes experience [*experimentum*], which some animals share in, but only to a small degree. For experience arises from the gathering together of a number of singulars received into the memory.

"This sort of collating is proper to man, and pertains to the cogitative power, called the particular reason, and which is collative with respect to singular intentions in the same way as the universal reason is so with respect to universal intentions.

"Now since from many things sensed and memory, animals become habituated to pursuing or avoiding something, they therefore appear to share to some extent in experience, but to a small degree only. Men, however, over and above experience, which pertains to the particular reason, have universal reason, by which they live as by that which is principal in them" (no. 15).

b. From Experience to Art

1) As particular reason produces experience, so universal reason, art. The many memories of one thing, united by the internal sense called the particular reason, produce what we call experience. Similarly, on the intellectual level, the gathering together of certain universal conceptions into a single coordinated unity produce what is called art. Just as the animals do better when, in addition to their natural instincts, they are also taught certain things for their own good or for the human being's, so too the human being does better when, in addition to the simple, untrained use of his reason, he acquires the methodical systematization of reason which constitutes art.

"Now just as experience is related to particular reason [i.e., as is a gathering-together to that which gathers it], and induced habit is to memory in the animals, so is art related to universal reason.

"Therefore, just as the perfect routine of life for animals is that which is the product of memory conjoined with habit, arising from their being taught or from whatever other way, so the perfect routine for man is that deriving from reason perfected by art. Some, of course, are ruled by reason without art, but such is an imperfect rule" (no. 16).

2) Experience compared to art.

a) Experience resembles art. Experience is constituted out of many single memories of some same thing, for example, of what bait certain fish like, what seeds certain birds like. With this experience one is enabled to act smoothly and efficiently in the cases past experience covers, as a lunch-wagon cook smoothly flips over pancakes. This ease resembles art and science to the extent that one says of people with such experience (for example, cracking eggs without breaking the yoke), "It's an art!" or "He has it down to a science!" Yet experience differs from art and science, in that the former is a coalesced memory of many singulars while the latter embody universal principles.

"The manner in which experience is caused is the following: from many memories of one thing a man grasps experience of something, the which experience enables him to act easily and rightly.

"And because experience affords the power of acting rightly and easily, it appears to be practically similar to art and science. For there is a likeness between them consisting in the fact that in both cases there is gathered from many occurrences a single grasp of some thing. But they differ in that through art universals are grasped, while through experience singulars" (no. 17).

b) Experience is the foundation of art. Many memories of singulars go to make up experience about some type of thing. This experience, in turn, constituted out of the memory of many singulars, becomes the foundation for the universal grasp which constitutes art.

"The manner in which art is produced from experience is identical with the former manner in which experience is produced from memory. For just as from many memories there is made one experiential science, so from many experiences which have been grasped, there is made the universal grasp of all similar cases. Whence art has this over experience: while experience is concerned with singulars only, art is about universals" (no. 18).

The inductive process involved in the art or science of medicine will furnish an example of the experience-art transition. Thus when successive experiential observation showed all the various people who had died from diabetes to have had deficient Islands of Langerhans in the pancreas, a universal connection was assumed to exist between these two factors: diabetes and insufficiency of insulin, the latter secreted by the Islands of Langerhans. This is similar to the example presented by Aristotle and expounded by Aquinas:

"When a man has taken into his knowledge that some certain medicine, whatever it may be, was good for Socrates and for Plato when these were suffering from some certain malady, as well as for many other singulars, this belongs to experience.

"But when someone grasps that this remedy is good for all who have a certain type of sickness, and are of a certain temperament, for example, that it is beneficial to those suffering from fever who are either of the phlegmatic or the bilious type, this already belongs to art" (no. 19).

c) Superiority of art over experience.

(1) Not in the realm of action. Insofar as action is concerned, art and experience are on the same footing, since action is of singulars, and experience knows singulars. Art, on the other hand, as such, arrives at its judgment of singulars from universal principles. Thus an older doctor might diagnose a patient's ailment from his experiential knowledge of previous cases with similar symptoms, while a younger doctor, lacking such experience, would have to diagnose the case from certain universal descriptions of the symptoms of various diseases given in the medical textbooks. As is well known, in such cases experience without

art has a way of being more discerning than art without experience—for it is not a universal, but a singular sickness, which is in question. (Obviously experience *and* art would be the ideal.)

"Whence, art being of universals and experience of singulars, if someone should have the notion of art without the experience he will indeed be perfect in the respect of knowing the universal, but, since he does not know the singular by reason of his lack of experience, he will often make errors in curing people. For curing pertains more to the singular than to the universal, belonging as it does to the former per se, to the latter only accidentally [i.e., one cures a singular man, not a universal one]" (no. 22).

(2) Rather in the realm of knowledge. Although in the purely practical realm experience has the advantage over art in dealing with the singulars which it knows and which an art which lacks experience does not, in the realm of knowledge, however and absolutely speaking, art ranks over experience. This is evident in the fact that art derives from experience in its origin, and represents an ultimate refinement of experience into universal principles. Consequently one who possesses an art, knowing the universal reason for some particular effect, knows the reason why. And since he knows the reason why, he is also able to transmit his art to others. Neither of these things can be true of him who has experience only.

(a) Art knows the cause and the reason why. Aquinas sets down the proof of this in syllogistic form:

"Those who know the cause and the reason because of which, are more knowing and wiser than those who do not know the cause but know only that it is so.

"But those who have experience know only that it is so, but do not know the reason because of which it is so.

"Craftsmen, however, know the cause and the reason because of which, and not merely that it is so.

"Therefore craftsmen [artisans, possessors of an art] are wiser and more knowing than those who have experience only" (no. 24).

Why should the craftsmen who know the reason why a thing is so be considered wise? An analogy is taken from the crafts themselves, wherein the craft which deals with the purpose and end, i.e., the final cause, of that which is done, dictates to the other crafts. Aquinas notes a threefold degree here: the art concerned with the matter is subject to that concerned with the form; the art concerned with the form is in turn subject to the art concerned with the use.

"Someone is called an architect as though designating the principal artisan (from *archos* meaning chief, and *techne* meaning art). Now that art is said to be the more dominant which has the more principal operation.

"The operations of craftsmen are, however, distinguished as follows. Certain operations are for the sake of disposing the matter of the artifact, as carpenters, by cutting and planing timbers, dispose the matter for the form of a ship. Another operation is ordained to inducing the form, as when someone, from timbers already disposed and prepared, puts the ship together. Still another operation is the use of the thing already constituted, and this is the principal one.

"Now of these the first is the lowest, since the first is ordered to the second and the second to the third. Whence the shipwright [who puts the ship together] is an architect with respect to him who prepares the timbers. The master, however, who uses the ship already made, is the architect with respect to the shipwright.

"And since matter is for the sake of form, and the matter should be such as befits the form, therefore the shipwright knows the cause as to why the timbers should be so disposed—which those who prepare the timbers do not know.

"Likewise, since the ship is for the sake of its use, he who uses the ship knows why such a form should be the one; for it should have the form it has as dictated by the use which is envisaged.

"Hence it is evident that from the form of the artifact is derived the cause of the activities concerned with disposing of the matter, while from the use is derived the cause of those activities concerned with the form of the artifact" (nos. 26-27).

(b) Art has the ability to teach. Because art knows the reason why, it also carries with it the ability to teach. Why is this so? It is so because teaching involves the causing of knowledge in another, and in order to do this one must be able to present the reason why what one says is true. If one does not do this, then the listener does not really learn but simply takes on faith that which he receives. He does not know why it is so.

"Just as, therefore, a sign that something is hot is its ability to heat, so too the sign of one who has science is that he is able to teach, which is to cause science in another.

"Now craftsmen are able to teach because, since they know the causes, they are able to demonstrate from them....But those who have experience only cannot teach, because they cannot lead one to science since they do not know the cause [science consisting in the knowledge of causes]. Should they transmit to others what they know through experience [for example, that some home remedy is good for poison ivy], it will not be accepted according to the manner of science but according to the manner of opinion or belief.

"Hence it is evident that craftsmen are more wise and knowing than those with experience only" (no. 29).

d) **Superiority of speculative art over practical.** It might at first seem implausible to suggest that it is not the useful arts, but rather those which have no usefulness, which are the most esteemed. But one has only to cast an eye on the contemporary scene to note that this is the case. Actors and actresses, singers, concert pianists, playwrights, painters, composers—all practitioners of arts which lay no claim to being useful—are honored and feted, while the outstanding figures in the useful arts, the inventors of the washing-machine, the can-opener, the gasoline engine, all go unknown and unsung. Why should this be so? It is so because the human being naturally desires to know—even if he is not clearly conscious of this—and consequently has little esteem for the practical arts which provide only the material necessities of life, but definitely a great deal for the fine arts, arts which come into being as providing not only repose from physical labors, but also a necessary repose in intellectual pursuits. Aristotle points this out as follows:

"At first he who invented any art whatever that went beyond the common perceptions of man was naturally admired by men, not only because there was something useful in the inventions, but because he was thought wise and superior to the rest.

"But as more arts were invented, and some were directed to the necessities of life [mechanical arts], others to recreation [fine arts], the inventors of the latter were naturally regarded as wiser than the inventors of the former, because their branches of knowledge did not aim at utility" (*Metaphysics*, I, c.l).

But even above the masters of the fine arts, the masters of still other arts are rated higher still. Thus Plato is universally esteemed higher than Shakespeare, Socrates than Cezanne, and Einstein over Debussy. In other words, it is the seekers of the highest causes of all, of the ultimate causes of things, whose art, tentative though it may be, is most revered. That it lays no claim to utility may be seen from the fact that the speculative sciences in general—the theoretical science of nature, the science of mathematics, the science of metaphysics—only began to come into being to the extent that the human being had already provided for the necessities of life, when, in other words, everything useful had already been taken care of and leisure was available. Thus Aristotle notes:

"Hence when all such inventions were already established [i.e., the useful or mechanical arts and the fine arts], the sciences which do not aim at giving pleasure or at the necessities of life were discovered [namely, the speculative sciences, preceded by the liberal arts], and first in places where men first began to have leisure. This is why the mathematical arts were founded in Egypt; for there the priestly caste was allowed to be at leisure" (ibid.).

Aquinas points out how this final statement is corroborated in Genesis 47:20-22, "So Joseph bought all the land of Egypt, every man selling his possessions,...except the land of the priests, which had been given them by the king; to whom also a certain allowance of food was given out of the public stores, and therefore they were not forced to sell their possessions."

c. Definitions of Habits

1) In the speculative intellect, which is ordained to truth: (a) understanding: the intellectual habit of first principles; (b) science: the habit of conclusions from lower causes; (c) wisdom: the habit of conclusions from first causes (insofar as it is of causes, it is likewise science par excellence).

2) In the practical intellect, which is ordained to a product: (a) prudence: the habit of acting rightly in actions which need not go out into external matter, i.e., moral actions, requiring a right will as well as reason; (b) art: the habit which directs making which does go out into external matter, such as that of building or cutting.

D. Conclusion

As has been seen, the human being naturally desires to know, and this knowledge, as it progresses, tends naturally and necessarily to be a knowledge of causes. It is also this knowledge of causes, in whatever degree, that causes a human being to be called wise in that degree.

Aristotle plots out the ascent from one wisdom to another towards that which is wisdom in the truest sense, namely, the knowledge of the first or supreme causes, as follows:

"The man of experience is thought to be wiser than the possessors of any sense perception whatever, the artist [craftsman] wiser than the man of experience, the master-worker [architect] than the mechanic, and the theoretical [speculative] kinds of knowledge to be more of the nature of wisdom than the productive [the practical]" (*Metaphysics*, I, c.l).

Chapter 2

The Wise Human Being and His Science, Metaphysics

(*Metaphysics*, I, c.2)

A. The six attributes of the wise human being
B. Metaphysics as fulfilling these attributes
    1. It knows all things
    2. It knows difficult things
    3. It has a greater certitude
    4. It is able to teach through causes
    5. It is desirable in itself
    6. It is in an ordering or directing position
C. Characteristics of metaphysics, the highest science
    1. For its own sake
    2. Truly free or liberal
    3. Divine more than human

The Wise Human Being and His Science, Metaphysics
(*Metaphysics*, I, c.2)

A. The six attributes of the wise human being
B. Metaphysics as fulfilling these attributes
C. Characteristics of metaphysics, the highest science

A. The Six Attributes of the Wise Human Being

In endeavoring to discern the requisites for the highest science, or wisdom, Aristotle suggests that one examine the various attributes which result in a person's being called wise. In the light of this, any science which can lay claim to the same attributes will rightly be called wisdom. They are:

1. The wise person must know all things.
2. He must know difficult things, not easily attainable by all.
3. He must have certitude concerning what he knows.
4. He must be able to give the causes of what is investigated—and so be able to teach.
5. His science must be desirable for itself, not wished for some practical purpose such as that of providing the necessities of life or for entertainment.
6. It must be in the ordering or directing position, not subordinated to some other science.

Placing all these attributes together, Aquinas collects the following description of the wise person:

"A man is said to be wise who knows all things, even difficult things, with certitude, and knowledge of the cause, who seeks science for its own sake, and orders and persuades others" (no. 43).

B. Metaphysics As Fulfilling These Attributes

As previously set forth, metaphysics, with its accompanying titles of first philosophy and divine science, is that science which, dealing with being in its universal sense, seeks the first and highest causes thereof, which causes, indeed, are none other than God and the separated substances. Because of its nature it fulfills, therefore, all the attributes of that which is to be wise.

1. It Knows All Things

The reason it knows all things is that he who knows *universals* knows in a way all things under them (as the idea of dog contains in a way all dogs), and metaphysics has as its subject-matter the most universal concepts, namely, being, one, potency and act, and so forth.

2. It Knows Difficult Things

The reason it knows difficult things is that whatever is *remote from the senses* is difficult to know, and metaphysics treats of the first and universal causes of things, which are most remote from the senses.

3. It Has a Greater Certitude

The reason it has a greater certitude is that the *less there is required in act* in the subject of the science, the more certain that science is; and metaphysics, unlike the practical sciences which must consider many singular circumstances which vary from case to case, considers in being, one, and so forth, aspects which are few and unvarying. It is thus more certain than those sciences which are by addition, even the other speculative sciences such as mathematics or natural philosophy.

"Arithmetic is more certain than geometry, for those things which are in geometry are by addition to those things which are in arithmetic. This is evident if we consider what both sciences respectively consider as their first principle [or starting-point], namely, unity in the one case and point in the other.

"For point adds position over unity, since it is being itself which, as indivisible, constitutes the notion of unity, which in turn, under the aspect of its having the notion of measure, becomes the principle of number. But point adds, over and above the notion of unity, that of position.

"The sciences of particular things are in turn posterior in nature to the more universal sciences, since the subjects of the former add to the subjects of the universal sciences. Thus it is evident that mobile being, which is the subject of natural philosophy, adds over and above being absolutely speaking, which is the subject of metaphysics, and quantified being, which is the subject of mathematics [comprising arithmetic and geometry]. Therefore that science which is of being, and of most universal things, is most certain of all.

"Nor is this contrary, namely, that it be said to be of fewer things, to the statement above that it knows all things. For that which is universal embraces, indeed, fewer things in act, but more things in potency.

"So much the more, then, is a science certain, as it requires a lesser number of things to be considered in act in the investigation of its subject-matter. Whence the operative sciences [e.g., the moral sciences, the mechanical arts] are most uncertain, since they must consider many circumstances in each thing to be done" (no. 47).

4. It Is Able to Teach through Causes

The reason it is able to teach through causes is that to teach is nothing other than to cause science in someone, through transmitting a knowledge of causes, and metaphysics is devoted to a knowledge of the first causes of all, and hence is most fitted to teach.

5. It Is Desirable in Itself

The reason it is desirable in itself is that one desiring to know for itself would naturally desire the most knowing science, but metaphysics is thus, being of the most immaterial (and therefore, as forms, most knowable) things, and of the first causes, through which other things are known but which are themselves not known through other things.

6. It Is in an Ordering or Directing Position

The reason it is in an ordering or directing position is that the science which considers the *end* directs the other sciences of things ordained to the end. But metaphysics, dealing with the highest causes, deals with the supreme final cause, that which is the ultimate good of the whole universe, namely, God. He is that good itself, and the order of the universe, by which it attains to God and which is its good. It is thus the ruling or architectonic science with regard to all the others.

C. Characteristics of Metaphysics, the Highest Science
1. For Its Own Sake

This is evident from the fact that it was only after an adequate supply of the necessities of life and the things that make for comfort and recreation had been obtained that, historically, human beings began the rational inquiry into the highest causes. The fact that this science originated *after* material necessities had been provided for shows that it did not come into being with a view to providing such.

What then was its purpose? To flee ignorance. In effect, when a man sees an effect of which he does not know the cause, for example, hears a loud explosion of which he does not know the origin, he considers himself ignorant in that respect—and seeks to banish that ignorance by discovering the cause of the effect in question.

This state of mind before an effect of which one does not know the cause is called wonder. Hence, says Aristotle, "it is owing to their wonder that men both now begin, and at first began, to philosophize." Wonder is, then, the beginning of philosophy. What is its end? To know the cause, whereby the original ignorance is thus banished.

What has been the historical sequence of the human being's wonder? Aristotle enumerates it as follows:

"They wondered originally at the obvious difficulties, then advanced little by little and stated difficulties about the greater matters, such as the phenomena of the moon and those of the sun and of the stars, and about the genesis of the universe."

Aquinas spells out these objects of speculation somewhat more in detail:

"They began to ask questions about more important and more hidden things, such as the changes in the moon, namely, its eclipse and the change in its appearance, which is seen to vary according to its different position with respect to the sun. Likewise they asked questions about those things that had to do with the sun, such as that of its eclipse, and its motion and its size. They also inquired about the stars, as to their quantity, and order, and other such, and about the generation of the whole universe. Some indeed stated it to have been generated by chance, others by an intellect, still others by love" (no. 54).

If wonder is the beginning of philosophy, what is the origin of the word *philosophy*?

"It should be noted that while at first the name *wisdom* [in Greek, *sofia*] was employed, now this has been changed into the name *philosophy* [from the Greek *philos* (loving) and *sofia* (wisdom)]. For they both stand for the same thing.

"For while the ancients who were devoted to the study of wisdom were called sophists, i.e., wise men, Pythagoras, on being asked what he claimed himself to be, did not wish to call himself a wise man as were his predecessors, since this seemed presumptuous to him, but rather he chose to call himself a philosopher, i.e., a lover of wisdom. From that time on the name of wise man has become changed into that of *philosopher*, and the name of *wisdom* into that of *philosophy*.

"Now this latter name adds something to the matter in question. For he is seen to be a lover of wisdom who seeks wisdom not for the sake of something else but for its own sake [as a true friend loves another for his own sake and not because of some utility to be gained]. For he who seeks some thing for the sake of another loves more that because of which he seeks than that which he is now seeking" (no. 56).

2. Truly Free or Liberal

That is said to be free which is not for the sake of another, as is a slave, but is for its own sake. Since this science of metaphysics is most genuinely for its own sake, as being about the ultimate final cause or the last end of all things, for which all other things exist, but which itself does not exist for the sake of something else, it is most truly free and liberal. This notion of liberal belongs not only to the highest science, but to all those arts and sciences which directly lead to it. These are inclusively the liberal arts of the trivium and quadrivium and the speculative sciences (natural philosophy, mathematics, metaphysics), to which the former are preparatory. Such an education would be called a liberal education.

Plainly, to seek knowledge for its own sake one would have to be free from worldly cares, one would have to have the leisure that is usually made possible by wealth and property. While the appurtenances of leisure such as, for example, wealth and property, are visible to the eye, the speculative sciences which they are destined to make possible are not. Hence, a liberal education comes somewhat to have the meaning of being the education of a person of property, who need not work. Such a person fulfills the visible aspect of doing no manual labor, of patronizing the fine arts, but whether he pursues the speculative sciences, is a lover of wisdom, is not examined too closely.

3. Divine More Than Human

A science which is for its own sake hardly befits the human being, who is subject to many needs, material and otherwise. In effect, he is impeded from pursuing knowledge of the highest causes by the need of securing the necessities of life. Then, even when he has attained to material sufficiency, the intellectual conquest of a knowledge of the highest things is a task in excess of the best human intellect. In a word, the human being is not master in relation to this highest science, which is for its own sake. Nevertheless whatever little one attains to in this realm exceeds whatever one can know in the other sciences.

Nor should the fact that this science of the highest causes is properly the possession of the divinity deter the human being from attaining to whatever is within his power. It is indeed divine in two respects: in one way as belonging properly to God; in another way as being about God, since it is of the first causes and principles. And God is understood by all as being the principle and cause of things. While all other sciences are more necessary for life than it, this divine science, then, which the human being, so to speak, borrows from God, is of all the sciences the most honorable.

Chapter 3

Pursuit of First Causes in the Past
(*Metaphysics*, I, cc.3-7)

A. Number of the causes
B. Opinions on nature of first causes
    1. Those omitting the formal cause
        a. Based on things manifest to the senses
            1) Solely a material cause
                a) One
                b) More than one: finite or infinite
            2) Proposing also an efficient cause
            3) Movement toward a final cause
        b. Based on things not evident to the senses
            1) Many principles
                a) Corporeal, i.e., atoms
                b) Incorporeal, i.e., numbers
            2) One single being, with denial of motion
                a) On the part of form: Parmenides
                b) On the part of matter: Melissus
        c. Summary
    2. Introduction of the formal cause: Plato
        a. Plato on the substance of things
            1) Ideas and species
            2) Mathematical substances
        b. Plato on the principles of things
            1) Principles
            2) The genus of cause in Plato's principles

C. Summary of philosophical opinions before Aristotle
    1. Material
    2. Efficient
    3. Formal
    4. Final

Pursuit of First Causes in the Past

(*Metaphysics*, I, cc.3-7)

The science of metaphysics, as has already been noted, sets out to attain to a knowledge, not of some particular area of being, but of being in its universality, and this in the light of an understanding of the first and universal causes upon which all being depends. Such a pursuit is not an intellectual luxury but corresponds, rather, to the natural, and therefore ineradicable, desire in the human being to attain to, and to be conjoined with, the supreme reality.

In setting out on such a pursuit it is only natural to endeavor to profit by the efforts other men have already made to attain to a knowledge of the first causes. At the same time one will note how these efforts of the past have in a certain way staked out all the possible avenues of approach to the problem—in such a way, in fact, that the most recent efforts will be seen to be, on inspection and reflection, modern variations on the themes first staked out by the ancients. Thus, to study them is to comprehend the moderns too.

A. Number of the Causes

Before beginning an examination of the first efforts to arrive at the highest and ultimate causes, one notes that all causes fall into one of four categories, first set forth by Aristotle in his *Physics*, II. Thus he begins his examination with the words: "Evidently we have to acquire knowledge of the original causes (for we say we know each thing only when we recognize its first cause), and causes are spoken of in four senses:"

1. the formal cause: that by which something is what it is.

    "The formal cause is the substance of the thing, by which one knows *what* each thing is. For it is evident, as is seen in *Physics* II, that we do not state anything to be of some specific nature until it has received its form. And that the form is a cause is evident from the fact that we reduce the question of why something is to a question of the formal cause as though to the ultimate reason, beginning with proximate forms and proceeding up to the ultimate one. Now it is plain that the question "why?" is one which seeks a cause and principle. Whence it is clear that the form is a cause" (no. 70).

2. the material cause: that out of which something is produced.

3. the efficient cause: that whence motion proceeds.

4. the final cause: that for the sake of which something is done.

    "The final cause is opposed to the efficient cause according to the opposition of beginning and end. For motion begins from the efficient cause and terminates at the final cause. Likewise this is that for the sake of which something is done, and which is the good of each nature.

    "The final cause is thus identified [by Aristotle] as to three things. It is (1) the terminus of motion, and as such is opposed to the beginning of motion, which is the efficient cause; (2) first in intention, by reason of which it is called that for the sake of which; (3) desirable in itself, by reason of which it is called good, since the good is that which all things desire.

    "Whence, expounding in what way the final cause may be opposed to the efficient, he [Aristotle] states that it is the end of generation and movement, whose beginning is the efficient cause. By these two [generation and movement] he is seen to introduce two different ends. For the end of generation is the form itself which is generated, and which is a part of the thing [e.g., the form of a house]. But the end of motion is something sought for beyond the thing which is moved [e.g., the actual use of the house to live in. The work which generates the house terminates in the finished house, but the purpose of the originating motion extends beyond this to the actual use of the house]" (nos. 70-71).

B. Opinions on Nature of First Causes
1. Those Omitting the Formal Cause
a. Based on Things Manifest to the Senses

1) Solely a material cause. Since matter is that which is most immediately obvious to the senses, it is only natural first to seek the ultimate cause of things in matter. There are four aspects of matter which lend themselves to its being considered the ultimate cause of all: (1) it is that out of which something is made, as a knife is made out of steel; (2) it is that from which, as from a starting-point, something is made, since the matter preexists to the making; (3) it is that into which all material things are resolved by corruption; (4) it remains while forms succeed themselves in it.

In modern times the efforts to resolve all sensible reality, both man and animal, both living and nonliving, into various random combinations of atomic or subatomic particles, are the same attempt to try to explain all things in terms of a sole material cause. This cause may be:

a) One. Historically speaking, and at least insofar as Western thought is concerned, *water* seems to have long ranked as a single primordial element. This is supposed to have been the opinion of Thales, a Greek, and traditionally the first philosopher—insofar as he is reputed the first one to attempt a rational inquiry into the causes of things, as against the more poetical and mythological presentations of his predecessors, such as Hesiod.

What could be the reasons for such a selection? Plainly moisture is closely bound up with material beings: unless a thing is moist, it dries up and turns to dust, particularly in the case of living things, which require moisture in their generation, live on moist things, and must remain moist to survive.

Nor is this opinion of Thales (circa 600 BC) so terribly outmoded, since today, in the scheme of evolution, life, including human life, is seen as emerging from the sea. It likewise antedated Thales, since in Greek mythology Okeanos and Thetis, gods of water, were the parents of generation, and the gods swore by the waters of the Styx.

"From the fact that they [the Greek poets] stated the gods to swear by water, they gave to understand that water was nobler than the gods, since a sacrament or oath is made by that which is the more honorable....Whence it is evident from this that they thought water to be prior to the gods themselves, whom they understood to be the heavenly bodies....If there is any opinion prior to this one concerning natural things, it is unknown to us" (no. 84).

It is interesting to note in our own day how the sun's energy, the source of our energy, is attributed to the fusion of hydrogen into helium—hydrogen which is so closely related to water that it is called in German *wasserstoff.*

Just as its connection with life suggests water as the primordial principle, so also the successors of Thales, such as Anaxagoras and Diogenes, posited *air* as the primordial element, in keeping with its necessity for breathing. Other philosophers, among whom was Heraclitus, posited *fire* as the basic element, possibly because of its subtlety.

b) <u>More than one: finite or infinite.</u> The first to posit more than one element was Empedocles, who posited a finite number—the traditional air, earth, fire, water—as against Anaxagoras, who posited an infinite number. His theory was that everything must be in everything, since everything seems to come out of everything, as the earth yields its varied fruits.

For Empedocles, the different things came about from different combinations of the enduring four elements; for Anaxagoras, they came about by the concentrating of one of the infinite elements over the others in any given thing.

2) Proposing also an efficient cause. The positing of an efficient cause, from which motion comes, is forced upon one's consideration by the very nature of things.

"No thing or subject transmutes itself, as wood does not transform itself to become a bed, nor is brass the cause of its own transformation whereby it becomes a statue. Rather, there must be something else which is to them a cause of transformation, namely, the artisan.

"Now those who posited one or several material causes stated that out of the same, as from a subject, the generation and corruption of things were produced. Therefore it is necessary that there be another cause, to explain change. And this is to seek another genus of principle and cause, called that from which motion proceeds" (no. 93).

The attitude toward motion of the early philosophers may be summed up as threefold:

1. The first were content to posit a material cause and did not trouble about a separate cause of motion.
2. Among their successors, those who could not find a suitable explanation for motion, and change in general, such as Parmenides

and Melissus, felt obliged to deny change entirely, and posit a single immutable reality. Their predecessors, even though they did not admit of the production of absolutely new things but only rearrangements in the accidental order of the basic element or elements, nevertheless did posit such an accidental transformation to take place by rarefaction and condensation.

3. Thirdly, there were those who set down a cause of motion by positing one element (such as fire) as active, and the other elements (such as air, earth, and water) as passive in respect to it. Thus fire became an efficient cause, the others a material cause. This Empedocles did.

3) Movement toward a final cause. An efficient cause as the cause of motion and change does not seem to suffice alone, for the term of motion or change is so often the good of that which is thus transformed or changed. Thus living things move toward a certain final perfection which is hard to attribute to motion moving merely blindly, since there is involved a series of complex steps, which are ordered to each other and which add up to the final result. Thus mere chance, mere cosmic trial-and-error, as posited by Empedocles to explain the different sorts of things, and as posited as the starting-point of evolution as commonly understood, did not seem sufficient to explain these good and happy results in things, which occur, unlike the products of chance as we know it (as for example, in the case of a winning number on a roulette wheel), not with the utmost rarity, but always for the most part.

What was the extension that had to be added, beyond a mere blind efficient cause, in order to explain the goodness in things? It was necessary to posit an intellect disposing and ordering.

This introduction of intellect as guiding the efficient cause is attributed to Anaxagoras, a disciple of Anaximines, who was in turn a successor of Thales. Others, such as Hesiod, one of the poets who preceded the philosophers, posited love as the unifying, ordering principle, bringing order out of chaos. (This opinion was likewise espoused by Parmenides as an explanation of an illusory sensible variety of things—as against a real and absolute unity.) All this makes sense.

"For also in us love moves us to actions, and this because it is the beginning of all the affections. Indeed, fear and sadness and hope do not proceed except from love. That love should draw together is evident from the following fact: love itself is a certain union of the one loving with the thing loved, since the one loving considers that which is loved as himself" (no. 102).

Empedocles, in his concept of a blind evolution of things, not only posited love as a unifying force, but hate as a dislocating force, and thus has the distinction of introducing contrariety into the production of things. This characteristic continues to be noted, for example, in the attribution of positive and negative electric charges to things. Empedocles is likewise, as already noted, the first to hold for four elements.

b. Based on Things Not Evident to the Senses

After an examination of opinions on the first cause of things which derive from things evident to the senses such as water, air, and fire, one now passes on to those opinions which began to lodge the first cause of things in things not perceptible to the senses. Here too principles may be many or immutably one. Further, they may be corporeal or incorporeal.

1) Many principles.

a) Corporeal, i.e., atoms. The contemporary concept of matter as constituted of particles which are discontinuous with each other, i.e., the theory of the discontinuity of matter, is a theory whereby everything is put together by means of particles whose different configurations, both within themselves and in conjunction with other things, constitute all the varying properties of matter. New elements are made by rearranging electrons, protons, and so forth. The particles do not touch but are linked together by fields of force. Thus one has porous matter, matter which is partly composed of the void, matter with holes in it.

This new matter is the old matter of Leucippus and Democritus, the inventor of the atom.

Certain philosophers considered a void necessary for motion, since a body could only move into a place which was empty or unoccupied. Since they felt they could not admit of the existence of a void or vacuum, they therefore felt obliged to deny motion and the diversity of things, in favor of a single, immutable, continuous unity. Democritus, on the other hand, since he was sure there was motion, likewise posited the void. And since he could see no reason for positing it in one place and not in another, he posited it in everything. Thus everything came to be discontinuous, to be composed of indivisible particles or atoms [from the Greek *a* (privative) and *tomos* (something cut), i.e., that which is uncut or indivisible] with void space between them.

"Thus, therefore [Democritus] stated the magnitude of each body to be constituted out of these indivisible bodies filling indivisible space, and out of certain void spaces lying between these indivisible bodies, which he called pores" (no. 113).

Thus, for Democritus, every body was composed of the nonvoid and the void, of being and nonbeing. (Karl Marx, who was later to explore in dialectical materialism the Hegelian concept of all being containing its contradiction, nonbeing, appropriately wrote his doctoral dissertation on Democritus.)

How did Democritus construct the diversity of matter out of his indivisible, point-sized atoms? How is matter constructed today? It is done by an arrangement of electrons around a nucleus in different configurations. As the electron is displaced, its position changed, as protons are added or subtracted, the element varies. For Democritus it was likewise an affair of arrangements of particles into various configurations (angular, circular, and straight) and into an order of particles to left or right, above or below, anterior or posterior, similar to polarization.

These particles, in addition, required no extrinsic efficient cause of motion. Democritus endowed them with a motion of their own, not unsimilar, perhaps, to that of today's electrons circulating around the nucleus, or to a concept of mass as nothing but latent energy.

b) Incorporeal, i.e., numbers. Today our heartbeats come out as lines on the cardiograph, our thoughts appear as lines on the electroencephalograph, enormous computers solve all sorts of problems in terms of the numbers one and two. This attempt to reduce all things to the language of continuous and discrete quantity, to lines and numbers, is not new.

While the Ionian philosophers, namely, Thales and his successors, Greeks living in Ionia on the coast of Asia Minor opposite Greece, sought to explain the nature of things in terms of sensible elements such as water and air, another Greek school of thought, that of Pythagoras, located in the south of Italy, endeavored to explain the nature of things in terms of nonsensible realities, namely, numbers. What prompted them to do this? It was no doubt the progress this school had already made in utilizing mathematical proportions, as incorporated in the multiplication table, the decimal system, the Pythagorean theorem; and it was only natural to try to find the same revealing proportions in

nature as a whole, to try to find for each thing a number which would
state its essence.

A study of musical harmony lends itself to this inclination. For
musical sounds which harmonize are seen, upon examination, to do so
according to fixed mathematical proportions. Just as sounds spaced
according to mathematical proportions on the musical scale (e.g., half
the length of a given string will yield a note exactly an octave higher)
are in harmony with each other, then, since the whole universe is obviously in harmony, why not suppose that the various celestial bodies are
spaced according to similar mathematical proportions—and even that
they, like the notes on a scale, yield to the knowing ear a certain celestial harmony, the "harmony of the spheres"? The great astronomer
Kepler who, unlike his contemporary, Galileo, placed the Copernican
system on a firm basis by his three famous Laws, was inspired to envi-
sion the distances between the planets after the manner of musical har-
monies. Among those immediately inspired by Pythagoras was Plato,
the teacher of Aristotle, who placed numbers as separate forms.

Whereas Empedocles introduced contrariety on the part of the efficient cause, namely, in love as a unifying force and hate as a disinte-
grating force, and his predecessors introduced it on the part of the formal cause, namely, by attributing the variety of things to rarefaction
and condensation of the same thing, the Pythagoreans were the first to
introduce contrariety into the material cause of things.

As has been stated, numbers were to be considered as the essences
of things. In these numbers, odd and even (source of the finite and the
infinite) constitute the basic differences of things. The odd numbers,
beginning with 1, are at the root of form and definiteness. This may be
seen in the fact that if the successive odd numbers are added to the first
basic square, which is 1 squared, the successive figures always remain
a square. Thus if 3 be added to 1, one has 4, the square of 2; if 5 then
be added to this, one has 9, the square of 3; and so forth. On the other
hand, if the first even number, 2, is added to 1, and then the second
even number, 4, is added to that, the figures evolving out of these ad-
ditions are constantly varying in shape. Thus even number is the
source of matter and indefiniteness, of infinity.

Starting from this, the Pythagoreans could evolve the contrariety of
things in greater and greater concreteness. Thus, starting from odd and
even, one has first the finite and the infinite. This leads in number to
the one and the many. From number comes magnitude, which is number in position: point (one) and line (two). The principles of position

are right and left—understood as perfect and imperfect respectively. Natural things add active and passive power over and above mathematical magnitude—the principles of these being masculine and feminine. In motion there is rest and motion, curved and rectilinear. In knowledge there is light and darkness. In the appetite there is good and evil. All these are derived from the original odd and even.

2) One single being, with denial of motion. Although nothing is more obvious than motion, and it is immediately evident to the senses, the inability to explain motion, however, has sometimes led to its denial. Thus, as has already been seen, to the extent that one considers the void or a vacuum necessary for motion, and at the same time an impossibility, one must deny motion, and thereby consider the variety in things, their changes in place, in size, in quality, an illusion. The apparent need for a void is somewhat similar to the need for a parking-space for a car to move into. In order for anything to move into it, it first has to be empty or void. This difficulty bedeviled Descartes.

Once one has been led, by the inability to explain motion without a vacuum, to posit all reality as one and immutable, one can no longer logically speak of cause and effect, since they imply multiplicity and distinction. Comparable conceptions of all things as one, and of all change and distinction as illusory, are found in Oriental philosophy and in the thinking of Spinoza.

a) On the part of form: Parmenides. Parmenides appears to have envisioned the absolute unity and immutability of things on the part of form. How did he argue to his position of absolute oneness? He reasoned thus:

Whatever is outside of being is nonbeing.
And whatever is nonbeing is nothing.
Therefore whatever is outside of being is nothing.
But being is one.
Therefore whatever is outside of one is nothing.

"In this respect he [Parmenides] considered the very notion of being, which is seen to be one, since it cannot be understood that anything be added to the notion of being to diversify it. Whatever would be added would have to be other than being. Whatever is such, is nothing. Hence being would appear not to be able to be diversified" (no. 138). Being therefore is not a genus, since genus is diversified by the addition of specific difference.

"They [Parmenides and followers] were deceived, however, because they looked at being as though it had one notion and one nature, as is the nature of a genus. But this is impossible. Being is not a genus but is said in many ways of diverse things [e.g., of substance and accident]. Hence it is stated in *Physics* I that the statement *Being is one* is false, for it does not have one nature, as does one genus or one species" (no. 139). In other words, the being in common which is one is not some single being but the universal concept of being, which is one as divided from nonbeing and undivided in itself. Actually existing being exists in particulars, from God to creatures, and in many different sorts and states, all sharing in the universal common notion of being and unity (see p. 259).

b) **On the part of matter: Melissus.** Melissus, on the other hand, appears to have wished to establish the immutable unity of things starting from matter. Thus he argues that being cannot be generated out of anything prior to being. This same ungenerated characteristic belongs to matter, out of which other things are generated. He reasons thus:

> Whatever is generated has a beginning.
> But being is not generated.
> Therefore it has no beginning.
> But what has no beginning has no end, and is therefore infinite.
> But if being is infinite, it must also be immobile, there being nothing outside the infinite to which it can move.

Melissus proves the ungeneratedness of being by arguing that being would have to be generated either from being or nonbeing. But it is not generated from the latter, since nothing can come from nothing; nor from the former, since then it would be before it came to be.

Melissus, considering being from the viewpoint of matter, to which it is proper not to be generated from anything preexisting, attributes infinity to it. Parmenides, on the other hand, considering being on the part of form, considers it finite or determined. Xenophanes, whose disciple Parmenides was, considered the whole of the heavens and called it God, in keeping with the tendency of the ancients to call the universe itself divine. Thus he made the composite of matter and form one. (It should be remembered, however, that Parmenides, while holding being to be absolutely one in reality, nevertheless allowed for its variety in appearance and consequently for cause and effect—the hot and fire being active in respect to the cold and earth as passive.)

c. Summary

"Now from the first philosophers it was had that the principle of all things was corporeal. This is evident from the fact that water and such things, which they laid down as the principles of things, are certain bodies. But they differed in this, namely, in that certain ones laid down this principle to be one only, as did Thales, Diogenes, and others like them. Others laid them down as more than one, as did Anaxagoras, Democritus, and Empedocles. But both groups, nevertheless, i.e., both those who laid down one principle and those who laid down more than one, laid down such corporeal principles in the manner of a material cause.

"Some, indeed, of them not only laid down a material cause, but with it added a cause whence motion begins—some setting it down as one, as Anaxagoras laid down intellect, and Parmenides love, while others set down two, as Empedocles set down love and hate....

"...[The Pythagoreans, starting from unity as being both finite and infinite, as the source of both odd and even number] concluded that number, which is constituted out of unities, was the substance of all things. The other natural philosophers, although they laid down unity and the finite or the infinite, nevertheless attributed these to some other nature as accidents are attributed to a subject, for example, to fire, or water, or some such. Furthermore they [the Pythagoreans] added something over and above the other philosophers in that they began to speak and define concerning 'what something is,' i.e., concerning substance and the quiddity of things [the formal cause]. They treated, however, of this in a most rudimentary way, defining only superficially" (nos. 145, 148-49).

2. Introduction of the Formal Cause: Plato
a. Plato on the Substance of Things

1) Ideas and species. Plato, coming after both the natural philosophers and the Pythagoreans, gleaned ideas from both.

At the time of Plato, whose student Aristotle was to become, the opinion of the natural philosophers, as expressed by their successors such as Heraclitus and Cratylus, was that all sensible things were constantly in a state of flux, and that consequently there could be no science of them. In keeping with this opinion, Socrates, the master of Plato, and himself a philosophical descendant of Anaxagoras, conceding that there could be no science of sensible things, abandoned the inquiry into the nature of things and concentrated on moral and ethical matters. In this field he was the first to seek out the universal, and to concentrate on definition.

Plato, his disciple, continued by seeking out the universal and definitions in natural things. He accepted, however, that the required immutability of universals and definitions could not be found in any sensible singular, since all such are in constant flux. He therefore lodged the universal and definition in certain ideas and species of sensible things. As ideas, these things served as models for sensible things and the source of their participated being; as species they were the principle of the knowledge of sensible things. Thus all sensible things were both caused by these ideas or species and known through them. In this sense, of all men there was a separated idea of man which was man in himself, and in relation to which all individual men were men by participation, participating the species.

The idea of participation had been derived by Plato from Pythagoras. The Pythagoreans considered that sensible things were certain imitations of numbers. Thus, numbers, by nature positionless, through acquiring position caused bodies.

2) Mathematical substances. Between the substance of sensible things and the separated species, Plato posited an intermediate realm of being, that of mathematics. Mathematical being differed from sensible things since these latter were corruptible and mutable while mathematics abstracted from motion, and consequently from change, and was immutable and immobile. Mathematical being likewise differed from the species in that in the species (e.g., man) there could be only one species of a given sort, able to be multiplied into many individuals in sensible reality (e.g., many individual men). In mathematical substance, however, one species could have several subspecies, e.g., in the species triangle, the subspecies scalene, isosceles, equilateral—each of which could then be multiplied in sensible reality in many individuals.

How to explain this positing by Plato of separated species and separated mathematics? It is explained by Plato's identification of our way of *knowing* things with the way of *being* of things. Thus we know by abstraction of the universal from the singular, which gives the intellectual species or universal idea. In mathematics we go further, obtaining, on the universal level, intelligible matter, i.e., in geometry we abstract from sense qualities, retaining only shape and size; in arithmetic, from what a thing is sensibly, to considering only units, independently of what those units may be in the sense order from the viewpoint of various sense qualities. Yet it is not necessary that things should actually exist outside the mind as they are known in the mind. When we abstract we take in certain aspects of external reality while leaving others behind. Thus the mind, as against the senses and the memory, abstracts a universal idea of man from the individual men which the senses encounter. Yet it recognizes that it is the individual man, not the universal idea of man, which actually exists. Similarly in mathematics the mind abstracts the concept of triangle from triangular objects which strike the senses, for example, the Pyramids, and conceives of triangle as constituted by lines which, while having length, have neither breadth nor thickness. This is obviously convenient for the mind, but the mind has no illusion that any triangle existing outside the mind could be of any such ethereal nature.

In a word, there is nothing wrong with the mind grasping things, for its own convenience and utility, in a different manner from that in which they exist in reality provided it does not conceive that the things actually exist that way. There is nothing wrong with the mind's abstracting provided that it knows it is abstracting. Plato, however, recognizing both that the mind abstracts universals, and that these universals have a real basis in things (for example, men are really alike in their common traits of humanity), and considering at the same time that this real basis could not be in the shifting sensible singular, felt obliged to lodge the species or universals neither in the mind, nor in sensible things, but in a separated realm of their own.

b. *Plato on the Principles of Things*

1) Principles. According to Plato, the separated species are the causes of all other beings. But what is the cause of the species? For Plato, in the Pythagorean line, it is unity. How are the different species evolved out of unity? This is done after the manner in which numbers vary by addition or subtraction of unity. This addition and subtraction constitutes for Plato the great and the small. Thus, just as unity, applied by addition or subtraction, constitutes the different species of numbers, so unity as form, working with the great and the small (addition and subtraction of unity) as matter, constitutes the separated species. In this is to be noted the fundamental identifying by Plato of the unity which is *convertible with being* (as everything is one, i.e., undivided, as God is one even without other gods, and human nature is one) with the unity which is the *principle of number* (number being defined as multitude measured by unity).

Both Plato and Pythagoras agreed that unity was the substance of things, and being itself; and this unity they identified with the unity which is the principle of number. Consequently, number, constituted by unities, in turn constitutes the different varieties of things.

They differed, however, in two respects. Whereas Pythagoras posited unity and finiteness on the part of form, and even and the infinite on the part of matter, Plato divides the matter of things into two, i.e., the great and the small. Thus where Pythagoras had the one infinite, Plato has the duality of the great and the small in the realm of material cause.

The other important respect in which they differed is that Plato posited numbers *outside* sensible things, both as to the separated species constituted out of the great and the small, and as to mathematics, which were a kind of intermediate number. (Thus there were for Plato both the separated species of things, constituted from unity, which were substantially number, and the numbers themselves.) But the Pythagoreans said that the numbers were the sensible things themselves, and did not posit intermediate numbers between sensible things and the separated species, nor separated species themselves.

What was the reason for this difference between Plato and the Pythagoreans? It would seem to lie in the fact that Plato was concerned with definitions and universals, which did not seem to be able to be attributed to sensible things, and which therefore had to be attributed to things existing apart. The Pythagoreans, on the other hand, had simply discovered mathematical properties in things themselves, and had not yet come to the logical problem of the formulation of definitions and to that of universals.

What prompted Plato to posit the duality of the great and the small as the matter of things instead of the single infinite derived from even? It seems that the Platonists were motivated in this positing of duality as the matter of things from the fact that *two* measures at least all even numbers. But this was not a felicitous choice in comparison to the attribution by all the natural philosophers of the duality of contrariety, not to matter, but to form. In effect, the one matter is susceptible of receiving many varying successive forms. Consequently, duality seems to exist more on the side of form than on that of matter. Plato's choice, however, was influenced, not by the consideration of a mutable matter in which various forms succeed themselves while the matter remains as subject, but rather by the abstract consideration of the single universal species which is multiplied and diversified by the different matters into which it is received.

2) The genus of cause in Plato's principles. Plato posited only two genera of causes, namely, the formal (the species) and the material (the great and the small). The species, derived from unity, are that by which a thing is what it is, the cause both of the knowledge of, and of the being of, sensible things. The matter, or that out of which, is the great and the small. In addition to these, Plato also assigned the causes of good and evil, as Anaxagoras and Empedocles had done before him: the species were the cause of good, matter the cause of evil. In this latter respect—the species as cause of good—there was a movement toward the formulating of the concept of a final cause.

C. Summary of Philosophical Opinions before Aristotle

As may be seen, the ancients did not come up with any other genus of cause than those which it remained for Aristotle to formulate clearly and explicitly for the first time in his *Physics*: namely, the formal, material, efficient, and final causes. The following is a summary of the treatment of each of these causes by the predecessors of Aristotle, and one which corroborates his own determination of their number and kind:

1. Material

"He [Aristotle] says therefore that they, namely, the earlier philosophers, all agree in attributing some principle to things in the order of matter. But they differ in two respects. First, in that certain of them laid down one matter, as did Thales and Diogenes and others like them; while others laid down several, as did Empedocles. Secondly, in that certain of them laid down the matter of things to be some body, as did the aforesaid philosophers, while certain others laid down something incorporeal, as did Plato, who posited duality. For Plato laid down the great and the small, which do not signify any body. The Italic philosophers, however, i.e., the Pythagoreans, posited the infinite, which likewise is not a body.

"But Empedocles laid down the four elements which are bodies. Likewise Anaxagoras laid down an 'infinity of like parts,' i.e., that infinite similar parts were the principles [i.e., everything was in everything]. And all these touched 'such a cause,' namely, the material. And also this was true of those who said that air or water or fire was the principle, or something intermediate in these elements, namely, more dense than fire, more subtle than air. For all such aforesaid philosophers laid down such a body to be the first element. And thus is evident what he [Aristotle] says, namely, that the philosophers, as to those things which have been mentioned, laid down the sole material cause.

2. Efficient

"Then he [Aristotle] gives the opinions concerning the efficient cause, saying that some of the aforesaid philosophers laid down, along with the material cause, the cause whence motion begins, as did any of those who laid down as the cause of things love, hate, and intellect; or who constitute other acting principles apart from these, as did Parmenides, who laid down fire as an agent cause.

3. Formal

"Subsequently he [Aristotle] gives the opinions concerning the formal cause, and he says that the cause through which one knows what the substance of a thing is, i.e., the formal cause, no one of them clearly attributes to things. If the ancient philosophers touched on anything which pertained to the formal cause, as did Empedocles, who laid down bone and flesh as having some certain notion by which they are such, nevertheless they did not lay down whatever pertained to the formal cause as befits the manner of a cause.

"But among the others, those most approached to a laying-down of the formal cause who posited species, and those notions which pertain to species, such as unity and number and other such. For the species and those things connected with species, such as unity and number, are not taken up or posited by them as the matters of sensible things, since they rather place matter itself on the side of sensible things. Nor do they posit them as the causes from which motion comes to things, for they are rather the causes to things of immobility. For whatever there is found of the necessary in sensible things, this they say to be caused by the species, and they stated them, namely, the species, to be without motion. Indeed they were laid down by them, as was said, in order that, existing in an immobile way, they [the species] might remain uniform, in such a way that definitions might be given of them and demonstrations made. But according to their opinions, the species lent to individual things their quiddity [or essence] after the manner of a formal cause, and unity in turn lent this to the species.

4. Final

"Then he [Aristotle] sets down the opinions of some concerning the final cause, saying that the philosophers in a certain way state the end for the sake of which transmutations and actions are produced to be a cause and in a certain way do not, nor do they state this in the manner that befits the being of a true cause. For those who state intellect or love to be a cause, state them as causes as a good. Now the cause of good cannot be anything but the good. Whence it follows that they laid down intellect and love to be a cause as the good is a cause.

"But the good may be understood in two ways. In one way as the final cause, insofar as something is done for the sake of some good. In another way, after the manner of an efficient cause, as we say that a good man does good. These philosophers, therefore, did not state the aforesaid causes to be good as though for their sake anything of beings existed or was produced, which pertains to the notion of final cause; but rather, because from the aforesaid, namely, intellect and love, there proceeded a certain motion toward the being and production of things, which pertains to the notion of efficient cause.

"Likewise also the Pythagoreans and the Platonists, who stated the substance of things to be one and being, also attributed goodness to one and being. And thus they stated such a nature, namely, the good, to be to sensible things the cause of their substance, either after the manner of a formal cause, as Plato laid down, or after the manner of matter, as did the Pythagoreans. They did not state, however, that the being of things or their production was for the sake of this, i.e., of one and being, which pertains to the notion of final cause. And thus, as the natural philosophers laid down the good to be a cause, not after the manner of a formal cause, but after the manner of an efficient cause, so the Platonists laid down the good as a cause after the manner of a formal cause and not after the manner of a final cause; while the Pythagoreans did so after the manner of a material cause.

"Whence it is evident that it happened to them in a certain way to state the good to be a cause, and in a certain way not to state it. For they did not state absolutely the good to be a cause, but accidentally. For the good, according to its proper notion, is a cause after the manner of a final cause. This is evident from the fact that the good is that which all things desire. But that towards which the appetite tends, is the end. The good, therefore, according to its proper reason, is a cause after the manner of an end.

"Those therefore lay down the good absolutely to be a cause who posit it as a final cause. But those who attribute to the good some other mode of causality, posit it as a cause, but accidentally, since they do so not by reason of the good itself, but by reason of that which good accompanies, namely, because something is, for example, active or perfective. Whence it is evident that those philosophers did not lay down the final cause except accidentally, since, namely, they laid down as a cause that to which it belonged to be an end, namely, the good, yet nevertheless they did not posit it to be a cause after the manner of a final cause, as has been stated.

"He [Aristotle] then arrives at his principally intended conclusion, namely, that the determination made above concerning the causes, as to what they were and how many [i.e., the four mentioned], was correct. For the aforesaid philosophers are seen to bear witness to this, being unable to add any genus of cause to those already mentioned. This utility, therefore [i.e., the corroboration of the causes established by Aristotle], arises from the recitation of the aforesaid opinions.

"Another usefulness which arises is the fact that thence it is clear that the principles of things are to be sought for in this science, being either all of those things which the ancients laid down and which have been determined above, or some of them. For this science chiefly considers the formal and final causes, and in a certain way also the moving cause.

"Nor should one only recite the aforesaid opinions, but afterwards one should pass on and state how each one of them spoke, and in what way well, and in what way ill; and how those things which are stated of the principles have any problem involved" (nos. 173-80).

Chapter 4

Critique of Early Thinking on First Causes
(*Metaphysics,* I, cc.8-10)

A. Of those who held natural or sensible principles
  1. One element
  2. More than one element
B. Of those who held other than natural or sensible principles
  1. Pythagoras
  2. Plato
    a. As to the substance of things
      1) Species
      2) Mathematical entities
    b. As to the first causes of things

Critique of Early Thinking on First Causes

(Metaphysics, I, cc.8-10)

A. Of those who held natural or sensible principles
B. Of those who held other than natural or sensible principles

A. Of Those Who Held Natural or Sensible Principles

What are the deficiencies in the theories concerning the first causes of things thus far presented?

1. One Element

Concerning those who supposed the first cause of things to be some one element, there are several inadequacies:

1. One of the most significant of these is that such a conception of the causes of reality leaves no room for immaterial being: everything is some form of body.
2. Something must be said of the cause of motion, since it is through motion that natural things evolve.
3. Nothing is said of form, that by which something is what it is.

2. More Than One Element

As to those, such as Empedocles, who posited more than one material element, and in them a certain contrariety to explain the differences of things, there is in their theories the basic defect of placing contrariety in the very foundation of things, which would involve either a first cause in conflict with itself, or first causes in conflict with each other. Anaxagoras was apparently the first to posit a first cause outside the realm of matter and contrariety, but not clearly. Likewise, by his concept of everything being precontained in everything, Anaxagoras approached the idea of prime matter, in which future forms of all material things are contained, not in act but in potency.

B. Of Those Who Held Other Than Natural or Sensible Principles
1. Pythagoras

It is appropriate for metaphysics to treat of those philosophers who laid down other than sensible causes of reality, since this science, unlike natural science, treats of all being, whether sensible or imperceptible to the senses. The Pythagoreans differed from the natural philosophers, who gave a material, sensible cause to things, by virtue of their attributing the first cause of things to mathematical entities in which there is no sensible motion. They agreed with the natural philosophers, however, in using these mathematical entities or numbers to explain a material world, considered as the sole existing world.

Their system lacked, however, any cause of motion, since its basic elements were the finite and the infinite, deriving from odd and even. Likewise numbers might explain the dimensions of bodies, but not their lightness or heaviness. Furthermore, Pythagoras seems to have made the same number both the first cause of things and the substance of the things themselves, whereas Plato later on was to posit two kinds of numbers, i.e., those which were the causes of sensible things, and those which were in the immaterial order.

2. Plato

Aristotle argues against Plato both as to what he says of the substance of things and as to what he says concerning their first causes.

a. As to the Substance of Things

1) Species. The complaint against the species, for example, the man in himself who is the cause of all individual men, is that they are simply a gratuitous invention, not based on any compelling necessity in the nature of things. Thus a problem is here solved, not by finding the cause of things, but by inventing new entities. Plato appears to have been impelled to posit the species by the need to base science on necessary, immutable grounds, which singular sensible things could not afford. But the resulting species would thereby be unable to account for changing, corruptible things. Likewise they would have to be not only of substances, such as man, but of accidents, such as blue—which would then be subsisting accidents without subjects. (Plato simply denied species for accidents.) Likewise, since the separated species of sensible things, and those things themselves, have something in common, there should be a species of this common note, such as a species of substance in itself, but Plato did not posit such.

Aristotle's chief complaint against the species is, then, that they solve nothing, either in the realm of corporeal things or in the realm of eternal things. The species cannot explain motion, since they are, rather, the cause of immobility. Nor do they help to know sensible things, which should be known through themselves. As separated species they have no proven connection with sensible singulars, neither can they be their causes. They are posited, rather, as gratuitous exemplars. This does not mean, of course, that there is no need for an exemplary cause, although it does eliminate the necessity for a species of each individual thing.

"It should be understood that this argument, even though it may destroy the separated exemplars laid down by Plato, nevertheless does not remove the fact of the divine knowledge being the exemplary cause of all things.

"For since natural things naturally intend to induce their likenesses into the things generated, it is necessary that this intention be reduced to some directing principle, which orders each thing to the end. And this cannot be other than the intellect to whom it belongs to know the end and the proportion of things to the end. And thus this likeness of effects to natural causes is reduced, as to its first principle, to some certain intellect.

"But it is not necessary, however, that it be reduced to other, separated forms, since there suffices for the aforesaid likeness that there be the aforesaid direction to the end, by which natural powers are directed by the first intellect" (no. 233).

2) Mathematical entities. As for the mathematical entities, the separated numbers, which Plato posited as intermediate between sensible things and the species, they too are posited as the principles of things in an oversimplified way. Thus unity is considered as constituting point; two, line; three, surface; four, body. Conversely, bodies are composed out of surfaces, surfaces out of lines, lines out of points, and points from unities, which constitute the numbers.

From the viewpoint of matter, magnitudes are constituted from lines, themselves composed from the drawn-out and the short, since the principles of all things are contraries. Since line is the first of the continuous quantities, to it first of all the great and the small were attributed, in order that, since these two are the principles of line, they may also be the principles of that which is subsequently constituted from line. But just as Plato produced everything by extension from points, so also he should have shown out of what points were produced, but this is not explained.

b. As to the First Causes of Things

In general, speaking of the principles of things, the Platonists omitted to speak of all the causes, omitting, for example, the efficient cause which is the cause of change. The species were posited as formal causes—yet they were not, since they were other than the substance of the thing, and separated from it. Likewise the final cause was not touched upon, yet it is because of this cause that every agent acting by intellect and by nature operates.

The Platonists thereby treated natural things as though they were mathematical things, omitting both the principle and the end of motion, the efficient and the final causes. An immutable species of the reality of motion would be an impossibility. Hence there is no explanation of motion nor assigned cause of it.

Insofar as the process of learning is concerned, if the species as ideas are the natures of all knowable things, and they are considered to be innately in us according to Platonic doctrines, then one does not learn anything. This ready-made knowledge which we remember is obviously not a fact. On the contrary, we clearly do not know those things we have not derived from sensible experience.

Chapter 5

The Human Being and Knowledge of Truth

(*Metaphysics*, II)

A. The human being and knowledge of truth
  1. Easy
     a. Everyone can speak some truth
     b. Everyone can benefit from combined efforts of all
     c. Everyone knows first principles
  2. Difficult
     a. On the part of things
     b. On our part
B. The knowledge of truth belongs chiefly to first philosophy
  1. Because it is speculative
  2. Because it treats first causes
C. The fitting manner of considering the truth
  1. The role of temperament and habit
     a. Let's be mathematical
     b. Draw me a picture
     c. Quote me an authority
     d. Show me appropriate certitude
     e. Let's not worry about small details
  2. Consideration proportionate to matter
     a. The general method found in logic
     b. An appropriate method for each science

The Human Being and Knowledge of Truth
(*Metaphysics*, II)

A. The human being and knowledge of truth
B. The knowledge of truth belongs chiefly to first philosophy
C. The fitting manner of considering the truth

Each of the particular sciences considers a certain particular truth concerning a determinate genus of being. Thus geometry is concerned with the magnitudes or sizes of things, arithmetic with numbers. But first philosophy considers the universal truth of things. Therefore it pertains to this science to inquire into the relationship between the human being and the knowledge of the truth.

A. The Human Being and Knowledge of Truth

The consideration of the truth is in a way easy; in another way it is hard.

1. Easy
a. Everyone Can Speak Some Truth

"[This ease is evident] first by this sign: that although no man may attain to a perfect knowledge of truth, nevertheless no man is so ignorant of the truth as not to know something of the truth. This appears from the fact that each one is able to enunciate something concerning the truth and nature of things, which ability is a sign of interior consideration.

b. Everyone Can Benefit from Combined Efforts of All

"Although that which one man is able to put out or add to the knowledge of truth by his labor and genius may be something small in comparison to the total consideration of truth, nevertheless that which is collected together out of all that which has been 'co-articulated,' i.e., searched out and collected, is made into something great, as may be seen in the various arts, which, through the labors and ingenuity of different men, have attained to a marvelous increase.

c. Everyone Knows First Principles

"In the consideration of the truth...those things through which one enters into the knowledge of other things are known to all, and none is deceived concerning them. Such are the first principles which are naturally known, as the principle that one cannot simultaneously affirm and deny [the same], and that every whole is greater than its part, and like things. Concerning the conclusions, however, into which, through such principles as through a door, one enters, it occurs often that one should err.

"The knowledge of the truth is, therefore, easy insofar, namely, as at least this small part which is the self-evident principle, through which one enters into the truth, is self-evident to all" (nos. 275-77).

2. Difficult

The difficulty in the consideration of the truth arises out of the fact that, concerning the truth, we cannot simultaneously have the whole and its part. In other words, we have to go either from the whole to a knowledge of the parts, from the composite and confused to the simple elements (the way of resolution) or from the parts to a knowledge of the whole, from the simple to the composite (the way of composition). In this process of going from one thing to another, we are impeded either by a deficiency on the part of the things to be known, or by a deficiency on the part of our intellect—just as a piece of wood may fail to burn either because it is wet, or because we do not have a strong enough flame.

a. On the Part of Things

Insofar as the difficulty on the part of things is concerned, there is the following consideration:

"Since each thing is knowable insofar as it is being in act,...those things which have deficient and imperfect being are, as to themselves, little knowable, as is the case with matter, motion, and time, because of their imperfection" (no. 280).

b. On Our Part

The principal source of difficulty is, however, on our part, as the following explanation shows:

"If the difficulty were principally on the part of things, it would then follow that we should know those things which are most knowable according to their nature. Now those things are most knowable according to their nature which are most in act, namely, immaterial and immobile things, which, nevertheless, are most unknown to us.

"Whence it is plain that the difficulty arises in the knowledge of the truth mostly because of the deficiency of our intellect. From which it comes about that the intellect of our soul is, in relation to immaterial things, which among all things are most manifest according to their nature, as are the eyes of bats to the light of day, which they cannot see, although they see dark things. And this is because of the weakness of their sight....

"Since the human soul is the last in the order of the intellective substances, it participates the least in intellective power. And just as according to nature it [the soul] is the act of the body, while the intellective power is not the act of a corporeal organ, so it [the soul with its intellect] has a natural aptitude for knowing the truth of corporeal and sensible things, which are actually less knowable according to their nature, because of their materiality, but nevertheless can be known through the abstraction of sensible things from phantasms.

"And since this mode of knowing the truth befits human nature accordingly as it is the form of such a body, and the things which are natural always remain, it is impossible for the human soul united to a body of this sort to know any more of the truth of things than that to which it can be lifted up through those things which it knows by abstracting from phantasms. It can in this way be in no way elevated to knowing the essences of immaterial substances, which are not proportioned to these sensible substances. Whence it is impossible that the soul united to such a body should apprehend the separated substances and know of them that which they are [i.e., their essences]" (nos. 282, 285).

B. The Knowledge of Truth Belongs Chiefly to First Philosophy
1. Because It Is Speculative

The knowledge of truth belongs to first philosophy or metaphysics because it is speculative, not practical.

"Theoretical, i.e., speculative [philosophy] differs from the practical as to its end. For the end of speculative philosophy is the truth: this indeed is what it intends, namely, the knowledge of the truth. But the end of practical [philosophy] is a work [or product, i.e., *opus*; hence the operative sciences], since even though 'practical' men, i.e., those who do something, intend to know the truth, as to how it is in certain things, they do not nevertheless seek it as the ultimate end. For they do not consider the cause of truth according to itself and because of itself, but rather order it to the end of the operation, or apply it to some determined particular thing, and some determinate time. If, therefore, in the light of these considerations we add that wisdom or first philosophy is not practical but speculative, it follows that it should rightly be called a science of truth" (no. 290).

2. Because It Treats First Causes

The knowledge of truth belongs chiefly to first philosophy among the speculative sciences because, among causes, it deals with first causes. The truth of the sciences comes from the causes they grasp. Other speculative sciences, such as geometry or arithmetic, grasp causes indeed, but it is first philosophy that considers first causes, and is therefore the science which is of the greatest truth.

Since it is the knowledge of causes which establishes the truth of things, it follows also that these very causes, as causes of truth, must themselves be true. Thus that which causes heat must itself be hot, i.e., have itself everything which it produces in another. Thus, too, the first causes will be most true.

In keeping with this, Aristotle makes an application to the causes of the heavenly bodies, namely, that these causes, as being causes of the immutable heavenly bodies, are most true:

"Hence the principles of eternal things [e.g., of the heavenly bodies] must always be most true (for they are not merely sometimes true, nor is there any cause of their being, but they themselves are the cause of the being of other things), so that as each thing is in respect of being, so it is in respect of truth" (c.2).

Aquinas here draws attention to the very important fact that Aristotle is in this place assigning a cause to the heavenly bodies, themselves the supreme bodies of the universe. Consequently, for him the universe is not the beginning of all things and divine, but it has a cause, namely, God:

"He [Aristotle] further concludes that the principles of those things which are always, namely, of the heavenly bodies, are necessarily most true, And this is for a twofold reason.

"It is so first of all because they are not 'sometimes true and sometimes not,' and thus they transcend in truth generable and corruptible things, which sometimes are and sometimes are not.

"Secondly this is so because nothing is a cause to them but they are the cause of being to others. And because of this they transcend in truth and being even the heavenly bodies which, although they are incorruptible, nevertheless do have a cause not only as to their motion, as certain have held, but also as to their being, as the Philosopher here expressly states.

"And this is necessarily so, since it is necessary that all composite things and participating things be reduced, as to their causes, to these things which have existence essentially. But all corporeal things are being in act insofar as they participate certain forms. Whence it is necessary that separated substance, which is form essentially, be the principle of corporeal substance.

"If, therefore, we add to this deduction that first philosophy considers first causes, it follows, as was had before, that it considers those things which are most true. Whence it is chiefly the science of truth" (nos. 295-97).

In the same vein one sees that as things are in being, so they are in truth. Thus, as a cause must have being in a more eminent way to cause the being of another, so a cause must have truth in a more eminent way to cause the truth of another. Likewise, as a thing is, i.e., mutable or immutable, so also will its truth be.

"From these considerations he [Aristotle] infers a certain corollary. For since it comes about that those things which are to others the cause of their being must be themselves most true, it follows that each thing, as it is to the fact of being, so likewise it is to the fact of having truth. For of those things whose being is not always in the same way, neither does their truth always remain. And those things whose being has a cause, likewise have a cause of their truth.

"And this [connection between being and truth] is so because the being of a thing is the cause of the true estimate which the mind has of the thing. For true and false are not in things but in the mind, as is stated in Book VI" (no. 298).

C. The Fitting Manner of Considering the Truth
1. The Role of Temperament and Habit

The consideration of the truth by a human being is closely linked with his habitual outlook. In other words we are inclined to believe those things which concord with our usual ideas, disbelieve those things which go against them. Thus we willingly believe good of our friends and are disinclined to believe evil of them—while acting conversely toward those we dislike. We are, then, influenced by our natures, and by those habits of thinking which have become like second natures. Thus, if people have acquired certain superstitions from childhood, such as those concerning black cats across one's path, or Fridays which fall on the thirteenth of the month, they are inclined to think according to them despite what reason says. The following are certain large categories of the human being's ways of thinking:

a. Let's Be Mathematical

"He [Aristotle] says that there are certain ones who do not accept what is said to them unless it is stated in a mathematical way. And this indeed befits, because of custom, those who have been brought up in mathematics. And since custom is like nature, this may likewise happen to some because of an indisposition, namely, to those who are of a strong imagination, not having a very elevated intellect.

b. Draw Me a Picture

"But there are others who do not want to accept anything unless there is proposed to them some sensible example, either because of custom or because of the dominion of the sensitive power in them and the weakness of the intellect.

c. Quote Me an Authority

"Others still are those who do not consider anything worth being presented to them without the testimony of a poet or some author. And this is also because of custom or because of a deficiency of judgment, since they cannot judge themselves whether an argument concludes with certitude, and therefore, as though not trusting their judgment, they seek the judgment of some notable.

d. Show Me Appropriate Certitude

"There are also some who wish all things to be stated to them with certitude, i.e., through a diligent inquiry of reason. And this occurs because of the goodness of an intellect which judges and seeks reasons, provided it does not seek certitude in those things in which certitude cannot be.

e. Let's Not Worry about Small Details

"There are some also who are saddened if anything is sought with certitude by diligent examination. And this can come about in two ways. One way can be because of impotency to understand: for such have a weak reason; whence they are not able to consider the order of the sequence of prior and posterior things. Another way can be because of micrology, i.e., reasoning on small things [i.e., they do not like to go into detail]. There is a certain likeness of this in an inquiry demanding certitude, and which leaves nothing unquestioned down to the smallest things. Now some imagine that just as in the reunions of diners it does not pertain to liberality to count even the smallest things in the reckoning, so too it betokens a certain importunity and illiberality should a man wish to discuss even the smallest thing in the knowledge of the truth" (no. 334).

2. Consideration Proportionate to Matter

The question of the fitting manner of considering the truth is proportionate to the matter one is studying. How can one know the fitting
manner for each science? Logic in general teaches the general method,
with each science at the beginning stating its own specific procedure.

a. The General Method Found in Logic

"Since different men look for the truth in different ways, it is necessary that a man be instructed as to which way, in each of the sciences,
those things are to be taken which are stated. And since it is not easy
for a man to grasp two things at once, but rather, while he pays attention to two things, he is able to grasp neither, it is absurd that a man
should simultaneously seek science, and the manner which befits science. And because of this he should learn logic before the other sciences, since logic transmits the common manner of procedure in all the
other sciences. But the mode which is proper to each of the sciences
should be transmitted in each science around the beginning" (no. 335).

b. An Appropriate Method for Each Science

Each of the sciences follows the method appropriate to the subject
treated:

1. metaphysics: most certain in itself, least attained by us;
2. mathematics: abstract, yet proportioned to us;
3. natural philosophy or physics: of variable things, true for the
   most part.

"Diligent and certain argument, such as is had in mathematics,
should not be sought in all things concerning which there are sciences,
but should be sought solely in those which do not have matter. For
those which do have matter are subject to motion and variation, and
therefore there cannot be had absolute certitude in all of them. For one
seeks in them not what is always and with necessity, but what is for the
most part. Immaterial things, however, are most certain in themselves,
since they are immobile.

"But those things which are immaterial in their nature, are not certain to us, because of the deficiency of our intellect, as was said before. Such are the separated substances.

"But mathematical things are abstracted from matter, and nevertheless they do not exceed our intellect; and therefore in them most certain argument is to be demanded. And since the whole of nature is concerned with matter, therefore this manner of most certain argument does not pertain to the natural philosopher [in all things]" (no. 336).

Chapter 6

The Subject of Metaphysics
(*Metaphysics*, IV, cc.1-2)

A. The subject is being and its per se accidents
B. The being studied is primarily substance
    1. Analogical predication in general
    2. As applied to being
    3. Metaphysics considers being analogically
    4. Substance is the prime analogate in being
C. This science also considers unity and its species
D. The sequence for studying being and one
E. The one that is two
F. How dialectics and sophistry treat being
G. Conclusion: scope of first philosophy

The Subject of Metaphysics
(*Metaphysics*, IV, cc.1-2)

A. The subject is being and its per se accidents
B. The being studied is primarily substance
C. This science also considers unity and its species
D. The sequence for studying being and one
E. The one that is two
F. How dialectics and sophistry treat being
G. Conclusion: scope of first philosophy

After an examination in the previous chapter of the human being's relationship to truth, it is now fitting to begin to examine the truth of things. As already stated there, one must first of all in each science consider the way in which that science proceeds, i.e., state its subject-matter, and the problems it has to solve, since the progress of a science is nothing other than progress in solving the problems laid out.

A. The Subject Is Being and Its Per Se Accidents

The subject of this science is being as being, and likewise the per se accidents of being as being, i.e., the accidents which belong to being as being. One of these is unity: everything that is being, is also one.

Other sciences are also of being, but of some particular being, for example, number, line, body, and so forth. This science is of being as it is being. Furthermore, this science is of those things which are in being per se. Thus the geometrician considers those things which are in triangle per se, such as to have interior angles equal to two right angles, and not those things which belong to it per accidens, such as that the triangle be made of wood or copper.

This science, therefore, does not consider all the things which are in being in the accidental order, because it would then consider the accidents sought in all the other sciences. All accidents, indeed, are in some being, but nevertheless not necessarily in it as it is being.

"For those things which are the per se accidents of the lower, are accidental to the higher, just as the per se accidents of man are not the per se accidents of animal. [Lower and higher here denote the logical order between species and genus, not an order of nature.]

"Now the necessity for this science which considers being and the per se accidents of being is apparent from the fact that such things as these should not remain unknown, since upon them depends the knowledge of other things, as upon the knowledge of common things depends the knowledge of proper things" (no. 531).

Hence this science seeks the first principles and the causes of being universally speaking, of being as being.

B. The Being Studied Is Primarily Substance

Although this science considers all being as such, and therefore both substance and accident, nevertheless it is primarily of substance, as being that to which the analogy of being, embracing everything that is being, is primarily reduced, as to the prime analogate.

1. Analogical Predication in General

"Whatever things receive the common predication of some one thing, even though not univocally so, but it is predicated of them analogically, pertain to the consideration of one science. But being is predicated in this way of all beings. Therefore all beings pertain to the consideration of one science which considers being insofar as it is being, namely, both substances and accidents....

"...Being, or that which is, is said in many ways. In keeping with this one must also realize that something is predicated of different things in many ways. Sometimes, indeed, it is predicated according to a notion which is absolutely the same; and then it is said to be predicated of them univocally, as *animal* is of horse and ox. But sometimes also according to notions that are wholly diverse; and then it is said to be predicated of them equivocally, as *dog* of the star and of the animal. Sometimes, too, according to notions which are in part diverse and in part not diverse. They are diverse in that they imply different relationships; but they are one in that these different relationships are referred to some one and the same thing. This then is said to be analogical, i.e., proportionate, predication, accordingly as each thing is referred, according to its own relationship, to that one.

"Likewise it should be understood that that one to which the diverse relationships are referred in analogical things is one in number, and not only one in notion, which latter is true of that one which is designated by a univocal name. And therefore he [Aristotle] says that being, even though it be said in many ways, nevertheless is not said equivocally, but with respect to one; and this indeed not to a one which is solely one as to notion, but which is one as a one certain nature. And this is evident in the examples given below.

"For he [Aristotle] lays down first an example where many are compared to one as to an end, as is evident in the case of the name *healthful* or *salubrious*. For *healthful* is not said univocally of a diet, medicine, urine, and an animal. For the notion of healthy as it is said of a diet, consists in the preserving of health. But as it is said of medicine, in the producing of health. While as it is said of urine, it is as of a sign of health. But accordingly as it is said of animal, its notion is of that which is receptive to, or disposed for, health. Thus, therefore, all that which is healthful or healthy is said in reference to one and the same health. For it is the same health which the animal receives, the urine signifies, the medicine causes, and the diet maintains.

"Secondly, he [Aristotle] gives the example of when many are compared to one as to the efficient principle. For something is called medicative, as indicating one having the art of medicine, e.g., an experienced doctor. Something could be called thus too because it is well disposed to having the art of medicine, as are men who are disposed in such a way that they may easily acquire the art of medicine. Hence, some by their own talent carry out certain medicinal procedures. Something else is called medicative or medicinal because it is necessary for medicine, as the instruments which doctors use may be called medicinal, and also the medicines which they use for restoring health. And likewise other things, similar to these, may be taken which are said in many ways" (nos. 534-38).

2. As Applied to Being

"And as it is with the aforesaid, so also being is said in many ways. Yet every being is said with respect to one first being. But this first is not the end or the efficient cause, as in the previous examples, but the subject.

"For some things are called being or are said to be, because they have being per se, as in the case of substances, which are principally and in a prior way called beings.

"But other things are so called because they are the passions or properties of substance, as are the per se accidents of each substance.

"Still other things are called beings because they are the way to substance, as are generations and motion.

"Other things again are called beings because they are the corruptions of substance. For corruption is the way to nonbeing, just as generation is the way to substance. And since corruption terminates at privation, as does generation at form, the privations of substantial forms are fittingly said to be.

"And likewise qualities or certain other accidents are called beings, since they are active or generative in respect to substance or those things which, according to some relationship of the aforesaid, are referred to substance, or according to any other way.

"Likewise the negations of those things which have a relationship to substance, or even of substance itself, are said to be. Whence we say that nonbeing is nonbeing, which would not be said unless being could in some way be said of negation.

"It should be understood, nevertheless, that the aforesaid modes of being can be reduced to four:

1. "For the one of them which is weakest is in the reason alone, namely, negation and privation, which are said to be in the reason since reason treats of them as though of certain beings, when it affirms or denies something of them. In what negation and privation differ, however, will be said below.
2. "Another which is near to this in weakness is the manner in which generation and corruption and motion are called beings. For they have something admixed of privation and negation. For motion is imperfect act, as stated in *Physics* III.
3. "A third is stated which has no admixture of nonbeing, but nevertheless it has a weak being, because existing not of itself but in another, as is the case with qualities, quantities, and the properties of substance.
4. "But the fourth genus is that which is most perfect, which, namely, has being in nature without the admixture of privation,

and has a firm and solid being, as though existing of itself, as is the case with substances. And to this being, as to the first and principal, all the others are referred. For qualities and quantities are said to be insofar as they are in substance; motion and generations insofar as they tend to substance or to one of the aforesaid; but privations and negations insofar as they remove any of the three aforesaid" (nos. 539-43).

3. Metaphysics Considers Being Analogically

"It belongs to one science to consider not only these things which are said 'according to one,' i.e., according to one notion which is wholly the same [i.e., univocal], but also those things which are said with respect to one nature according to different relationships [i.e., analogically]. And the reason for this is because of the unity of that to which these are referred; just as it is evident that one science, namely, medical science, considers all healing things." (no. 544).

4. Substance Is the Prime Analogate in Being

"Each science which is of several things which are said with respect to one first thing is properly and principally of that first thing upon which the others depend according to being, and because of which they are named as they are. And this is universally true. But substance is this first thing among all beings. Therefore the philosopher, who considers all beings, should have first and principally before him in his consideration the principles and causes of substances. Therefore, consequently, this science's consideration is first and principally of substances....

"...All substances, insofar as they are beings or substances, pertain to the consideration of this science. But insofar as they are such-and-such a substance, such as lion or ox, they pertain to the special sciences" (nos. 546-47).

C. This Science Also Considers Unity and Its Species

One and being signify one nature according to different notions or reasons. That is, they are not synonymous, as are *clothing* and *raiment,* which are said of the same thing. Rather they represent two different aspects of a same thing.

Although being and one refer to different aspects, they are nevertheless both identical with the one same thing to which they are referred. This is shown by the fact that to say *a man*, and *a being which is a man*, denotes the same thing. This same is true if one should say *a being which is a man* and *one man*. (Note how in French *un homme* means both a man and one man.) Likewise a man is generated and corrupted, but that which is generated and corrupted is always a being and also one being. Thus, by the addition of the note of being or one, no new nature is added to man.

But being and one differ as to notion; otherwise they would be wholly synonymous. They are not, however. The name *being* is imposed as denoting the act of existing, while the name *one* refers to indivision. (For one is being which is undivided.)

Now it is the same thing which has being, and an essence through that being, and is undivided in itself. Whence these three names, *thing* (as signifying an essence), *being*, and *one*, signify absolutely the same thing, but according to different notions.

Insofar as being is concerned, it means the thing itself, even though the existence of the thing, which makes it a being, is different from its essence. For being thus applied does not signify something superadded after the manner of an accident, but rather as constituted out of the principles of the essence. It is the essence gone from potency to act.

Insofar as one is concerned, this is not the one which is the principle of number. For nothing which is in a determinate genus follows upon all beings. Whence that one which is determined to a special genus of being, namely, to the genus of discrete quantity, is not seen as being able to be converted with universal being.

"The one, therefore, which is the principle of number, is other than that one which is converted with being.

"For the one which is convertible with being designates the being itself, adding, over and above, the notion of indivision which, since it is a negation or privation, does not posit any nature added to being. And thus it in no way differs from being according to reality, but solely according to reason. For negation or privation are not beings of nature, but of reason, as was said.

"But the one which is the principle of number adds, over and above substance, the notion of measure, which is the proper passion of quantity, and is found first in unity. And it is said by way of the privation or negation which is according to continuous quantity. For number is caused out of the division of the continuum. And therefore number belongs to mathematical science, whose subject cannot be outside of matter" (no. 560).

D. The Sequence for Studying Being and One

Since first philosophy—or simply philosophy as being the philosophy par excellence, dealing with first causes—is primarily concerned with being and one as said of substance, it follows that there will be as many parts of this philosophy as there are of substance, and which are, namely, that dealing with material, and that dealing with immaterial, substance.

"Since the parts of substance are ordered in respect to each other, immaterial substance being naturally prior to sensible substance [i.e., with a priority of nature, as man is prior to animal], it is therefore necessary that among the parts of philosophy [following the division of substance] there be some first.

"That part, nevertheless, which is concerned with sensible substance is first in the order of learning, since we must begin learning from the things which are more known to us (and concerning this substance it is determined in *Metaphysics* VII and VIII).

"But that part which is of immaterial substance is prior in dignity and intention (concerning which it is treated in *Metaphysics* XII).

"Nevertheless, whatever is first, it is necessarily continuous with the other parts, since all the parts have as their genus, one and being. Whence it is in the consideration of one and being that the different parts of this science are united, although they be of different parts of substance" (no. 563).

E. The One That Is Two

The unity which is convertible with being, by which every being is one, must not be confused with that one which is the principle of number (as in the sequence 1, 2, 3 . . .).

"One implies the privation of division, not of the division which is according to quantity; for that division is determined to one particular genus of being and cannot fall in the definition of one.

"But the one which is convertible with being implies the privation of formal division as this is brought about through opposites—the prime root of which is the opposition of affirmation and negation. For those things are divided from each other which are such that this is not that.

"First, therefore, one understands being itself, and then consequently nonbeing, and then division, and then consequently one which removes division, and then consequently multitude, in the notion of which falls division (just as indivision does in the notion of one). Several things divided in the aforesaid way cannot, however, fulfill the notion of multitude unless first to each of the divided things there is attributed the notion of one" (no. 566).

F. How Dialectics and Sophistry Treat Being

A sign that it belongs to the first philosopher or metaphysician to consider being and the common accidents of being lies in the fact that both the dialectician and the sophist, who have a certain resemblance to the first philosopher, treat of them:

"Now they [the first philosopher and the dialectician] agree in this, that it belongs to the dialectician to consider all things. But this could not be unless he were to consider all things accordingly as they come together under one heading; since of one science there is one subject, and of one art there is one matter concerning which it is operative. Since, therefore, all things do not agree except in being, it is plain that the matter of dialectics is being, and those things which belong to being, concerning which the first philosopher also considers.

"Likewise sophistics has a certain likeness to [first] philosophy. For sophistics is 'seeming,' or apparent, wisdom, not being really so. But that which has the appearance of some thing must have some likeness to it. And therefore it is necessary that the philosopher, the dialectician, and the sophist consider the same things.

"Nevertheless, each differs from the other. The philosopher differs from the dialectician according to power. For the consideration of the philosopher is of greater power than that of the dialectician. This is because the philosopher proceeds concerning the aforesaid things demonstratively. And therefore it belongs to him to have science concerning the aforesaid, and he knows them with certitude. For certain knowledge or science is the effect of demonstration. But the dialectician proceeds concerning all the aforesaid things from probable bases, whence he does not produce science, but a certain opinion.

"The reason for this is because being is twofold: namely, the being of reason and the being of nature. Now the being of reason is said properly of these intentions which reason finds in the things considered, such as are the intentions of genus, of species, and such like things [e.g., the predicables or ways of predicating], which, indeed, are not found in the nature of things, but are consequent upon the consideration of reason. And such things, namely, the beings of reason, are properly the subject of logic.

"But such intelligible intentions are equated to the beings of nature, by virtue of the fact that all the beings of nature fall under the consideration of reason. And therefore the subject of logic extends to all things, concerning which the being of nature is predicated. Whence he [Aristotle] concludes that the subject of logic is equated to the subject of philosophy, which is the being of nature. The philosopher, therefore, proceeds from the principles of this being to prove those things which should be considered concerning such common accidents of being [as one]. But the dialectician proceeds to their consideration from the intentions of reason, which are extraneous to the nature of things. And therefore it is said that the dialectician is tentative, since to attempt (*tentare*) is properly to proceed from extraneous principles.

"But the philosopher differs from the sophist...on the grounds of choice and pleasure, i.e., by what he desires in life. For the philosopher and the sophist order their life and actions to different things. The philosopher, indeed, orders his to knowing the truth; but the sophist to having the appearance of knowing, although he does not know" (nos. 572-75).

G. Conclusion: Scope of First Philosophy

"It is plain that it pertains to the one science to consider being as it is being, and those things which are in being per se. And from this it is evident that this science not only considers substances, but also accidents, since being is predicated of both. And it considers...the same [i.e., one in substance] and different; like [i.e., one in quality] and unlike; equal [i.e., one in quantity] and unequal; negation and privation and contraries—which we stated above to be the accidents of per se being [i.e., substance]. And not only does it consider these...but it also considers prior and posterior, genus and species, whole and part, and others of the sort, since these also are accidents of being as being" (no. 587).

Chapter 7

The First Principles of Demonstration
(*Metaphysics*, IV, cc.3-8)

A. Does the first philosopher treat these principles?
   1. How do other sciences treat of them?
   2. What are these first principles?
B. The absolutely first principle: contradiction
   1. Conditions of an absolutely first principle
   2. The principle itself
C. How defend this principle against deniers
   1. Those holding contradictories as simultaneously true
     a. General arguments
       1) What principle does one use against deniers?
       2) Various arguments against deniers
         a) Example showing all things must be one
         b) A sign from things sought and avoided
         c) Another sign: All things not equally false
     b. Special arguments for different cases
       1) Those who have doubts
         a) Leading to contradictories as simultaneously true
         b) Leading to whatever appears to be, to be true
           (1) Reasons for the doubt
             (a) The nature of the doubt
             (b) The causes of the doubt
           (2) Solution of the doubts
             (a) On mutability of sensible things
             (b) On belief that whatever appears is true
       2) Those who doubt whatever cannot be proved

2. Those holding contradictories as simultaneously false
3. Summation
   a. Generic causes of denial of first principles
   b. Origin of such denial
   c. Consequences of such denial
   d. Procedure against such denial

The First Principles of Demonstration
(*Metaphysics*, IV, cc.3-8)

A. Does the first philosopher treat these principles?
B. The absolutely first principle: contradiction
C. How defend this principle against deniers

A. Does the First Philosopher Treat These Principles?

The answer is in the affirmative, since these principles apply to all being, and not just to some particular category of being.

"Whatever things are in all being, and not in some separate genus of being only, such things pertain to the [first] philosopher. But the aforesaid principles are such. Therefore they pertain to the consideration of the philosopher....

"The reason why all the sciences use them he [Aristotle] assigns as follows, namely, because each subject genus receives the predication of being. Now the particular sciences use the aforesaid principles not according to their common note insofar as they extend to all beings, but so much as suffices for them, i.e., according to the genus which is the subject of the science, concerning which the science brings demonstrations. Thus natural philosophy uses them as they extend to mobile beings, and not beyond.

"[A sign that this consideration belongs to first philosophy is that] no one intending to transmit from the start the science of some particular being has attempted to say anything concerning the first principles, as to whether they are true or not. Neither the geometer nor the arithmetician has done so, even though they use these principles more than any other....Whence it is evident that the consideration of the aforesaid principles belongs to this science" (nos. 590-92).

1. How Do Other Sciences Treat of Them?

Actually, even though it belongs properly to first philosophy or metaphysics to treat, as the science of being in common, of the principles common to all the sciences, nevertheless, both physicists and mathematicians often do treat *ex professo* of such principles as *Being is not nonbeing*, and *The whole is greater than the part*. Why is this? It is to the extent that they mistake their science as the ultimate science, mistake the being of their science as the ultimate in being.

"The ancients did not think there was any substance beyond corporeal mobile substance, concerning which the physicist treats. And therefore they believed that they alone were to determine concerning the whole of nature, and consequently concerning being—and thus also of the first principles which are to be considered together with being.

"But this is false, because there remains a science superior to natural science. For nature, i.e., the natural thing having in itself the principle of motion, is in itself one certain genus of universal being. But all being is not such, since it was proved in *Physics* VIII that there exists a certain immobile being.

"Now this immobile being is superior to, and more noble than, mobile being, concerning which natural science considers. And since it belongs to that science to consider being in common to which it pertains to consider the first being, therefore the consideration of being in common pertains to another science than natural science. And it will likewise belong to it to consider such common principles. For physics is a certain part of philosophy—but not the first, which considers being in common and those things which belong to being as such" (no. 593).

2. What Are These First Principles?

The first principles which are in the domain of first philosophy or metaphysics are the self-evident principles known to all, which are at the base of all our thinking.

"Self-evident propositions are those which are immediately known upon their terms being known. This occurs in those propositions in which the predicate is placed in the definition of the subject, or the predicate is the same as the subject.

"But it occurs that some proposition as to itself is self-evident; nevertheless it is not self-evident to all, namely, to those who ignore the definition of the predicate and the subject....

"But those things are self-evident to all whose terms fall upon the conception of all. Such things are the common things, since our knowledge arrives from the common to the proper, as is stated in *Physics* I. And therefore those propositions are the first principles of demonstration which are composed out of common terms, such as *whole* and *part* (e.g., *every whole is greater than its part*) and such as *equal* and *unequal* (e.g., *things equal to one and the same, are equal to each other*). And the same is true of similar things.

"Now since such common terms belong to the consideration of the philosopher, so these principles belong to the consideration of the philosopher. But the philosopher determines them not by demonstration, but by showing the notions of the terms, as, for example, what *whole* is and what *part* is, and so of the others. But once this is known, the truth of the aforesaid principles becomes manifest" (no. 595).

B. The Absolutely First Principle: Contradiction

Among all the first principles which the first philosopher must examine and defend, clearly that must come first in his consideration which is the principle upon which all others depend, and which, since certitude is reduced back to the certitude of one's principles, must be the most certain of all.

1. Conditions of an Absolutely First Principle

What must be the characteristics of this most certain principle? They are three:

"The first condition is that one must not be able to lie or err concerning it. And this is evident, because, since men are only deceived concerning that which they do not know, then that concerning which one cannot be deceived, must be most known.

"The second condition is that it be 'not conditional,' i.e., not held by virtue of any supposition, as are those things which are laid down by some kind of agreement....And this is so because that which must be had by anyone understanding any beings whatsoever 'is not conditional,' i.e., is not a supposition, but must be self-evident.

"The third condition is that it be not acquired through demonstration, or by any other like manner, but that it come as though by nature to the one having it, as though it were naturally known and not acquired. For from the very natural light of the agent intellect, first principles are made known; and they are not acquired through reasoning, but solely by virtue of the fact of their terms being made known.

"This indeed comes about through the fact that from sensible things there is had memory, and from memory experience, and from experience the knowledge of those terms which, once they are known, there are known those common propositions which are the principles of the arts and sciences. It is plain, therefore, that the most certain principle, or the most firm, must be such that one cannot err concerning it, that it not be supposed, and that it come about naturally" (nos. 597-99).

2. The Principle Itself

What is this most certain and firm principle to which these characteristics belong? It is the principle *It is impossible for the same thing to be and not be true of the same thing* with the addition *under the same aspect*—and any other qualifications necessary to exclude apparent difficulties. It is impossible for anyone to think that the same thing both is and is not, although one can say it, as Heraclitus did.

This principle is likewise clearly not from any supposition, whereas all other principles suppose it.

"Since the operation of the intellect is twofold, namely, that one by which it knows what something is, and which is called the understanding of indivisibles [simple apprehension], and that other by which it composes and divides [judgment, followed by reasoning], in both of these there is a beginning.

"In the first operation of the intellect, indeed, there is a certain first thing which falls upon the conception of the intellect, namely, that which I call *being*. Nor can anything be conceived by the mind in this operation without understanding being.

"And since the principle *It is impossible to be and not be at the same time* depends upon the understanding of being, as the principle *Every whole is greater than its part* does upon the understanding of whole and part, therefore this principle [*It is impossible for the same thing to be and not be at the same time*] is naturally first in the second operation of the intellect, namely, that of the intellect composing and dividing.

"Nor can anyone understand anything according to this operation of the intellect unless this principle has been understood. For just as whole and parts are not understood unless being is understood, neither is this principle *Every whole is greater than its part* understood unless the aforesaid most firm principle has been understood" (no. 605).

C. How Defend This Principle against Deniers

Plainly this first principle of all *It is impossible for a thing both to be and not be* cannot be demonstrated or proved from some higher principle, since it is the first of all, and presupposed to all others.

"If anyone should wish to demonstrate absolutely the aforesaid principle, he would seem to beg the principle, since nothing can be taken for its demonstration except things which would depend upon the truth of this principle, as is evident from what has been previously said" (no. 609).

Rather, the principle of contradiction is defended against its deniers, not directly from some other principle, but by showing the fallaciousness of arguments brought against it.

Those who implicitly or explicitly deny the principle of contradiction are those who affirm contradictories to be simultaneously true, or those who affirm them to be simultaneously false (i.e., affirm a middle between two contradictories).

1. Those Holding Contradictories As Simultaneously True
a. General Arguments

1) What principle does one use against deniers? If someone does not admit the principle of contradiction, namely, that a thing must either be or not be, and not both simultaneously, one cannot use this principle in convincing him, but one must use something else that is admitted—even though in reality what is admitted be actually less evident than the principle of contradiction, provided that it be admitted.

"[In refuting all such opinable things] one cannot take as a principle that someone is willing to suppose something 'to be' determinately or 'not be,' i.e., one cannot take as a principle some proposition which would assert something of a thing or deny it of it, for this would be to beg the principle, as was said. But it is necessary to take for a principle that a name means something, both to him who expresses it, insofar as he understands himself speaking, and to him who hears him.

"But if someone should not concede this, then such a one will not have something to say, either to himself or to another. Whence it will be superfluous to dispute with him.

"But if he does concede it, there will be immediately a demonstration against him: for there is immediately able to be found something which is defined and determined, which is signified by a name, and which is distinct from its contradictory, as will be evident below.

"Nevertheless, this will not demonstrate the aforesaid principle absolutely speaking, but it will be solely an argument sustaining it against those who deny it. For he who 'destroys meaning,' i.e., his speech, by saying that a name means nothing, has really to maintain it since the very thing which he denies he cannot express unless by speaking and meaning something" (no. 611).

2) Various arguments against deniers. Those who deny first principles, and in particular the principle of contradiction, and wish to say that a thing can both be and not be at the same time and under the same aspect, and that therefore the same thing may be truly both affirmed and denied of something, find themselves in certain inextricable self-contradictions. The defense of the principle of contradiction does not, in effect, consist in proving it, since it is itself the most evident of all principles and there is none more evident than itself from which it might conceivably be demonstrated. On the contrary, just as all concepts involve the general concept of being, so too all principles involve previous acceptance of the principle *It is impossible for the same thing both to be and not be.*

The defense of this principle consists, then, in showing that it is impossible not to hold it, no matter what one says, and that one cannot contradict it without at the same time denying one's own contradiction. All the arguments in defense of the principle will be seen to hinge on the acknowledgment of the fact that one's words mean something: if they do, then it is impossible for one to use them to deny the principle of contradiction; if they do not, then it is not logical for one to speak.

a) Example showing all things must be one. As an example of what far-reaching absurdities one gets oneself into by trying to maintain that affirmation and negation about a same thing may be equally true, one may cite the result that then all things must be one! How is this so? Supposing that it is true to say of someone that he is man, then he is also nonman. But if the denial of himself is true of him, the denial of other things must be even more true. Therefore one can say that this man is nonman—and also nonelephant. But if the denial of elephant is true of him, then also the affirmation of elephant is—since denials and affirmations are equally true. Therefore *Man is elephant* is true, and likewise *Man is mountain* and *Man is flower* and so forth. Thus, since everything may be predicated of everything, all things must be one and the same.

   b) **A sign from things sought and avoided.** On the other hand, a sign that we do not for one minute consider all things to be the same, may be seen from the things which we seek and avoid. In effect, if all things were the same, all equally true, one would then ask a professor why he went home for supper, since *to go home for supper* and *not to go home for supper* are one and the same. It would be useless to ask whether one liked one's steak rare or medium, whether one desired one teaspoonful of sugar or two in one's tea—since to have one's steak rare or not to have it so would be the same thing anyway; to have one teaspoonful of sugar, or not to have one (i.e., to have none or to have three) would all be the same thing. Obviously, someone engaged in strenuously defending the thesis that affirmations and negations are equally true, and who would in an intermission have the occasion to go out for lunch, would tolerate no such nonsense on the part of a philosophically-inclined waiter.

   c) **Another sign: All things not equally false.** Another point that might be presented is, even on the supposition that all things are equally true and false, that some things would be considered more true or more false than others. In effect, one would not consider it equally true to say that two was even and that three was even; nor would one consider it equally false to say four was five and four was one thousand. But some statements could not be considered more true than others, or more false than others, unless there were something absolutely true in comparison to which something would be more true and less false.

b. Special Arguments for Different Cases

   Actually all those who express doubts concerning first principles do not do so for the same reason: (1) Some do so because they have been confronted by certain sophistic arguments which they are unable to refute, and who consequently feel that they must accept their opponents' conclusion; (2) others do so by a certain rebelliousness, claiming the right to hold anything may be simultaneously true or false unless someone can prove that it cannot be.

"Certain people fall into the aforesaid positions [namely, that contradictories are true, and that consequently, since some men hold
something to be while others hold it not to be, things are as they appear
to each] in two ways.

"For some do so out of doubt. When they are confronted with certain sophistic arguments from which the aforesaid positions appear to
follow, and they are unable to resolve them [i.e., the arguments], they
concede the conclusion. Whence their ignorance is easily curable. For
they do not have to be opposed, nor does one have to meet the arguments they give, but rather one addresses himself to their mind, in order, namely, to dissipate the doubt from their mind through which they
have fallen into such opinions. And then they abandon such positions.

"But others pursue the aforesaid positions, not because of any doubt
which brings them to such, but solely 'for the sake of expression,' i.e.,
out of a certain impudence, wishing to hold such impossible arguments
for their own sake, since their contraries cannot be demonstrated. And
the remedy for these is argument or rebuttal 'which is in the statement
made,' i.e., through the fact that a statement uttered means something.
Now the significance of an utterance depends upon the significance of
words. And thus one must return to this principle, namely, that names
mean something, as the Philosopher made use of this above" (nos. 663-
64).

1) Those who have doubts.

a) <u>Leading to contradictories as simultaneously true.</u> How do
some people come about holding contradictories to be simultaneously
true? For some it arises out of sensible things, in which there is generation and corruption and motion. How does it arise? They see that
from some one thing contraries arise—as, for example, out of water,
which extinguishes fire, comes oxygen, which nourishes it. Consequently, things must contain their contraries, and both be and not be,
for example, be inimical to fire, and not be inimical.

"What is produced, is produced out of something preexisting. For
that which is not cannot become, since nothing is produced from nothing. Therefore a thing would have to be with contradiction simultaneously within itself; since, if out of the same thing there is produced
both that which is hot and that which is cold, there is consequently produced that which is hot and that which is nonhot.

"Now because of this reason Anaxagoras stated that all things were
mixed into all things. For from the fact of seeing that anything was
made from anything, he thought that nothing could be produced from

something other unless it had already been there previously. And Democritus appears to have agreed with this reasoning. For he laid down that the void and the full were conjoined in every part of a body. These indeed are related as being and nonbeing. For the full is being, while the void is nonbeing" (nos. 665-66).

How does one solve this difficulty? First of all, it is not a difficulty arising out of willfulness, but a difficulty of the mind. Therefore one should clear up the difficulty in the mind, showing how in a way one speaks rightly and in a way one does not, because of not seeing the matter clearly.

"Those who opine the aforesaid unfitting things should be answered according to the mind. Therefore to those...who think contradictories to be simultaneously true for the above reason we say that in a way they speak rightly, and in a way they do not know what they are saying, speaking unfittingly.

"For being is said in two ways: being in act and being in potency. When, therefore, they say that being is not produced from nonbeing, in a way they speak the truth, and in a way not. For being is produced from nonbeing in act, yet being in potency.

"Whence also in one way the same thing can be both being and nonbeing simultaneously, and in a way it cannot. For it occurs that the same thing is [two] contraries in potency, but nevertheless not 'perfectly,' i.e., in act. For thus lukewarm is in potency both hot and cold, yet neither in act" (no. 667).

b) Leading to whatever appears to be, to be true.

(1) Reasons for the doubt.

(a) *The nature of the doubt.* What causes some to hold that whatever appears to be, must be true? Their reasoning is as follows, based, as previously, on sensible things. In effect, men are found to have contrary opinions concerning the same sensible things. For example, what seems sweet to some, is bitter to others. Likewise what seems tasty to a cow, such as hay, does not seem tasty to us. Even to the same man things which ordinarily have a distinct taste may seem tasteless when he has a cold.

In all this variety, how can one tell what is the true opinion and what is the false one, as in the case when one person says the soup is salty and another says that it is not? The one has no more right to affirm his opinion than the other. Therefore, either both opinions are true, or both are false, since the reasons for holding them both or rejecting them both are equally valid in both cases.

Therefore, Democritus decided that either there was nothing determinately true in things, or that if there were, it was not manifest to us, since we receive knowledge of things through the senses, and the judgment of the senses is not certain.

What of the solution that one will take as the true judgment of the senses that which is the judgment of those in good health, and as the true judgment of the truth that which is the judgment of those wise and intelligent? This seems to be somewhat like legislating the truth, making it depend on a variable majority, or on a specialized vote. Since opinions differ at different times, as was the case concerning the advisability of Prohibition, then, in effect, what is true and good at one time, can become false and evil at another—by vote.

(b) The causes of the doubt. The cause of the doubt may be on the part of the *senses*. The basic thinking behind such a doubt is the thinking which sees no difference between sense and intellect. The predecessors of Aristotle did not at first distinguish between sense and intellect. Consequently, things were true as they appeared to the senses. Thus, if the sense should err concerning one of the common sensibles, such as motion or number, for example, thinking a train to be moving when it is not, or that one is touching several things when in reality one is touching only one; or if the sense should be indisposed and give a different judgment than usual—all this led to saying that one could do no better than to say that things were as they appeared at the present moment.

Thus, for Empedocles, if a man's physical complexion changed, his judgment of things changed with it. Today this opinion would be held under the form of saying that as man's intelligence evolves, he will see things in a different light from that in which he sees them now—and that all truth is, therefore, a provisional, changing thing. Parmenides seems to have felt the same as Empedocles. Anaxagoras, likewise, appears to have held that things were as one received them. Homer depicts Hector as seeing things one way when whole, in another way when wounded and delirious. All of which opinions make the pursuit of some determined truth an illusory enterprise.

The cause of the doubt may be on the part of *sensible things* themselves. How do sensible things lend themselves to this outlook? It is because of the presence in them of matter, which of itself is not determined to one particular form, causing the knowledge of sensible things to be proportionately mutable and indeterminate. Nevertheless it is not true to say that there is nothing determinate in sensible things.

"For although matter of itself is undetermined in relation to many different forms, through form it is determined to one mode of being. Whence, since things are known through their form more than through matter, one should not say that a certain determinate knowledge of things cannot be had" (no. 682).

Another reason for holding for the mutability of all knowledge is because sensible nature appeared to be in motion, and, as such, impossible to be stated in any fixed, definitive way. How far did this opinion lead?

"Cratylus held this opinion [attributed first to Heraclitus, that all things were in motion and that consequently nothing could be determinately true], who eventually came to the madness of opining that one should not say anything by a word, but in order to express what he wished, he moved only his finger. And he did this because he believed that the truth of the thing which he wished to enunciate had already passed away before he could finish his statement. But he could move his finger in a shorter time. This same Cratylus reprehended or scolded Heraclitus. For Heraclitus had said that a man cannot enter twice into the same river, since before he can enter a second time, the water which was in the river has already flowed on. But he [Cratylus] considered that a man cannot even enter once into the same river, since before he can even enter once, the water of the river has flowed on and other water has taken its place. And thus not only a man cannot speak twice of some thing before its disposition be changed, but he cannot even speak once" (no. 684).

(2) Solution of the doubts.

(a) On mutability of sensible things. What is the correct approach toward the mutability of sensible things? The opinion that nothing definite can be said of things in motion has many flaws. For example, when a thing is in motion from one terminus to another, it is true to say of it that it is not in either terminus, but in a state of change. But to say that something is not, when it is not, is to state a determinate truth. Likewise when something is moving toward a term, it has already something of the true of that term, since everything which is finally produced has been previously in production. Likewise in all change there has to be something unchanging, some subject, just as a man cannot move from place to place unless it is the same man who is at the beginning and end of the motion.

Likewise one is not really taking a full view of nature if one judges all sensible things to be in a constant state of flux because some things, namely, terrestrial things, are such, while the heavenly bodies move indeed but show no great quantitative or qualitative changes. Likewise, too, if it is proved that there is a certain unmoved First Mover, then one cannot suppose all of reality to be in motion so that nothing determinately true may be said.

Finally, this position that all things are in motion destroys the first opinion, that contradictories are simultaneously true of the same; since if something simultaneously is and is not, it follows more that all things are at rest, rather than in motion. For nothing changes to that which is already present in it, as what is white does not change to white. But if the same thing is both true and not true of something, all things are in all things—since all are one—and therefore nothing can be changed.

(b) _On belief that whatever appears is true._ What is the correct approach toward those who hold for the truth of that which appears? First of all, when a sense seems to vary concerning some certain object, for example, when it states that to be tasteless during a cold which usually is judged to have a certain savor, this is not necessarily a fault of the sense, but possibly of the relaying of the sense impression to the internal sense, and which is dependent upon the state of the internal sense organs. If they are not properly disposed, the perception of the sensation by the internal senses of imagination and common sense (i.e., the reception of what is called the phantasm, that motion produced by the sense in act toward the internal senses) may be vitiated.

These adjustments and recognitions of the occasional indispositions of the senses are made naturally, just as one does not normally think for a minute that because an object seen from a distance looks small, that it really is small. In a word, we very definitely do not judge things according to mere appearances. Nor do we really hold that the judgment of an indisposed sense is equally valid with that of the same sense when well. When one cannot taste or smell certain things during a cold, one does not thereby consider that the things have changed or are variable, but rather that the senses are indisposed.

A further indication that we do indeed consider ourselves able to discriminate in the judgment of our senses between that which is actually so and that which has merely an appearance of being so is the way we act subsequently to dreams. In effect, someone might dream that he was in a hotel in Paris, but when he wakes up he does not start planning his day as to whether or not he should visit the Eiffel Tower that afternoon—which he could do if it was natural for him to judge the appearances of his dream on the same footing as the data of his senses when awake.

In a word, people may doubt about these things in speech (namely, whether we must say things are as they appear at the time to each), but they plainly do not doubt them in their mind, whether they avert to this or not. Thus, between men, one does not accept what appears to the layman concerning a sick man's symptoms, and what appears to an experienced doctor concerning the same, as having equal value. We do not accept that things are as they appear to anyone at all, anytime, and the subsequent admission that the same things can simultaneously be and not be, for example, be sweet and not sweet, as judged by the tastes of two different people. Nor among the senses, do we accept the judgment of a sense concerning that which is not its proper object (for example, sight judging something to be hot because of steam) with the judgment of the sense whose proper object it is, for example, touch. Nor do we consider judgments concerning common sensibles (i.e., motion, rest, number, shape, size) by a given sense necessarily as accurate, without the cooperation of other senses, as is the judgment of the sense concerning its proper object. If we should vary in our judgment as to the sweetness of some given thing, or as to its odor or weight, we nevertheless consider that there is some objective standard of these, and that it is not the thing that is varying, but our judgment of it.

To assume that things are as they appear at a given moment destroys the natures of things, since a thing could then be and not be at the same time, according to the different impressions it might create. For example, the same virus would be microbe to some, nonmicrobe to others, and equally as much one as the other. At the same time, since the senses are the measure of the reality of a thing under this supposition, then, things are as they are sensed. If a given object ceases to be sensed by someone, as when we turn our backs on a mountain, then it ceases to exist. Obviously, the being or reality of a thing is not bound up with the knower's sensation of it. Although the knower cannot sense unless the object of sensation first exist, the object of sensation does not conversely depend for its existence upon being sensed.

2) Those who doubt whatever cannot be proved. There are those who are led into error by others to the extent of believing that they can hold nothing definitively unless it be first of all proved. The sophists keep them in their doubts by proposing such sophistic difficulties. Thus the victims, while willing to believe that one should accept the judgment of a well sense over a sick one, of a wise man over an ignorant one, of what one sees waking over what one sees dreaming, will nevertheless have been deceived into thinking that these things cannot be decided. The reason is that there is no way of proving demonstratively, i.e., through an argument proceeding from self-evident principles, that certain senses are well while others are sick, certain men wise while others ignorant, certain things dreams while others real.

In the meantime, neither the sophistic deceivers nor their victims are really deceived in reality, as their acts show:

"For although they lay this down [that nothing is sure unless proved] and ask for it in speech, nevertheless they are not deceived in this as to the mind, to the point of believing that the judgment of a sleeping man and a man awake are alike true. This is evident from their actions, as was said" (no. 709).

That to seek demonstration of everything is unreasonable is seen from the fact that there can be no demonstration of the principle upon which all demonstrations depend. The fact that it cannot be demonstrated is, however, demonstrable. "For there is a demonstrative argument which proves that not all things can be demonstrated, since otherwise one would proceed to infinity" (no. 710).

However, such intellectual difficulties do not bother those who simply feel that anything may be said which cannot be disproved. These wish, from the admission that whatever appears is true, to lead to the admission of contraries being simultaneously true. How are they to be handled? Actually their position supposes certain concessions which need not be admitted—should one decide to discuss with them propositions that are actually impossible to be held, no matter what one might say.

The basic position is that all things are as they appear to the one sensing them. To concede this would mean to concede that nothing exists absolutely, i.e., independently of sensation, but solely as sensed. Such being the case, two persons' contrary opinions concerning the same thing would be equally true, and therefore of everything contradictories would be true. Actually, however, it makes no sense, and there are no grounds on which to concede that things are only as seen. This would mean, for example, that all the flowers which are "born to blush unseen," all the gems of "of purest ray serene," which the "dark, unfathomed caves of ocean bear," actually do not exist—since they are not seen by anyone. To concede this gratuitously would obviously be foolish. Let the one who wishes to hold such a thing supply a plausible motive for holding an opinion which no experience justifies.

It should be noted, in terminating, that the impossibility of contradictories being simultaneously true likewise excludes the possibilities of contraries being simultaneously true of a same thing (since every contrary includes the contradictory of that of which it is the contrary). Thus if water cannot be simultaneously hot and nonhot, neither can it be that extreme of nonhot which is cold. It could, however, be both potentially—as water may be lukewarm and neither hot nor cold actually, yet both potentially. Likewise a thing might be one contrary as to one part, another as to another, for example, black as to hair, white as to teeth.

2. Those Holding Contradictories As Simultaneously False

The reverse of holding both contradictories to be true, is to hold both contradictories to be false. This would come about by supposing that something might not only not be one or the other, for example, hot or nonhot, or both, but some third something in-between. This might seem a logical possibility, abetted by the fact that there can be a middle between two contraries, for example, between having sight and being blind, since a stone is neither. Nevertheless one cannot find a middle between contradictories, as, for example, between something being either true or not true. In effect, what else can it be except one of these two? If one should say that a thing could be partly true and partly not-true, it is plain that the two, true and not-true, are not being referred to the same aspect.

3. Summation
a. Generic Causes of Denial of First Principles

What, generically, are the causes of the denial of self-evident first principles? They are two:

"The first is the inability to resolve sophistic arguments leading to the denial, and the consequent feeling that one must therefore accept such arguments.

"The second is because one wishes to find a demonstrative argument for all things, and therefore refuses to admit, and subsequently denies, whatever cannot be proved. But first principles, which are the common conceptions of all, cannot be proved. Therefore they deny them, and so fall into impossible positions.

"[From what basic principles should one proceed against such opinions? Aristotle] says that one should proceed from the definition of *true* or *false*, or some other names....For they must concede the definitions of things, if they set down that names mean anything. For the notion signified by the name is the definition of the thing. But if they do not concede all [names] to mean something, then they are no different from the plants, as was said above" (no. 733).

b. Origin of Such Denial

From the viewpoint of an origin in philosophical inquiry, the idea of everything being said to be true may be derived from the outlook of Heraclitus; the outlook of everything being false, from the outlook of Anaxagoras. In effect, for Heraclitus everything was in movement, and therefore both was and was not. Hence all things were true, i.e., both their affirmation and their denial. For Anaxagoras, everything was contained in everything, and therefore nothing was precisely anything. Hence all things were false, i.e., neither this nor that.

c. Consequences of Such Denial

From the viewpoint of their philosophical consequences, these denials lead to a destruction of logic and to a destruction of physics. Now it is up to the first philosopher or metaphysician to dispute against such arguments, since he must defend the principles of all the sciences, they being all in turn founded on the principle of contradiction, the principle that an affirmation and negation cannot be simultaneously true, and that there can be no middle between them. The principles of the other sciences follow upon the notion of being, which is the primary subject of first philosophy.

Thus true and false, which belong to logic, follow upon being as perceived by the mind. Consequently an error concerning being and nonbeing will lead to an error concerning true and false. For there is truth when that is said to be which is, or not to be which is not, and falsehood conversely.

Likewise an error concerning being and nonbeing leads to an error concerning motion and rest which belong to the subject-matter of physics or the science of nature, since nature is defined as the principle of motion and rest in natural things. For that which is in motion, as such, is not yet; while that which is at rest, is.

Thus, if errors concerning being and nonbeing are destroyed, subsequently the errors concerning true and false, motion and rest, are destroyed.

d. Procedure against Such Denial

In proceeding against all such errors concerning being and nonbeing, one cannot assume that something clearly is or is not, but rather one must proceed from the fact that names mean something, which being so, one proceeds to definitions. Thus, from the definition of true and false, one can show that not all things can be true, for example, contradictory statements, nor can they all be false.

Here one may note that he who states all things to be true, states the contradiction of his own statement to be true; he who states all things to be false, states his own statement to be false.

If one should wish to make exceptions for these statements, for example, say that all things are false except one's statement to that effect, actually this leads to the possibility of an infinity of true statements: thus if it is true to say, "This one statement is true," it is also true to say, "The statement that this one statement is true, is true," and so on. In the realm of motion, if everything were at rest, then nothing would change and the truth would always be the same. But this cannot be, since the man who thinks or says such a thing, at one time was not, now is, and later will not be (thus, the proposition *This man is* is neither always true, nor always false). Likewise if everything should be in motion, nothing will be true, because what is true, is already, but what is in motion is not yet. Therefore everything would be false—which has been shown to be impossible. At the same time, even that which moves, always is in a certain way, since it changes from something to something, which latter something preexists in a way in that which changes, and remains in the term. Likewise, as has been seen, the subject of change must remain in order for there to be a change.

Does this mean, therefore, that all things are sometimes changing and sometimes at rest? No, rather there are also certain mobile things which are always in motion, as are the heavenly bodies; while there is a certain mover, namely, "the first, which is always immobile and always in the same disposition, as is proved in *Physics* VIII" (no. 748).

Chapter 8

The Vocabulary of Philosophy
(*Metaphysics*, V)

A. Causes
  1. In general
    a. Principle
      1) Origin for us of idea of principle: local motion
      2) Principle as meaning what is best for us
      3) Extended meanings of principle
      4) Common note of principle
    b. Cause
      1) Species of causes
        a) Enumeration of different types of cause
          (1) Material
          (2) Formal
          (3) Efficient
          (4) Final
          (5) Additional points about causes
            (a) There may be many causes of one thing
            (b) Causes may be causes of each other
            (c) The same thing may be the cause of contraries
        b) Whatever is called cause, is one of above types
          (1) Material
          (2) Formal
          (3) Efficient
          (4) Final
      2) Modes of causes (relations of cause to caused)
        a) Prior and posterior
        b) Per se and per accidens

(2) Being in the mind only

(3) Being as divided into potency and act

b. In particular: substance, chief concern of science

  1) Four ways in which substance is said

    a) Particular substances

    b) Their form

    c) Their terminations

    d) Their definition

  2) Ways reduced to particular substance and form/species

    a) Particular substance

    b) Form and species

2. Parts of subject of this science

  a. The parts of one

    1) Prime parts

      a) The same

      b) Diverse

      c) Different

      d) Like

      e) Equal and unequal

    2) Secondary parts of plurality

      a) Opposite

      b) Contrary

      c) Diverse in species

  b. A consequence of one: prior and posterior

    1) Prior in becoming

      a) In continuous things

        (1) According to order in place

        (2) According to order in time

        (3) According to order in motion

      b) In discrete things

    2) Prior in knowledge

      a) As universals are prior to singulars

      b) As accident is prior to composite of subject and accident

      c) As passions of prior things are called prior

    3) Prior in being

      a) In the order of commonness or dependence

      b) In the order of substance to accident

      c) As being is divided into potency and act

    4) Reduction of previous ways to three ways of prior in being

c. The parts of being
  1) As being is divided by act and potency
    a) The four meanings of potency
      (1) Active potency
      (2) Passive potency
      (3) Power to do something well
      (4) Power to resist change
    b) The four meanings of possible
    c) The meanings of impotent
    d) The meanings of impossible
    e) Metaphorical use of power in geometry
    f) Reduction of above meanings to active potency
  2) As being is divided into the ten predicaments
    a) Quantity
      (1) The species of quantity: multitude and magnitude
      (2) The modes of quantity
        (a) Per se
        (b) Per accidens
    b) Quality
      (1) The modes of quality
        (a) Substantial or specific difference
        (b) Immobile and mathematical things
        (c) Alterations
        (d) Dispositions to good or evil
      (2) Reduction of modes to specific difference and passion
    c) Relation (toward something)
      (1) Relation according to itself
        (a) Relations following number and quantity
          1* Following number absolutely
            a* Exceeding and exceeded
              1> Number to unity: exact multiples
              2> Number to number: multiples and a fraction
              3> According to proportion, not number
            b* More and less
          2* Following unity absolutely
        (b) Relations according to active and passive
        (c) Relations according to knower and known
      (2) Relation according to accident
C. Passions or properties of subject of this science
  1. Things pertaining to perfection of being

a. Perfect
    1) The perfect itself
      a) According to itself
      b) With respect to something else
    2) Conditions for the perfect
      a) Terminus
      b) Per se
        (1) Secundum quod (that according to which)
        (2) Per se (according to itself)
        (3) Disposition
      c) Having or habit
        (1) Twofold sense of having or habit
        (2) Things consequent upon having or habit
          (a) After the manner of opposition
            1* Passion: as imperfect to perfect
            2* Privation: as direct opposition
              a* Aptitude of subject
              b* Negation
          (b) After the manner of an effect
b. Whole
    1) Meaning of from
      a) To be made from something properly and primely
      b) To be made from something according to part
      c) To be made from something because of order alone
    2) Meaning of part
    3) Meaning of whole
      a) Whole in common
        (1) Whole, in comparison to the defective
          (a) Universal whole
          (b) Integral whole
        (2) Defective, as opposed to whole
      b) That whole which is genus
        (1) Ways in which genus is said
        (2) Ways something is said to be of diverse genus
2. Things pertaining to the defect of being
  a. False
    1) How said in things
    2) How said in definitions
    3) How said of human beings
  b. Accident

The Vocabulary of Philosophy
(*Metaphysics*, V)

A. Causes
    1. In general
       a. Principle
       b. Cause
       c. Element
    2. In particular: nature
    3. Something pertaining to cause: necessary
B. The subject of this science
    1. The subject
       a. In common: being and one
       b. In particular: substance, chief concern of science
    2. Parts of subject of this science
       a. The parts of one
       b. A consequence of one: prior and posterior
       c. The parts of being
C. Passions or properties of subject of this science
    1. Things pertaining to perfection of being
       a. Perfect
       b. Whole
    2. Things pertaining to the defect of being
       a. False
       b. Accident

This science, namely, metaphysics or first philosophy, treats of things common to all, about which the same name is predicated, not univocally, but analogically. Thus being is predicated both of substance and of accident. The ten supreme categories of being, or most general genera of being, comprising substance and nine kinds of accident, are treated in the *Predicaments*, or *Categories*, of Aristotle, his first logical

work. These are *what* is predicated. The predicables, or *ways* of predicating (see p. 79 above), are also treated in the same work. In keeping
with the latter, animal is predicated of man as a genus, rational as a
specific difference, both falling under the category or predicament of
substance.

In analogical predication there is, nevertheless, one basic meaning
from which the others derive according to a prior or posterior close-
ness. Thus healthy is said basically of the living animal, and then, by
derivation, of the food which makes it healthy, or the heart beat which
is a sign of health.

Consequently, before embarking upon the study of the matter of
first philosophy, it is necessary first to establish the basic meanings of
the terms which are essential to such a study. These terms are, because
of the universal nature of first philosophy, terms which are indispensable for all inquiry into the truth of things.

What are the words whose meaning must be investigated? Since
the aim of every science is to learn the causes of its subject matter, and
through them demonstrate the properties of the subject, the terms to be
grasped will fall under three headings: those related to the causes;
those related to the subject and its parts; those related to the properties
of the subject.

A. Causes
1. In General
a. Principle

In treating of the words designating causes, Aristotle first treats of
words designating causes in a general way, then of one designating a
specific type of cause, namely, the word *nature.*

In treating of the words designating causes in a general way, Aristotle follows the sequence: principle, cause, element. Why this order?
The reason is because this is the order of generality: principle is more
general than cause, cause more general than element. Thus the starting
post in a horse race is indeed a principle or starting point, but it is not a
cause. Similarly, the sculptor of a statue is a cause of it, but he is not
an element of it. That is reserved for the intrinsic causes, such as the
bronze or marble out of which the statue is made.

What is the relationship of principle to cause? Since principle is
more general, cause must add something to principle which narrows

the scope of the latter. While every principle or beginning implies a certain order of before and after, cause implies, over and above this, a certain influx toward the being of the caused. Thus, while the moment of sunrise is the principle or beginning of the day, the first in an order of events constituting the day, nevertheless it is not the cause of the day. On the other hand, the impact of the bat against the baseball is not only the principle or starting point of the ball's motion toward center field, it is also the cause of it.

1) Origin for us of idea of principle: local motion. Since all our knowledge comes from the senses, the origin of the idea of principle will be that derived from the first and most obvious principle or beginning that we see. Where do we most obviously see an order of before and after leading to the idea of principle? Plainly it is in local motion, by which a thing is seen to start from some place and move towards another.

In this origin of the idea of principle from local motion, three factors may be noted: it is the before and after of magnitude, (i.e., of continuous quantity) which supplies the measure of the before and after in local motion, which in turn supplies the measure of the before and after of time.

1. Magnitude. It is because one is able to mark off a succession of intervals against a certain extended magnitude that one is able to identify motion as the moving body goes through one after the other. If a body did not displace itself against a certain extended background, one would not be conscious of its motion.
2. Motion. Likewise the motion is measured against the background. Thus one says that a moving object is at such-and-such a place, that a horse is rounding the curve, coming down the homestretch, and so forth.
3. Time. Finally, just as motion is measured against magnitude, time is measured against motion. Thus, when one says it is twelve o'clock noon, one means that the sun in its apparent motion has attained that part of the heavens to which there corresponds the time of noon. The circular expanse of the heavens around the earth constitutes an extended magnitude which can be marked off in the imagination into twenty-four sections. The sun in its apparent motion then moves through these sections one after the other. Six o'clock in the morning, nine o'clock, noon,

mean simply that the sun is present in the sixth, ninth, or twelfth of the imaginary sections marked off against the sky.

Time, then, is measured by measuring motion; and motion in turn is measured by measuring the magnitude against which it displaces itself. Consequently magnitude or spatial quantity, as the starting point of motion, supplies the first idea of principle.

The word *principle* is then extended to other things on the basis of their similarity to the spatial principle or beginning. Thus the premises of a syllogism are called the principles of the conclusion, and the basic propositions on which a science depends, the principles of the science.

2) Principle as meaning what is best for us. A second meaning of principle, closely derived from the first is to call that a principle or beginning or starting point, from which one begins best. Thus, it is customary to say that the starting point of our knowledge is from what is best known to us—which is not, as has been made clear, that which is best known in itself. We also speak of putting one's best foot forward. In this vein a novice skier might choose to descend, not from the top of the hill, the absolute principle or starting point of the descent, but from somewhere near the middle, the best starting point for him. In circular motion, which has no specific starting point, the starting point is the point where it is best to begin, e.g., in starting a round-the-world trip.

3) Extended meanings of principle. By extension from the basic case of local motion, that is called a principle whence any generation or production of a thing proceeds, with or without local motion. This may be intrinsically or extrinsically.

1. Intrinsic. The intrinsic principle of a house would be its foundation; of a ship, its keel, the part from which the rest of the ship takes shape.
2. Extrinsic. Extrinsically speaking the principle would be (a) that from which the motion evolving a thing begins, e.g., the sun as the principle of the growth of a plant; an insult as the principle of a fight; (b) a will which is able to produce something, such as the will of the ruler or superior in regard to his subjects; (c) the arts as the principles of the artifacts which proceed from them.

Moving on into the intellect, that may be called a principle which is the beginning of the mind's discourse from one thing to another.

Causes are principles as initiating the movement toward the being of the caused.

4) Common note of principle. "He [Aristotle] says that it is common to all the aforesaid ways that that should be called a principle which is first, either in the being of a thing, as the first part of a thing is called a principle; or in the becoming of a thing, as the first mover is called a principle; or in the knowledge of a thing" (no. 761).

These principles differ, however, in that, as noted, some are intrinsic—such as the nature and form of a thing, or the element or matter of a thing; some are extrinsic—such as the plan of a thing in an intellect, or the intention in a will.

The final cause, the end for the sake of which something is done, the good which one seeks or the evil one avoids, are principles both of knowledge and motion. Thus, if a man's intention were to get ahead at any price, this could cause him to conclude to the necessity of flattering some powerful man in a given case, and to actually execute this. The good desired becomes a principle both in reasoning and in action. Consequently, in natural things, in moral things, and in artificial things, demonstrations are drawn chiefly from the end.

b. Cause

1) Species of causes.
a) Enumeration of different types of cause.

(1) Material. In one way, that is said to be a cause out of which something is made, and which exists within it. Such is the case of the bronze out of which a statue is made, or the flour out of which bread is made. This differs from privation which, while being a principle, is not that out of which. Thus the principle of a wall's being painted green is for it first to be nongreen, i.e., to have the privation of green. The painting must start from this, but this privation is not a component of the green wall; it is not that out of which the green wall is made. This is true, however, of the green paint. Not only are the species of these things causes, as bronze is of a statue, but also their genera, as metal, or even matter, are causes of the statue.

(2) Formal. In another way, that is said to be a cause which is the species and exemplar, namely, the formal cause. When it refers to the intrinsic form of a thing, it is called the species; when it refers to the extrinsic model, this extrinsic formal cause is called the exemplar. Such were the ideas of Plato. Since everything acquires its nature, ei-

ther generic or specific, through its form, and this generic or specific nature is that which the definition, stating what the thing is, signifies, it follows that the form is the basis of the definition through which one knows what a thing is. As in the case of matter, not only that which is specific, but also that which is generic, enters into the expression of the formal cause. Thus, not only does rational animal state the form of man, but also (partially) animal. This form, through which a thing acquires its nature, and which is expressed in the definition stating what a thing is, is not an isolated form, but a form implying matter, which is implied obliquely in the definition. Thus soul is called the act of an organic physical body having the potency of life. Soul is not pure act, but act of a body.

(3) Efficient. In a third way, that is said to be a cause which is that whence the beginning of change and rest first comes, since in natural things that which is the cause of the natural motion of a thing, as in growth, is likewise the cause of its coming to rest at a due term. Thus the father is the cause of the son, the adviser is the cause of the action taken by advice. In addition to this, there is the one who disposes the matter for the form, as the woodsman hews out a log for a cabin; the one who aids the principal agent, as a soldier goes off on a scouting mission as part of the general's campaign. In this latter respect, all secondary agents act according to the end and form of activity which is given them by the principal agent, as the architect gives this to the housebuilder, and God, the First Intellect, gives this to the whole of nature. To this genus of cause is reduced that which makes anything to be in any way, whether substantial or accidental: thus the parents cause the child to be in the substantial order, fire causes the water to be hot in the accidental order.

(4) Final. The fourth way in which something is said to be a cause is as the end, namely, that for the sake of which something is done, is called a cause. The identification of the end as a cause, i.e., the recognition of the final cause, was not immediate with the first philosophers. Yet the question, "Why?" and the question, "For the sake of what?" seek a cause. Thus, if one were to ask someone, "Why are you taking a walk?" and he were to answer, "For the sake of my health," it would be considered that he had supplied a cause of the walking. Thus the end or purpose for which something is done is truly a cause. This is true not only of the ultimate end, but of intermediate ends. Thus a student might study elocution in order to become a good speaker, in order to be elected to the US Senate, in order to be in view to be chosen as a

presidential candidate, in order to be elected as president. Each one of these steps is the end of the step preceding it, just as each step is the efficient cause of the one following it. These steps may be either actions or things—just as the thing of a bridle or saddle is produced for the action of riding, which in turn might be used for the thing which is the gold obtained in a highway robbery.

(5) Additional points about causes.

(a) There may be many causes of one thing. This clearly follows from what has preceded, and occurs not in the accidental order only, but in the strict sense—not, however, in the sense of many causes of the same nature (unless as in the case of parents of a child, several causes combined are required), but in the sense of essentially different causes. Thus the sculptor is the cause of a statue, and so is the bronze, and so is the desire to win an art exhibition, and so is the model after which the statue is designed.

(b) Causes may be causes of each other. Thus, being elected to office may be the final cause for giving speeches; whereas giving speeches may be the efficient cause of being elected to office. Here again, the same cause cannot be the cause of itself, just as there cannot be two same causes of one thing. In this mutual intercausation, the causes group themselves into two pairs.

"Now the efficient and the final correspond with each other, because the efficient is the beginning of motion, while the final is the terminus. And likewise matter and form correspond: for the form gives being, while matter receives it.

"Therefore the efficient is the cause of the end, while the end is the cause of the efficient. The efficient, indeed, is the cause of the end as to existence, since by moving the efficient leads to this, that the end should be. But the end is the cause of the efficient, not as to being, but as to the reason of its causality. For the efficient cause is a cause insofar as it acts—but it does not act except as this is caused by the end. Whence the efficient cause has its causality from the end.

"But the form and matter are causes of each other as to being. The form, indeed, is so of the matter insofar as it gives it to be in act; while the matter is so of the form insofar as it sustains it. Now I say both of these to be causes to each other of being either absolutely or in a certain respect. For the substantial form gives being to matter absolutely. But accidental form does so in a certain respect, to the extent that it also is a form. Matter likewise sometimes does not sustain the form according to being absolutely, but accordingly as it is the form of this thing, having being in this thing, as is the case of the human body in relation to the rational soul" (no. 775).

*(c) **The same thing may be the cause of contraries.*** This is possible, not in the sense of the same positive cause producing contrary effects, but in the sense of the same cause producing one effect by its presence, another by its absence. Thus, when the teacher is present she is the cause of order in the classroom; in the same vein, her absence is the cause of disorder.

b) **Whatever is called cause, is one of above types.**

(1) Material. Letters are said to be the causes of syllables; matter, the cause of artificial products; the chemical elements, the causes of compounds; parts, the cause of a whole; premises, the cause of a conclusion. All these fall under the heading of a cause out of which something is made, i.e., the material cause. This is true of propositions, not from the viewpoint of their power to produce the conclusion—in which sense they are in the nature of an efficient cause—but from the viewpoint of their containing the terms out of which the conclusion is made. In general, whatever is in the nature of a subject for the form, is in the nature of a material cause. Sometimes this matter out of which is some one thing, sometimes several. The bronze out of which a statue is made is a case of the former. Cases of the latter are the men in an army, or the households in a city, which constitute a unity or whole of order, namely, the army or the city. Sometimes the elements are not united by order only, but by contact or connection also, as in the case of the parts of a house, the result of which is a composite. Finally the parts may undergo alteration, as do chemical elements such as hydrogen and oxygen in constituting the chemical compound, water. All these elements or parts, which are that out of which the result is made, come under the heading of material cause.

(2) Formal. That which gives identity to the result, which states what the thing is—the statue, the army, the house, the water—comes under the heading of formal cause.

(3) Efficient. From another viewpoint, the doctor, the counselor, the sperm cell, and in general every maker, as being a principle of motion and rest, is called a cause. And this is in the order of efficient causality.

(4) Final. The fourth manner of causing is that by which that which is an end or good is called a cause. That for the sake of which something is done is considered the best and is the end of the others. Should one object that that for the sake of which one acts is not always

good, as in the case of the thief acting to steal someone's money, it should be noted that whether the end is really good or only seemingly good, one always acts for it as good. No one ever pursues what he considers to be bad for himself, since he cannot pursue except what he desires, and only that which is desirable is called good. Even though the good or the end, or, in a word, the final cause, may be last in being in certain cases, it is nevertheless always first in causality.

"Although the end may be last in being in certain things, nevertheless it is always prior in causality. Whence it is called the cause of causes, since it is the cause of the causality of all the causes. For it is the cause of the causality of the efficient cause, as has been stated. But the efficient cause is the cause of causality both of the matter and the form. For it causes the matter, by its motion, to be receptive of the form, and the form to be in the matter. So consequently the end is also the cause of the causality both of the matter and the form. And therefore the most powerful demonstrations are taken from the end in those things in which something is done for an end, as in natural, and moral, and artificial things" (no. 782).

2) Modes of causes (relations of cause to caused).

a) <u>Prior and posterior</u>. This may be the relation of two different causes in the order of nature; or of the same cause considered in two different ways in the order of reason. In the former case one would have, for example, the sun as a prior and remote cause in the growth of plants, the seed as a posterior and proximate cause. This is at the root of Aristotle's classical statement *Man is begotten by man and by the sun as well* (*Physics*, II, c.2). One has an example of the second case when one says that in a prior way, as a universal, a composer composed the Fifth Symphony, while in a posterior way, as a particular, Beethoven composed it. Here the two causes, composer and Beethoven, differ in reason but not in reality.

b) <u>Per se and per accidens.</u> The per se cause of a statue is a sculptor; the per accidens cause is the man who happens to be the sculptor, e.g., John. This is so because, while John is not necessary in order that there be a statue, a sculptor is. As has already been seen, per se causes may be prior or posterior, remote or proximate. So also of per accidens causes. Thus, if John is the per accidens posterior cause of a statue, man, the species of John, or animal, the genus of John, are prior per accidens causes. Likewise the per accidens causes may be remote or proximate: since to predicate an accident of an accident is a more remote form of predication than to predicate it of the subject by virtue of which it may be predicated of the accident. Thus it is more remote to say of John, the sculptor, that *a sculptor is a musician*, than to say, *John is a musician*.

Something may be said to be the accidental cause of something else in two ways: in one way, insofar as that which happens to the cause is called an accidental cause, as a musician may be said to be the builder of a house if the builder happens to be a musician; in the other way, insofar as that may be called the accidental cause of something which is the per se cause of something else. Thus a fisherman's deliberate spadework for worms, while being the per se cause of finding worms, may be the accidental cause of discovering a buried treasure. This accidental effect may happen in one of three ways. One way is if the accidental result has a necessary connection with the per se effect, as in the case of a man opening a water faucet and the following flow of water. Another way is if the order is neither necessary nor usual, but rare—as in the case of finding treasure being connected with digging for worms. Finally, the connection may be merely in opinion, as in the case of a man who says that the earth quakes when he walks out the door because he walked out of the door and the earth happened to quake at that moment.

c) **In potency and in act.** In this respect one has the distinction between the builder as cause of the house when actually building it, and when being able to build it (when at home resting).

d) **Simple and composite.** Just as the causes may be prior and posterior, per se or per accidens, proximate or remote, so, of course, may be the effects. Thus the sculptor is the cause, not only of this statue, but of a statue, and, even more universally, of an image; he is likewise the cause of the whiteness of the statue, since he chose the marble to which the whiteness belongs. Finally, just as one may say that John made the statue, or a sculptor made the statue, singly, so one may say in a composite way that John, the sculptor, made the statue, joining the per accidens and the per se causes.

It should be noted in considering these various modalities of a same type of cause that whereas some effects in act require causes in act, as a house cannot be actually being built here and now unless someone is actually building it, and if the house is not actually being built, then there is no actual cause of its building; nevertheless the potential cause may remain even when the effect is not being produced.

c. Element

Just as principle is more universal than cause (in that, while every cause is a principle, not every principle need be a cause) so cause is more universal than element—since element represents a certain species of cause, namely, a material cause.

1) Definition of element. Four characteristics are combined in an element properly speaking:

1. It must be a cause in the sense of that out of which, which places it in the category of material cause.
2. It must be a principle out of which something is made primarily or basically. Thus a wall may be made from cement, but the cement is not an element, because the cement itself is made from something else more basic.
3. It must be existing within or intrinsic, i.e., not something which passes once the thing is made, as when musician is made out of the privation, nonmusician.
4. It must have some certain species which is not divided into other species—by which it differs both from prime matter, which has no form or species, and from substances such as water, which is divisible into species such as hydrogen and oxygen, themselves (if considered indivisible into other species) being able to be considered as elements.

Thus an element may be defined: that out of which something is composed, first, existing within it, indivisible as to species into any further species.

2) Exemplifications of definition.

a) In letters. The letters of the alphabet may be called the elements of words.

b) In natural bodies. That into which chemical compounds, such as water, are resolved, is called an element, as in the case with hydrogen and oxygen. (It should be noted that when one states an element cannot be further divided as to species, this excludes quantitative division, since the compound, water, is not divided quantitatively into different species, but solely chemically.)

c) In demonstrations. One may consider the basic syllogisms of a science, whose conclusions serve as premises for other syllogisms, and to which other proofs are reduced, as elements. Thus the basic syllo-gisms of Euclid in geometry are called the *Elements* of Euclid.

d) By extension. Whatever is small in quantity, and simple in the sense of not composed of others, and indivisible, and deemed useful for many things, comes to be called an element. Thus the contemporary search for the ultimate subatomic particles considered to constitute matter is a search for elements and is so called in modern terminology. Genera have the nature of elements, since as such they are no further divided, but the species are constituted out of them by the addition of specific difference.

3) Common note in element. This common note is to be that first out of which something is constituted.

2. In Particular: Nature

Whereas the words, *principle, cause,* and *element,* signify causes in a general way, the word *nature* does so in a more particular way. It might seem that the word *nature* belongs primarily to the natural sci-entist's domain, but actually it is seen to be applicable in some way to all substance—and hence to belong to the first philosopher.

a. Different Meanings of Nature

There are five principal ways in which nature is taken. The basic meaning of the word *nature* is derived from nativity, the birth of living things. Thus too in Greek, the word *phusis,* source of *physics* and *physical,* and to which the Latin word *natura* corresponds, means, when the *u* is short, the production of things in common, when the *u* is long, the production of living things, i.e., of plants and animals. (Consequently, the terms *physics* and *natural science,* derived from the corresponding roots in Greek and Latin respectively, are synonymous.)

"By virtue of the fact that nativity (or birth) itself was first called nature, a second mode followed, namely, that the principle of genera-tion out of which anything [i.e., inanimate as well as animate being] is generated, as from an intrinsic principle, should be called nature.

"And through the likeness of nativity to other motions, the meaning of this word proceeded farther, so that nature should be said, in a third way, as that whence there is the principle of motion in any being ac-cording to nature, provided it be in it as such and not accidentally. For example, in the doctor who is sick there is the principle of a cure, namely, the art of medicine, but not, nevertheless, insofar as he is sick, but insofar as he is a doctor. But he is cured, not insofar as he is a doctor, but insofar as he is sick. Thus the principle of motion is not in him insofar as he is moved....What is born is always conjoined [according to quantity and continuity, and not according to quality] to that from which it is born. Therefore nature never means an extrinsic principle, but according to all its meanings it means an intrinsic principle.

"Now from this third notion of nature there follows a fourth. For if the principle of motion of natural things is called nature, and the principle of motion in natural things appeared to some to be matter, it follows that matter should be called nature—which, indeed, is a principle of the thing both as to being and as to becoming. It likewise is considered without any form, nor is it moved by itself but by another. And therefore he [Aristotle] states that that is called nature out of which some being first is or is made....

"...Since, however, the motion of natural things is caused more from form than from matter, there therefore came a fifth way, according to which the form itself is called nature....They [the ancients] were led to lay down the form as nature for the reason that whatever things exist or are made naturally are not said to have a nature—although the matter exists out of which it belongs to them to be made or to exist—unless they have a proper species and form by which they attain a species. The name *species* appears as standing for the substantial form, and *form* for the figure which follows upon the species and is a sign of the species. If, therefore, the form is nature, nor can anything be said to have a nature except when it has a form, therefore that which is composed out of matter and form is said to be a nature, i.e., to be according to nature, as are animals and their parts, such as flesh and bone and such....

"...Just as form and matter are called nature, since they are a principle of generation, which [generation] is called nature according to the first imposition of the name, so too species and substance are called nature, since they are the end of generation. For generation terminates at the species of the generated, which results from the union of form and matter.

"And from this, according to a certain metaphor and extension of the name, every substance is called a nature, since the nature about which we spoke, which is the terminus of generation, is a certain substance. And therefore every substance has a likeness with that which is called nature....By reason of this way the word *nature* is distinguished among the common names. For it is thus common as *substance* is common" (nos. 809-23).

b. Reduction of All Meanings to Form

1) According to order in giving names. "Names are imposed by us accordingly as we understand, since names are signs of our understandings of things. But we sometimes understand prior things by posterior things....For since the forms and powers of things are known from their acts, generation or nativity received the name *nature* first and then lastly form did.

2) According to order of being. "But according to the order of things, in a prior way the notion of nature belongs to form, since, as was said, nothing is said to have a nature except as it has form.

"Whence it is evident according to what has been said that 'first and properly substance is called nature', i.e., the form of things having within themselves the principle of motion as such [that is, not accidentally].

"For matter is called nature because it is capable of receiving form. And generations have the name of *nature* since they are motions proceeding from the form, and again to forms. And itself, namely, the form, is the principle of the motion of things existing according to nature, either in act or in potency.

"For the form does not always cause motion in act, but sometimes in potency only, as when the natural motion is impeded by some external factor, or even when natural action is impeded through a defect of the matter" (nos. 824-26).

3. Something Pertaining to Cause: Necessary

A cause is that upon which something else necessarily follows. Hence a discussion of necessary pertains to the discussion of cause.

a. Kinds of Necessity

1) In a certain respect. The first way is when that is called necessary without which something cannot live or exist. This, although it is not the principal cause of the thing, is nevertheless concomitant, as, for example, breathing for an animal, or eating.

The second way is when something is called necessary without which some good cannot be attained. Thus the tired man may say he needs a good drink; it is necessary to him not in the sense that he cannot live without it, but in the sense that he needs it for well-being, as a remedy to his fatigue.

The third way is when that is called necessary which is the result of violence, and is against either the natural inclination in some natural things (as when a stone is prevented from falling to the ground) or is against the will in a rational creature—as when a man is prevented from going to the rescue of his friend by being chained. In this respect the necessary in question is against natural appetite or will, and as such it is both saddening and inculpable. Thus a man might say that he had to shoot a hostage because those were his orders. (The necessity invoked, however, might not be admitted.)

2) Absolute. Fourthly there is the necessary absolutely speaking: that which cannot be otherwise. The previous examples of necessary represent necessity only in a certain respect.

b. Sources of Necessity

1) Absolute: matter and form. "Now the absolutely necessary differs from the other types of necessity. For absolute necessity belongs to a thing according to that which is intimate and proximate to it, whether it be the form, or the matter, or the essence itself of the thing—as we say animal to be necessarily corruptible, since this follows upon its matter insofar as it is composed out of contraries. We likewise say an animal is necessarily sensitive, since this follows upon its form; and an animal to be necessarily an animated sensitive substance, since this is its essence.

2) In a certain respect: end and efficient cause. "But the necessary in a certain respect and not absolutely is that whose necessity depends upon an extrinsic cause. Now extrinsic cause is twofold, namely, the end and the efficient cause. But the end is either the being of the thing absolutely, and necessity taken from this end pertains to the first way; or being well, or having some good, and from this end there is taken necessity according to the second way.

"Now the necessity which is from an external mover, pertains to the third way. For violence is present when something is moved by an external agent to something other, to which it does not have an aptitude by its proper nature. For should it be ordered according to its nature to receiving the motion from the external agent, then the motion will not be violent, but natural—as is evident of the motion of the heavenly spheres by the separated substances, and of the motion of lower bodies by the higher" (nos. 833-35).

c. All Forms of Necessary Reduced to Absolute Necessity

All the modes of necessary are reduced to the mode of absolute necessity. As to the third mode, for example, when a thing does something against its own proper inclination, it is because, in a way, it cannot do otherwise. Likewise in respect to the first and second ways, that without which a thing cannot live or cannot be well, they reflect the basic necessity by which for something it is impossible to be otherwise.

This basic type of absolute necessity is also the necessity which is had in demonstrations, since the conclusion of a demonstration in the strict sense of the word is that which cannot be otherwise. This requires necessity in the premises.

"Since a demonstration causes one to know absolutely, which is not except through the cause, it is also necessary that the principles, from which the syllogism is made, be necessary as being impossible to be otherwise. For from a nonnecessary cause there cannot follow a necessary effect" (no. 838).

d. Three Conclusions

First, from the fact that in demonstrations the premises are the cause of the conclusions and both are necessary, it follows that things are necessary in a twofold way: some have a cause of their necessity; others have no cause of their necessity, but are necessary of themselves. This is against those who say that one should not seek a cause of necessary things, as is had in *Physics* VIII.

Secondly, there must be one first necessary thing, from which other things have their necessity, since one cannot proceed to infinity. This necessary being must be simple, since composite things are mutable and therefore may be in several ways—and consequently do not fulfill the condition of being impossible to be otherwise.

Thirdly, since necessary principles will be simple and immobile, there cannot be any violence in them, since violence implies mutability.

Thus the necessity which the immaterial substances have is not that of violence.

B. The Subject of This Science
1. The Subject
a. In Common: Being and One

1) One.
a) <u>One per accidens.</u> One may be said either per accidens or per se. Accidental unity is constituted either when an accident is compared to a subject, or when one accident is compared to another. A case of the first is the unity constituted by John the musician; a case of the second is the unity constituted by the just musician. In the first case, the accident, musician, is referred to the subject, John, to constitute an accidental unity; in the second case, by virtue of the accident, just, and the accident, musician, being referred as accidents to some one subject, they are accidentally referred to each other, because of this connection with a common third. In the case of a singular substance, such as John the musician, the accidental unity cannot be predicated of another; in the case of the universal, man, the accidental unity, musical man, may be predicated of another, as in the statement *John is a musical man.*

b) <u>One per se.</u>
(1) The natural division of one.
(a) <u>Five ways in which things are called one.</u> The first way in which things are said to be one in themselves is when they are continuous as to extension. Sometimes this continuity is supplied through something else, sometimes it is intrinsic.

A case of continuity *through something else* would be a bundle of wood reduced to unity by a continuing piece of wire around it. This continuity could be either in a straight line (in the continuity of a ladder being supplied by the single straight pieces on either side or in that of several sheets of paper by the reflex continuity of a staple) or in a curved line, in that of a barrel by the curved continuity of the hoop around the staves. Since this continuity through another may be either by art (as in the above cases) or by nature (as in the case of the bones of the leg being made continuous by virtue of the enveloping continuous skin of the leg), and in the second case the continuous binding factor cannot be extraneous from the nature of the thing, this second case more closely approaches absolute continuity of the thing itself.

In keeping with the above is the requisite that that which is continuous move with one motion. Thus, if a bundle of sticks moved with different motions in different parts, to that extent it would not be considered one bundle. Of course, while there is only one basic motion, or motion per se, there may be other accidental motions, as in the case of a man who is walking or moving per se along the deck of a ship toward the stern, while the motion of the ship itself is carrying him accidentally in the opposite direction. Likewise this one motion must be indivisible as to time, that is, at the same time one part of the continuum cannot be moving and the other at rest. (This does not mean, however, that one part of the continuous thing must be going past the same point at the same time as another part, as the head of a nail being driven into a piece of wood does not have to reach the surface of the wood at the same time as the point of the nail is crossing the surface; all parts move at the same time, but the prior part in space passes a given point at a prior time.)

Those things are said to be continuous *intrinsically or in themselves* which are not said to be one by contact.

"For those things which are in contact [as are two cogs in a machine] do not have unity of continuity through themselves but through some bond which conjoins them [such as the frame of the machine]. But those things which are continuous, are called one according to themselves, although they may have reflexion. For two reflex lines are continuous at one common terminus which is the point in the place where the angle is made" (no. 856).

Even though reflex things may be continuous—as in the case of a continuous leg, which nevertheless bends, or is reflexive, at the knee—still those things are more one which are continuous without reflexion. For a reflex line may have one motion and two motions. Thus one can consider a line with an angle moving in a single direction, as in the case of the V of an arrowhead; or with one part at rest and the other in motion, as if one were to close an angle by moving one of its sides inwards, similar to the case of bending one's arm up below the elbow, while leaving the upper arm at rest. Because of this, the individual bones are more truly continuous in themselves than the whole constituted by the several bones linked together, even should their points of contact be actually joined and continuous by tissue.

The second way in which things are said to be one in themselves, or per se, is when they are not only continuous as to quantity, but also indifferent in form. Thus, if a piece of copper is soldered to another piece of copper, the fused joint between the copper and the solder is continuous, but the unity constituted is a unity of quantity, not of nature. The water contained in a glass, however, is not only one in continuity, but also one in nature. Likewise things may be said to be one in some even more common base, as bourbon and scotch might be said to be one by virtue of their common alcohol.

The third way, that by which things which are one in genus are called one, has a similarity with the second way. In effect, in the previous case, things are said to be one which have one basic nature, not differing as to form, as several liquids could be called one if reduced to one basic liquid such as alcohol; in the present case, things are called one which have one basic genus, subsequent to which they differ as to form, as man and horse have the basic genus, animal, subsequent to which they differ by their specific differences, such as rational for man. This third way, too, resembles the way things may be one in prime matter, while differing by different substantial forms—although it is plain that while the genus resembles matter, as lacking ultimate determination, nevertheless it is actually an element of the form, namely, that which the mind states first in definition as being better known because more common.

However, things may be said to be one in genus in two ways: in one way, insofar as they represent species of some one genus, as man and horse are one in the genus, animal; in another way, insofar as they may be said to be the same one generic thing. Thus equilateral triangle and isosceles triangle cannot be called the same (one) triangle, because they differ as triangles, but they can be called the same (one) figure because they do not differ by the differences by which figure differs and is divided into circle, triangle, rectangle, and so forth. In other words, things may be called the same superior genus of which they are not differentiations, unlike the case of the inferior genus. Thus man and horse could be called the same living substance, since they do not differ by the differences by which living substance is differentiated, namely, by sensitive (animal) and nonsensitive (plant).

The fourth way in which things are called one in themselves is that by which things which have one definition are called one. This may be absolutely so, as two men are one in the same definition of man; or only in a certain respect, as ox and horse agree in the same one definition of animal—which does not, however, fully state their total essence.

The fifth way, in which things are most absolutely one, is when the understanding of them is absolutely indivisible, which therefore excludes a composition of material and formal principles. For example, man, even though understood as one substance, is nevertheless understood as composed of matter and form. Our intellect does not grasp such simple things as composed of principles, but more after the manner of negation (thus point is that which has no part) or by relation to composites (thus unity is the principle of number). Such things are indivisible, as to time, place, and motion. They are thereby most one, especially that which is one in such a way in substance, since an accident which is one in this way, such as point, is still in composition with some substance in which it ultimately exists.

(b) Reduction of all five ways to indivision absolutely. "Those things which are wholly indivisible are said to be most one. Indeed, it is to this mode that all the others are reduced, for it is universally true that whatever things do not have division are called one insofar as they do not have division. For example, those things which are not divided in that which is man, are said to be one in man, as are Socrates and Plato. And those things which are not divided in the notion of animal, are said to be one in animal. And those things which are not divided in magnitude or measure, are said to be one according to magnitude, as are continuous things.

"And from this one can derive also the number and diversity of the ways of being one set down above, since what is one is either indivisible absolutely or indivisible in a certain respect.

"If indeed absolutely, then it is the last way, which is the principal one.

"But if it is indivisible in a certain respect, it is so either according to quantity only or according to nature. If according to quantity, then it is the first way. But if according to nature, it is so either as to the subject, or as to the division which is on the part of form. If it is so as to subject, it is either according to a real subject, and then it is the second way; or according to a subject of reason, and then it is the third way. But the indivisibility as to form, which is the indivisibility of notion, i.e., of definition, makes the fourth way.

"Now from these ways certain other ways are further derived. For many things are called one because they make one, as several men are said to be one from the fact that they pull a boat. Likewise certain things are called one from the fact that they undergo some one thing, as many men are one people, from the fact of being ruled by one king. Certain other things are called one from the fact that they have some one thing, as the many possessors of some field are one in their domain over it. But certain things are called one from the fact that they are some kind of unity, as many white men are called one, because each of them is white" (nos. 866-68).

With respect to all these secondary ways, however, that is still principally one which is so according to substance, whether in quantity only, or also as to subject, whether it be the real subject or the genus, or whether it be so by the whole definition, as in the fourth and fifth ways.

On the other hand, things are plural in number, or counted in the plural, which either are not continuous, or do not have one subject, or do not agree in one definition.

A further type of unity is that derived not so much from indivision, as from division, in the sense of something which requires a certain order of parts, and is therefore, in this sense, divided, and is not called one until the order of parts is as it should be.

"From this it is evident that the circular line is most one, since it not only has continuity, as does the straight line, but it also has totality and perfection, which a straight line does not have. For that is perfect and whole to which nothing is lacking—which, indeed, occurs with the circular line. For no addition can be made to it, as is the case with the straight line" (no. 871).

(c) A property of one: to be a measure. One, by virtue of its indivision, has the characteristic of being a principle of knowing things. In effect, one is the first measure of number, by which every number is measured. But measure has the nature of a principle, since through measure the things measured are known. But things are known through their proper principles. Therefore one is the principle of what is known or knowable concerning any thing, and is in all things a principle of knowledge (insofar as it has the aspect of measure).

This one which is the principle of knowledge is not the same in all genera of things. For example, in words it is a letter; in weights it is some minimum weight such as the ounce; in motion it is some first measure which measures others, namely, that most simple motion which is the apparent diurnal motion of the sun, from which our time is derived, and which is therefore used for timing other motions.

What is common to all these ways is that whatever is the first measure is indivisible according to quantity or according to species. Therefore, what is one and first in the genus of quantity must be indivisible according to quantity. If it is wholly indivisible according to quantity and does not have position, it is called unity. Point is that which is wholly indivisible as to quantity but does have position. Line is that which is divisible according to one dimension only; surface according to two; body according to all three.

It should be understood that to be a measure is the proper notion of one accordingly as it is the principle of number. This is not the same as the one which is converted with being. The notion of this latter one consists solely in indivision, whereas that of the former in measurement. Although the notion of measure belongs primarily to one which is the principle of number, nevertheless it is extended by a certain likeness to one in all the genera (as Aristotle shows in *Metaphysics* X). In this respect, then, the notion of measure is found in every genus:

"Now this notion of measure follows upon the notion of indivision, as was stated. And therefore one is not said entirely equivocally of that which is converted with being, and of that which is the principle of number—but according to prior and posterior [i.e., analogically]" (no. 875).

(2) The logical division of one. According to the sequence found in logic, certain things are, first of all, one in <u>number</u>. These are those whose matter is one. "For matter, accordingly as it stands under signate [i.e., real and specific] dimensions, is the principle of the individuation of the form. And because of this, it is from matter that the singular has its being as something one in number divided from others" (no. 876).

Things are one in <u>species</u> which have the same definition, through genus and specific difference.

Things are one in <u>genus</u> which have one mode of predication or one common predicament. Thus substance is predicated in a different way from quality or action, but all substances are predicated in one way, i.e., as not existing in a subject.

Things are one in <u>proportion or analogy</u> which agree in this, that this is to that, as some other thing is to some other thing. This may be taken in two ways, either in the sense of the two having different relations to a common one, as healthy, said of urine is related as a sign of health, while of medicine as a cause of health; or in the proportion of two to different things, e.g., calmness to the sea, as stillness to the air. For calmness is the repose of the sea, and stillness that of the air.

In all these modes of one, the subsequent mode follows upon the prior without conversion. For whatever things are one in number, are also one in species, but not conversely. And so of the others.

(3) How many is said. Since in as many ways as one of two opposites is said, so is the other said, it follows that in as many ways as one

is said, in so many ways is many said. One starts with things which are not one—and are therefore many—as not continuous, going on to others which are not one, but many, because they have different definitions. As to the fifth way, of things one because they are absolutely simple and indivisible, the opposite, being divisible, does not constitute something many in act, but only in a certain respect and potentially so.

2) Being. Being is said both in itself and according to accident. Such a division of being is not that of being into substance and nine accidents, had in the predicaments, and which is a division of being itself. Rather, this is a division of being accordingly as something is said or predicated of something per se, or only accidentally, as constituting only an accidental being—as *man* and *white* constitute an accidental unity in *The man is white.*

a) Being per accidens. This type of being is had in three ways: when an accident is predicated of an accident; when an accident is predicated of the subject; when the subject is predicated of the accident.

1. One has a case of the first (accident of accident) when it is stated, "This musician is white." Here, because some accident, namely, musician, happens to be predicated of a subject, and likewise white happens to be predicated of that subject, the two may be predicated of each other.
2. One has a case of the second (accident of subject) when it is stated, "This man is a musician"—because musician happens to be predicated of him.
3. One has a case of the third (subject of accident) when it is stated, "This musician is a man." Here, because the subject is predicated of that to which the accident, which is set down as the subject, happens (namely, man), it may be predicated of the accident. (This is similar to the first case.)

What is common to all three cases is that in every case *is* means nothing other than happens to be. In other words, the unity thus constituted, and therefore the being, is not an essential nature such as man or blue, but rather an accidental combination which need not be—just as in the case of accidental causes, one may say that a musician builds a house because the builder happens to be a musician, or in the case of accidental effects one may say that the doctor cures himself because the patient happens to be a doctor. In neither of these cases, that of the

musician-builder or that of the doctor-patient, is the unity or being a
unity of nature, a per se unity.

b) **Being per se.**

(1) Being outside the mind: ten predicaments. This is perfect being, unlike being in the mind or being in potency. It is the being represented in each of the ten predicaments. These ten predicaments are not
species of some common genus, being. The reason for this is that the
difference which, by addition to the genus, constitutes the species, is
outside the essence of the genus, as rational is outside of, or in addition
to, animal.

"But nothing can be outside the essence of being which, by addition
to being, constitutes some species of being, for what is outside of being
is nothing, and cannot be a difference" (no. 889).

The ten predicaments signify, then, not ten genera to be further
contracted by species, but the ten ways of predicating being of a given
subject, consequent upon ten different ways of being.

"It should be understood that the predicate may be related to the
subject in three ways:

"In one way when it is that which is the subject, as when I say that
Socrates is animal. For Socrates is that which is animal. And this
predicate is said to signify *first substance*, which is particular substance, concerning which all things are predicated.

"In a second way as the predicate is taken as that which is in the
subject. Now this predicate either is in it per se and absolutely, as following the matter, and thus there is *quantity*; or as following the form,
and thus there is *quality*; or is in it not absolutely, but in respect to another, and thus there is *to another* (*relation*).

"In a third way as the predicate is taken from that which is outside
the subject—and this in two ways:

"In one way as to be wholly outside the subject. If it be not a measure of the subject, it is predicated according to the manner of *having*
(*habitus*), as when it is said that Socrates is shod, or clothed. But if it
be a measure of it, since the extrinsic measure is either time or place,
the predicate is taken either on the part of time—and thus there will be
when; or on the part of place—and thus there will be *where*, the order
of parts in place not being considered. If this also be considered, there
will also be *position* (*situs*).

"In another way accordingly as that from which the predicate is
taken is in a certain respect in the subject. If indeed this be according
to its principle, it is so predicated as *action*. But if it be according to

terminus, it will thus be predicated as in *passion*. For passion terminates in the subject which undergoes it" (nos. 891-92).

In all of this it should be remembered that the predication of being in a proposition—or its negation—always exists whether the verb *to be* appears or not.

"For each and every verb is resolved into the verb *to be* and a participle. For it in no way differs whether one should say, 'The man is convalescing' or 'The man convalesces'—and so of others. Whence it is evident that in as many ways as predication is made, in so many ways is being said" (no. 893).

(2) Being in the mind only. Here being and *is* signify the composition of a proposition made by the intellect composing and dividing. In this case being signifies the truth of a thing. The truth of a proposition may be called truth through a cause—for accordingly as the thing is or is not, so is the proposition true or false.

"For when we state something to be [as stated], we signify the proposition to be true. And when we say it not to be, we signify it [the proposition] is not true. And this is so whether the proposition is affirmative or negative" (no. 895).

"It should be understood, however, that this second way [i.e., is true, as indicating truth of a proposition] is compared to the first [actual being or nonbeing of the thing], as effect to cause. For from the fact that something is in the nature of things, there follows truth and falsehood in the proposition.

"But since the intellect considers something which is in itself nonbeing as a certain being (as, for example, negation and such) therefore sometimes being is said of something in this second way [namely, the statement is true] and not in the first [namely, the thing is]. For blindness is said to be in the second way, in that the proposition is true which states that something is blind—but nevertheless it is not stated to be true in the first way. For blindness does not have any being in things, but is more a privation of some being.

"Now it is accidental to each thing that something should be truly affirmed of it by the intellect or by a word. For the thing is not referred to knowledge, but conversely. But the being which each thing has in its own nature is substantial. And therefore, when it is said, 'Socrates is,' if this *is* be taken in the first way [i.e., 'Socrates has being'], it is in the nature of a substantial predicate. For being is superior [i.e., as a kind of supreme genus] to each and every thing, as animal is to man. But if it be taken in the second way [*is* when in predication with something true about Socrates], then it is of the nature of an accidental predicate" (no. 896).

(3) Being as divided into potency and act. In this respect, being is more common than perfect being, or being in act. For being in potency is being in a certain respect and imperfect.

"Every predicament is divided by act and potency. And just as in things which are outside the mind, some thing is said to be in act and some other thing in potency, so in the acts of the mind, and in privations, which are beings of the mind only. For someone is said to know both because he is able to use knowledge, and because he actually uses it....And not only is this so in accidents, but also in substances. For we say that Mercury, i.e., the image of Mercury, is in the stone in potency, and we say the middle of a line to be in a line in potency. For any part of a continuum is in the whole potentially. (Now line is placed among substances according to the opinion of those setting down mathematical things as substances, which he [Aristotle] has not yet refuted.)...But when something is in potency, and when it is not yet in potency, must be determined elsewhere, namely, in *Metaphysics* IX" (no. 897).

b. In Particular: Substance, Chief Concern of Science

1) Four ways in which substance is said.

a) <u>Particular substances.</u> Such are simple bodies or elements, e.g., hydrogen, oxygen, and so forth; and the composites made from them, e.g., water, salt, and so forth; and in turn the living things made from these, e.g., plants, animals and their parts such as hands, feet, and the like.

"All the aforesaid are called substance because they are not said of any subject, but other things are said of them. And this is the description of first substance in the predicaments" (no. 898).

b) <u>Their form.</u> The intrinsic cause of the existence of substances, namely, the form, is likewise called substance. Thus the soul may be called the substance of an animal.

c) <u>Their terminations.</u> According to the Platonists and Pythagoreans, that which is found in everything and without which it cannot exist, is the substance of a thing. Thus, if surface is destroyed, body is destroyed; if line is destroyed, surface is destroyed; if point is destroyed, line is destroyed. Conversely, bodies are considered as composed out of surfaces, surfaces out of lines, and lines out of points. Whence point is a part of, and the substance of, line; line of surface;

and so forth. According to this position, number appears to be the substance of all things—since if number be removed, nothing remains in things; whatever is not one, is nothing; and likewise what is not in plural number is nothing.

"But this mode is not true. For it is not necessary that that which is commonly found in all, and without which the thing cannot be, should be the substance of the thing. Rather, it can be some property following upon the substance of the thing, or a principle of the substance. This error was true of them especially as to one and number because they did not distinguish between one which is convertible with being, and one which is the principle of number" (no. 901).

d) Their definition. The quiddity or whatness of a thing, which the definition signifies, is called the substance of each. Now this quiddity or essence of the thing, the notion or reason, which the definition expresses, differs from the form, which was called substance in the second way, as humanity does from soul.

"For the form is a part of the essence or quiddity of the thing. But the quiddity or essence itself of the thing includes all the essential principles. And therefore the genus and species are said to be the substances of those things of which they are predicated, in this last way. For the genus and species do not signify the form only, but the whole essence of the thing" (no. 902).

2) Ways reduced to particular substance and form/species.

a) Particular substance. This substance, which is the ultimate substance in propositions, and is not predicated of any other, is first substance. This substance which is this something, is subsistent in itself, is separable as distinct from all and not communicable to many. Particular substance differs from universal substance in these three ways:

1. Particular substance is not predicated of any inferior, as is universal substance;
2. It subsists of itself, while universal substance subsists only by virtue of particular substance;
3. It is separable and distinct from all, while universal substance is in many.

b) Form and species. Nevertheless, these two also, as expressed in the second and fourth ways, are called substance. They agree in that in both cases that is stated to be, by which something exists.

"But form refers to matter, which it causes to be in act; while quiddity refers to the supposite [the actually existing substance], which is signified as having such an essence" (no. 904).

Matter, however, is omitted as not signifying substance in act. Nevertheless, it is included in the first way, "since particular substance owes its being as substance and as individual in material things, to matter" (no. 905).

2. Parts of Subject of This Science
a. *The Parts of One*

First the parts of one will be treated, then the names signifying something consequent upon the notion of one, namely, prior and posterior. Concerning the names signifying the parts of one, and its opposite, many, first there will be treated those signifying the prime parts, then those signifying certain secondary parts. The prime parts of one are: same (one in substance); like (one in quality); equal (one in quantity). The corresponding parts of many are: diverse, unlike, unequal.

1) Prime parts.

a) The same. Things are said to be the same *accidentally* in three ways:

1. in one way, as when two accidents, such as white and musical, are said to be the same, because they are true of the same subject.
2. in another way, as when the predicate, e.g., musical, is said to be the same as the subject, e.g., man, because it is predicated of the subject.
3. in another way, as when the subject, e.g., man, is said to be the same as the predicate, e.g., musical being, as when it is predicated of it, i.e., *This musical being is man.*

For whatever is predicated of something is signified as being the same as it; thus, when it is said, "The man is a musician," *musician* and *man* in this case are one and the same thing.

(It should be noted that this type of accidental sameness requires singular subjects, since what is true of a universal subject must be predicated universally, which is the property of that which belongs per se, not accidentally. What is true of every man as such could not be predicated accidentally, but would be necessarily connected with man.

Conversely, the nature of that which is accidentally predicated, such as musician, is to be predicated of the singular.)

Things are said to be the same *per se* in the same ways as things are said to be one per se. These may be reduced to two ways. Things may be called one:

1. whose matter, either according to subject or species, is one, e.g., chair and table are the same oak, two chairs are the same furniture (the second and third ways of one per se; see p. 123 above);
2. whose substance is one, either by virtue of continuity (e.g., the same wood throughout a board, i.e., the first way), or by virtue of unity and indivisibility of definition [i.e., several men are the same as to definition; all points, defined by negation (that which has no part) are the same; all number ones, as principles of number, are the same (i.e., the fourth and fifth ways)].

Consequently, identity is unity or union, and things said to be the same may be:

1. different things, said to be the same because in some respect they are one;
2. one thing, considered as more than one by the intellect for the sake of a relation.

"For a relation cannot be understood except between two extremes, as when something is said to be identical with itself. For then the intellect uses that which is one according to reality, as two. Otherwise it could not designate the relation of some same thing to itself. Whence it is evident that if relation always requires two extremes, and in such relations there are not two extremes in reality, but according to intellect only, the relation of identity will not be a real relation, but of reason only, according to which something is said to be the same absolutely. It is otherwise, however, when some two things are said to be the same either in genus or in species.

"For if the relation of identity were some thing over and above that which is called the same, the thing also which is the relation, since it in turn is identical with itself, for a similar reason would have another relation, which would be identical with itself, and so on to infinity....But in things which are according to intellect, nothing prevents this. For when the intellect reflects upon its own act, it understands itself understanding. And this very thing it can likewise understand, and so on to infinity [i.e., indefinitely]" (no. 912).

b) Diverse. Things may be said to be diverse in the three following ways:

1. in species—as ass and ox are diverse;
2. in number—as differing according to matter, in the case of two individuals of one species, e.g., Socrates and Plato;
3. according to the definition declaring the substance of the thing—as, in some one and the same thing, such as Socrates the musician, Socrates is by definition diverse from musician.

In a word, since diverse is opposed wholly to the same, for every way of saying the same, there will be a corresponding way of saying diverse—and all may be reduced to the three ways cited above.

c) Different. Those things are properly called different which are not wholly diverse, but agree in some aspect, whether:

1. in number, as Socrates sitting and Socrates standing;
2. in species, as Socrates and Plato—the same in species, but different in number;
3. in genus, as man and ox;
4. in proportion or analogy, as quantity and quality in being.

Things which agree in species, differ only according to accidental differences, as Plato and Socrates differ only according to height, color of hair, and so forth. Things, which agree in genus and are different according to species, differ with substantial differences.

"Those things are most properly called different which are the same as to genus, and diverse according to species. Now every genus is divided into contrary differences; but not every genus is divided into contrary species. For the species of color are contrary, namely, white and black, and the differences also, namely, congregative [of light] and dispersive. But while the differences of animal are indeed contrary, namely, rational and irrational, nevertheless the species of animal, such as man, horse, and the like, are not contrary" (no. 917).

d) Like. Things are said to be like or similar which have the same qualities, such as heat or shape, or undergo like things, such as being pushed, or undergoing in some generic way. Things are most alike which agree in most closely related qualities, as steel is more like iron than tin is. In a converse way, things are said to be unlike or dissimilar.

e) **Equal and unequal.** These terms are not discussed, since multiplicity of meaning is not so evident in them.

2) Secondary parts of plurality.

a) **Opposite.** After an examination of diverse and different comes an examination of the secondary parts of plurality, namely, opposite, contrary, and diverse in species. First of all, things may be said to be opposite in the following four ways: contradictories, contraries, privation and having, and relation.

> "Something is placed opposite another or in opposition to it
> 1. either by reason of dependency, and thus they are opposite relatively;
>   or else by reason of removal, since, namely, one removes the other. This, indeed, occurs in three ways:
> 2. for either it wholly removes it, leaving nothing behind, and thus there is negation [contradiction];
> 3. or the subject alone is left, and thus there is privation;
> 4. or it leaves the subject and genus, and thus there is a contrary. For contraries are not only in the same subject, but also in the same genus" (no. 922).

How may things be recognized as opposite? Things may be recognized as opposite:

1. by comparison to motion, since in all motion the terminus from which is opposed to the terminus to which. Therefore those things from which motion is, are opposed to those to which motion is, as white is generated from nonwhite, and fire from nonfire.
2. from the subject, in that things which cannot be simultaneously in the same thing which is receptive to them, are opposed, either in themselves, or in those things in which they are. Thus the same body cannot be both white and black; nor can man and ass be said of the same; nor pale and white, to the extent that pale contains black.

b) **Contrary.** Properly, things are said to be contrary which, while being opposed, agree in the same genus, the same subject, or the same power. Thus those are contraries which differ most in the same genus, such as white and black in the genus of color; in the same subject, such as well and sick in an animal; in the same power (or mental habit), such as congruent and noncongruent in grammar.

Commonly speaking, things are called contrary whose difference is the greatest, either absolutely or in the same genus, or in the same species.

Just as being and one are divided according to the ten predicaments, so also are those things which are their parts, such as the same and its opposite, diverse, and contrary, which is contained under diverse.

c) Diverse in species. Things may be said to be diverse in species in five ways: as two things in the same genus:

1. not divided by opposite differences—as whiteness and science in the genus, quality;
2. as divided by some difference, whether contrary or not—as biped and quadruped;
3. as having contrary differences, such as white and black in the genus, color; man and ass in the genus, animal;
4. as differing in the ultimate and most special species, as man and horse in animal—and all such properly differ as to species when they are alike in genus;
5. as being several accidents in the same subject and yet differing from each other, since there cannot be several accidents of the same species in the same subject.

In a converse way, things are said to be the same in species.

b. A Consequence of One: Prior and Posterior

One implies a certain order, inasmuch as to be one is also to be a principle. The principle, or beginning, in any genus is that which is first in the genus. Prior is said of that which is closer in act to some determinate principle. This principle, in relation to which something is said to be prior, may be so absolutely and according to nature—as the father is the principle of the child; or relatively so—in relation, for example, to knowledge, or perfection, or dignity or some other such; or also according to place.

Since prior and posterior are said by relation to some principle, and principle is that which is first in being, or becoming, or knowledge, prior and posterior will be divided in the same way, beginning with becoming.

1) Prior in becoming. Things may be prior in becoming according to the order of motion, which follows the order in quantity and magnitude.

a) In continuous things.

(1) According to order in place. According to this order, that is prior which is closer to some determined place, whether this place be determined as the middle in a given magnitude or an extreme. The order itself may be either natural or arbitrary. In one case, chemical elements may be ordered according to their natural densities, so that the denser elements would be prior when starting from the bottom of the scale, the less dense elements prior when starting from the other end. In the other case, the top of a heap of stones could be prior in one way, the bottom of the heap prior in another way. Thus, whatever is closer to the recognized or chosen principle will be prior, what is more remote will be posterior.

(2) According to order in time. In respect to the past, those things are called prior which are farther away from the present now—as the Revolutionary War is called prior to the Civil War. In respect to the future, those things are called prior which are closer to the present now—as someone might be told, "Prior to going to bed, kindly put the cat out." Thus time is measured in both directions from the present now.

(3) According to order in motion. In this respect, that is naturally prior which is closer to the first mover—as the child is prior to the man, since it is closer to the first mover, the one generating. That is prior in the order of voluntary things which has the greater power—as the king is prior to his subordinates, since they move only when he moves first.

b) In discrete things. Noncontinuous things, which are united only by order, will be called prior and posterior according to their position in that order, whether starting from an extreme or from the middle. As to extremes, one milestone might be called prior to another from the viewpoint of a traveler approaching a city, while the same milestone would be posterior to that other for a traveler departing from the city. As to the middle, the scores on a target are given priority starting from the middle, or center, of the target.

2) Prior in knowledge. Things may be prior in knowledge in the order either of intellectual knowledge or of sense knowledge. This may occur in three ways:

a) <u>As universals are prior to singulars.</u> "Universals are prior to singulars [in intellectual knowledge], although in sense knowledge the converse occurs. For there singulars are prior. For reason is of universals, while sense is of singulars.

"Whence it is that sense does not know universals, except accidentally, in that it knows the singulars concerning which the universals are predicated. For it knows man insofar as it knows Socrates who is man. The intellect, on the contrary, knows Socrates insofar as it knows man. Now that which is per se is always prior to that which is per accidens" (no. 947).

b) <u>As accident is prior to composite of subject and accident.</u> "According to reason [i.e., in the intellectual order], 'accident is prior to the whole,' i.e., to the composite of subject and accident; and musical man cannot be known without the notion of that part which is musical. In the same way all other simple things whatever are prior, according to reason, to the composite, while with sense it is the opposite. For to sense the composites are offered first" (no. 948).

c) <u>As passions of prior things are called prior.</u> Here and elsewhere the word *passion* as used generically in Aristotelian terminology refers to an undergoing, in the sense of something being received passively, as, for example, wood is burned. In the present context it refers, in the example, to something basic or prior being received intrinsically in line, namely, to be straight, as before being left or right. (Passion, as commonly used in English, refers to a particular undergoing, namely, an imprint received in the sense appetites from something apprehended as sensibly good or bad, causing initial desire or fear. For passion as predicament, see p. 130 above.)

"For example, straightness is considered prior to leftness. For straightness is a per se passion of line, while leftness is so of surface—but line is naturally prior to surface. According to sense, however, surface is prior to line, and the passions [or properties] of composites to the passions of simple things" (no. 949).

3) Prior in being.

a) <u>In the order of commonness or dependence.</u> Things are said to be prior in this respect which are able to exist without the others, while the others cannot exist without them. And this is that prior which is not convertible with its consequent in the order of being, as stated in the

Predicaments. This is the priority which Plato attributed to universals with respect to singulars, to surface with respect to body, to line with respect to surface, and to number with respect to all other things.

b) In the order of substance to accident. Substance is said to be prior to accident, whose subject it is.

c) As being is divided into potency and act. In the order of potency, half may be said to be prior to whole—and in general, any part may be so said to be. Likewise matter is prior to form in this sense. But according to act the aforesaid are said to be posterior. For they do not come into act except by the dissolution of the whole into its parts. Therefore, when the whole is potential and in the process of coming to be, the parts exist first; but when the whole now exists in act, the existence of the parts in act, dependent upon the dissolution of the whole, is posterior.

4) Reduction of previous ways to three ways of prior in being. "He [Aristotle] concludes that all the modes of prior and posterior may be reduced to these last modes, and especially to the first of them—as that is called prior which is able to exist without the others but not conversely....All prior things can in some respect be without the posterior, and not conversely" (no. 953).

c. The Parts of Being

1) As being is divided by act and potency. At present only the meaning of potency is discussed, the meaning of act not being able to be fully discussed until after the nature of forms is manifested in *Metaphysics* VIII-IX. Concerning potency, first the various meanings of potency are given, then, as with every analogous term, they are all reduced to one prime meaning. Both potency and impotency are treated, and, under potency, likewise possible.

a) The four meanings of potency.

(1) Active potency. This is described as the principle of motion or change in another as other. The principle of motion or change here is not that already in the thing, namely, the matter, or the formal principle from which motion follows—as downward motion, the form of heaviness—but that which acts on something other, as other.

"Whatever is moved, is moved by another. Nor does anything move itself except by parts, insofar as one of its parts moves another, as is proved in *Physics* VIII. Potency, therefore, accordingly as it is the principle of motion in that in which it is, is not included under active potency, but rather under passive. For heaviness in earth is not a principle of its moving, but rather that it be moved. Therefore the active potency of motion must be in other than that which is moved, just as building power is not in that which is built, but rather in the builder" (no. 955).

(2) Passive potency. This is described as the principle of motion or mutation from another as itself other.

"That principle by which it befits something to be moved or to undergo something from another is called passive potency" (no. 956).

"That is said to undergo (*pati*) improperly which receives some perfection from something, as to understand is called a certain undergoing. But that is said properly to undergo which receives something accompanied by a transmutation of itself from its natural state....Now this cannot be done except through some contrary....But when something receives that which is fitting for it, it is said to be perfected, rather than to undergo" (no. 958).

(3) Power to do something well. This is described as the principle of doing something, not simply in any way whatsoever, but well, or according to one's wishes. Thus conversely, of a person who can't speak well, one says that he can't speak. On the other hand, things that can undergo something well are stated as being able—as gasoline is called inflammable.

(4) Power to resist change. Thus are described all habits or forms by which something is rendered wholly impassible, or immobile, or not easily moved. In other words, since to be easily moved or changed seems to indicate a lack of power, those things which are not easily moved, not easily overcome by their contraries, are said to be immobile states; soft or sickly signify their opposite and impotence.

   b) **The four meanings of possible.**

1. potent or able corresponding to the first mode of potency—meaning able to do something, either directly or through another, as a king through his servant;
2. able to undergo something, presupposing some disposition in the thing, some passive potency whereby it can undergo a change, a change presupposing a weakness on the part of that undergoing, whereby it is unable to resist the active potency acting upon it;
3. potent according to the fourth mode of potency—whereby something cannot be overcome or changed from without;

4. potent according to the third mode of potency—in the sense of that which is able to act well, or simply to act. Thus one might say, "That horse can really run!"—meaning that it can run well.

c) The meanings of impotent. By contrast with potent and its connotation of an active or passive disposition toward doing or undergoing something well, or simply without qualification, impotent implies the privation, or absence in an apt subject, of such a disposition. Thus something is said to be impotent as to sight, or unable to see, which should have the power of seeing but lacks it.

d) The meanings of impossible. In one way that is said to be impossible by contrast with the meanings of possible stated above, namely, as not having the potency presupposed.

In another way, something is said to be impossible because of the repugnance of terms in propositions.

"For since to be able is said in order to being, then, just as being is said not only of what exists in the nature of things, but also according to the composition of a proposition as there is in it truth or falsehood, so too possible and impossible are said not only because of the potency or impotency of the thing, but also because of the truth or falsehood in the composition or division of propositions.

"Whence that is called impossible whose contradictory is necessarily true—as for the diameter [diagonal] of the square to be commensurable with its side is impossible, since this particular proposition is false, whose contrary is not only true, but also necessary, and which is, indeed, to be not commensurable. And because of this, to be commensurable is necessarily false, and this is the meaning of impossible" (no. 971).

In this respect, that is said to be possible whose contrary is not necessarily true, nor necessarily false—as for a man to sit is possible, since not to sit, the opposite thereof, is not necessarily true, nor necessarily false. This mode of possible is divided into three ways:

1. "For that is said to be possible in one way, which is false, but not necessarily so—as for a man to sit when he is not sitting, since its opposite is not true of necessity.
2. "In another way, that is said to be possible which is true, but not of necessity, since its opposite is not false of necessity, as for Socrates to sit when he is sitting.

3. "In a third way something is said to be possible which, although it is not true, nevertheless may be true shortly" (no. 973).

e) Metaphorical use of power in geometry. "The square of a line in geometry is called the power of the line according to this like-ness—for just as out of that which is in potency there is made that which is in act, so from the production of a line upon itself, there re-sults its square. For example, we might say that three has power to nine, since nine results from the production of three upon itself. For three times three is nine" (no. 974).

f) Reduction of above meanings to active potency. All modes of possible are said with reference to the first, active potency, namely, that principle of permutation in another as other. For it is to this potency that passive potency corresponds, likewise the potency of doing well, and the potency to resist corruption and remain immutable. As this applies to potency and possible, so the opposite applies to impotency and impossible.

2) As being is divided into the ten predicaments.

a) Quantity. That is said to be a quantum or quantified which is divisible into those things which are within.

This is not the division of mixed bodies, or compounds, which are divided into their elements which existed there virtually, and in which division there is required also a certain alteration or chemical change.

Likewise it is not a division into essential parts, namely, matter and form, neither of which is intended to exist by itself.

(1) The species of quantity: multitude and magnitude. "Now both of these [i.e., multitude and magnitude] have the notion of quantified, insofar as multitude is numerable and magnitude is measurable. For mensuration belongs properly to quantity.

"Multitude is that which is divisible according to potency into non-continuous parts. Magnitude, however, is that which is divisible into continuous parts. This indeed occurs in three ways, and according to this there are the three species of magnitude. For if it be divisible ac-cording to one dimension only into continuous parts, there will be length. But if in two, width. If in three, depth.

"Furthermore, when plurality or multitude is finite, it is called num-ber. But a finite length is called line; a finite width, surface; a finite depth, body. For if a multitude were infinite, number would not exist, because what is infinite cannot be numbered. Likewise if there were infinite length, there would not be line, for line is a measurable length.

And for this reason there is set in the notion of line that its extremities are two points. The same is true of surface and body" (no. 978).

(2) The modes of quantity.

(a) Per se. Quantity per se may be considered, first, after the manner of a substance and subject, as in the case of line, surface, number. Each of these is substantially quantum, in that quantity is placed in their definition. Thus line is continuous quantity, divisible according to length, and finite, and so on for the others.

Secondly, quantity per se may be considered as a habit or passion of such a subject, e.g., of line, which is substantially quantity. This may be so of specific types of quantity: e.g., large and small, considered as passions of number; prolonged and short as passions of line; wide and narrow as passions of surface; deep and shallow as passions of body. One could also include here heavy and light according to the opinion of those who consider the number of atoms to be the cause of weight in bodies (as did Democritus, although according to Aristotle, weight and lightness pertain not to quantity, but to quality, as will be seen).

Certain other properties are said commonly of any continuous quantity, such as the terms *big* and *little, more* or *less*—whether absolutely speaking or relatively to something. Likewise they may be transferred to other things than quantity. Thus one speaks of a heavy color, a light sound, and so forth.

"Now it should be known that quantity is, among the other accidents, closer to substance. Whence some think quantities to be substances, namely, line and number and surface and body. For quantity alone, after substance, has division into proper parts. For whiteness cannot be divided; and consequently neither is it understood to be individuated except through its subject. Whence it is that in the sole genus of quantity some things are signified as subjects, others as passions" (no. 983).

(b) Per accidens. In one way something is said to be quantified for the sole reason that it is an accident of some subject which is quantified. It is in this way that white or musical is quantified.

In another way, something is said to be quantified, not by virtue of the subject it is in, but because it itself is quantitatively divided according to the division of another quantity:

"Motion and time, which are called certain quantitative and continuous things because of the fact that those things of which they are, are divisible, are themselves divided according to the division of the latter. For time is divisible and continuous because of motion; but motion because of magnitude—not, indeed, because of the magnitude of that which is moved, but because of the magnitude of that in which something is moved. For from the fact that that magnitude is quantified, the motion too is quantified. And because the motion is quantified, it follows that time is quantified. Whence, these may be called, not only quantities per accidens, but rather *in second* (*per posterius*), insofar as they receive the division of quantity from another prior being" (no. 985).

Time is here considered a per accidens quantity, whereas in the *Predicaments* it is considered quantity per se (as an extrinsic measure of things). But in the *Predicaments* the species of quantity are divided according to the different elements of measuring, whereas here they are considered according to the being of quantity, in which respect, time is quantitative accidentally, as is motion. Place, like time, is posited in the *Predicaments* as a species of quantity because it has another notion of measurement but does not have an accidental quantitative being after the manner of motion and time, and hence is omitted here.

b) Quality.

(1) The modes of quality.

(a) Substantial or specific difference. This is the difference by which one thing differs from another substantially, and it enters into the definition. The specific difference is, in effect, predicated as a certain kind of whatness (i.e., *in quale quid*). Thus the answer to "What kind of animal is man?" is: "A certain kind of animal, i.e., two-footed." This meaning of quality is not set down in the *Predicaments*, since in this respect, i.e., as specific difference, it is not under the predicament of quality but under that of substance. But here there are being discussed all extended meanings of the word *quality*.

(b) Immobile and mathematical things. Mathematical things, indeed, abstract from motion (and are hence immobile), as will be stated in Book VI. Mathematical things are numbers and magnitudes. Both are said to be qualitative or such-and-such. Thus, if one asks of what kind surfaces are, the answer is square or triangular or the like. If one asks of what kind numbers are, the answer is composite (i.e., measurable by some other number) or prime (i.e., measurable by unity alone, such as 3, 5, 7, 11).

The composite numbers are likened to surfaces insofar as multiplication resembles a line being extended back on itself: thus 2 times 2 may be called 2 squared. They may also be compared to solids: thus, 2 times 2 times 2 may be called 2 cubed. Whatever is in number beyond its basic substance, such as 2 in the examples above, may be called its quality. Hence squared and cubed here represent certain qualities of 2. (This is the fourth species of quality in the *Predicaments*.)

(c) Alterations. These alterations are the passions of mobile substances, such as hot, cold, and the like. (This is the third species of quality mentioned in the *Predicaments*.)

(d) Dispositions to good or evil. Thus virtue and vice, science and ignorance, health and sickness, are all qualities. (This is the sense of the first species of quality set down in the *Predicaments*.)

(The second species of quality in the *Predicaments* [potency or impotency] are not discussed here since, even though they are called qualities, they are rather, as to being, contained under potency as already treated above.)

(2) Reduction of modes to specific difference and passion. Quality is said most basically, first, of difference of substance, i.e., of specific difference. It is this difference in numbers, for example, and mathematical things, that makes them of such a kind. (Even though the word *substance* is used of mathematical entities such as numbers, lines, and so forth, no more is meant than that they are treated after the manner of substance, as being subjects—this being mentioned as a prerogative of quantity.)

The second basic sense in which quality is used is of the passions of things moved, and also of the consequent differences of motion. Such are, for example, hot and cold, and heating and cooling. Just as difference of substance extends to mathematical entities, so alterations extend to things being disposed well or ill.

"Nevertheless, well and ill pertain most to quality in animate things, and especially in things having *prohaeresis*, i.e., election [choice]. And this is because good has the notion of end. Now those things which act through election, act because of an end. But to act because of an end belongs chiefly to animate things. For inanimate things act or are moved because of an end, not as knowing the end, or causing themselves to act for an end, but rather as they are directed by another, who gave them the natural inclination—as an arrow is directed to an end by the archer.

"Now irrational animate things know indeed the end, and desire it with animal appetite, and move themselves locally to the end as though having judgment concerning the end. But the appetite of the end, and of those things which are because of the end, is determined for them by natural inclination. Because of this they are rather made to act than acting. Whence, neither is there in them free judgment.

"But rational things, in whom alone there is choice, know the end and the proportion of those things which are for the end. And therefore, just as they move themselves to the end, so also to desiring the end, or those things which are for the sake of the end, because there is in them free choice" (no. 1000).

c) **Relation (toward something).** In the continuing reflection on the ten predicaments, and after substance and the accidents of quantity and quality, there is now treated the accident of relation. In contrast to quantity and quality, which are predicated as determinations of the subject, relation pertains to a reference in the subject to something other. For example, a man is called father, not because of some quantity or quality in himself, but with respect to a child. This relationship is something real, but should the child cease to exist, the relation, father, no longer actually exists.

(1) Relation according to itself. There are three ways in which relation in itself may be viewed. The first of these has to do with number and quantity. Thus, when something is called double, this implies a relation to something other which, conversely, will be half of that which is double. In the same mode what is triple is related to that which is one third of it. Likewise that which is containing to that which is contained. When a glass contains water, the water is contained by the glass, 4 is contained by 5, and so forth.

The second sense is that in which some things are said to be relative according to action and passion, or active and passive potency. Thus heater is related to heatable in the natural order; sawer to sawable in the artificial order; and universally every active thing to everything passive.

The third sense of relation is that in which something measurable is said to be relative to a measure. This is not the mutual measurement according to quantity mentioned in the first way, whereby double is said of half, and conversely, half is said of double, but is rather the measurement according to being and truth. In this respect the thing known measures the knower, but not conversely, just as the exemplar measures the image, but not conversely. "The truth of science is measured by the scientifically knowable thing. For from the fact that the thing is or is not, the expression known is true or false, and not conversely" (no. 1003).

The reason for the three above modes is as follows. Since relation, which consists in things, consists in a certain order of one thing to another, there must be as many types of these relations as there are ways for one thing to be ordained to another.

Now one thing is ordered to another:

1. "either according to being, as the being of one thing depends upon another, and this is the third mode [as knowledge depends on what is known];
2. "or according to active and passive power, accordingly as one thing receives something from another or bestows something on another, and thus one has the second way [as what is burned is related to what burns it];
3. "or accordingly as the quantity of one thing is able to be measured by another, and thus there is the first way [as 4 is the double of 2, and 2 the half of 4]" (no. 1004).

The quality of a thing, however, as such has regard only to the subject in which it is. It is only insofar as it takes on the character of active and passive potency and becomes a principle of action and passion, or by reason of quantity attributed to it, as one thing is said to be more white than another, or similar to some other quality, that the note of relation enters in.

Other genera of being follow relation, rather than cause it. Thus when consists in some certain relation to time; where to place; position (or *situs*) to order of parts; having to the relation of the one having to that which is had.

(a) Relations following number and quantity.

1* Following number absolutely. Numerical proportion is not restricted to discrete quantity, or number, but applies also to all those measurements in continuous quantity which are in some way derived from number. Thus two lines might be said to be in the proportion 2:3.

Numerical proportion is either equal or unequal, and the latter may be in the proportion either of exceeding and exceeded or more and less.

a*Exceeding and exceeded. This may be either in the proportion of number to unity or that of number to number, a proportion which is either determinate or indeterminate.

1> *Number to unity: exact multiples.* This is the case where one number is an exact multiple of the other, e.g., 2:1, 6:3, and so forth. In general these proportions do not have names, but some have specific names, e.g., double, triple, and so forth. In this first sort of proportion, any case of it is always found first in some number with respect to unity.

"For example, the proportion of double is found first between 2 and 1. Whence from this proportion it receives its notion and name. For double proportion is said of two things to one. And because of this, if one number is double with respect to the other, nevertheless this is accordingly as the lesser number takes on the notion of one, and the larger the notion of two. For 6 is in double proportion to 3, insofar as 3 is to 6, as 1 is to 2. And it is similar in triple proportion, and in all the other species of multiplicity" (no. 1015).

2> Number to number: multiples and a fraction. This is the case in which one number contains the other, plus one or more parts of the other—and is therefore not an exact multiple of the other. Examples of this are the relations 3:2, 5:3, 5:2, 8:3. The greater number contains the smaller or is a multiple of the smaller, plus some part or parts of the smaller.

These proportions cannot be considered in terms of number to unity, since the greater number contains the smaller, plus one or more parts of the same—because unity cannot have a part. Thus the proportion is rather of number to number. Some of these, at least in Latin, have special names (e.g., *sesquialtera*—3:2); in general they are undetermined.

3> According to proportion, not number. "It occurs that some continuous quantities have proportion to each other, but not according to some number, either determinate or indeterminate. For of all continuous quantities there is some proportion; nevertheless it is not [necessarily] numerical proportion. Indeed of any two numbers there is one common measure, namely, unity, which, taken a certain number of times, gives any number whatsoever. But there is not found to be one common measure of any continuous quantities whatsoever.

"Rather, certain continuous quantities are incommensurable—as the diameter of the square is incommensurable with the side. And this is so because there is not proportion between it and the side as the proportion of number to number, or of number to one" (no. 1020).

b* More and less. This is the case of the containing and the contained: here the proportion is not expected according to any number, all numbers having a common measure which is unity. Rather, the relation of containing to contained is said accordingly as something is so much and more, leaving undetermined whether it is commensurable or not. "For every quantity, whatever sort may be taken, is either equal or unequal. Whence, if it be not equal, it follows that it is unequal and containing, even though it be not commensurable" (no. 1021).

2* Following unity absolutely. This proportion is not according to the proportion of number to unity. Thus certain relatives are said according to unity absolutely: things are said to be the same, whose substance is one; alike, whose quality is one; equal, whose quantity is one. Since one is the principle of unity and measurement, these relatives have some relationship to number, but they are said according to unity absolutely speaking, i.e., represent how a thing is in some respect one with another. This oneness is exemplified in the following comments: "I'll take the same as he does." "The twins wore look-alike dresses." "The candidate demanded equal time with his opponent."

(b) Relations according to active and passive. These relations are either in terms of active and passive potency, or the acts thereof, which are to act and to undergo. Thus able to heat is active potency, while heatable is passive potency; heating and being heated are the corresponding actualities.

On the other hand, in things according to number, since they abstract from motion, there is no action except according to similitude—as when one speaks of multiplying, dividing, and so forth.

Action and passion, however, are spoken of according to different times; namely, past, present, and future.

(c) Relations according to knower and known. The distinctive characteristic of these relations—between sense and the sensible, intellect and the intelligible, science and the scientifically knowable—is that they are not reversible. Knowledge refers to something new constituted in the knower related to the known, but in the known nothing has changed. There is no relation of the known to the knower.

"To see and understand, and such actions (as will be stated in Book IX), remain in the agents, and do not pass out into things which undergo them. Whence the visible and the knowable do not undergo anything from the fact that they are understood or seen. And because of this, they are not referred to others, but others are referred to them.

"And it is the same in all other things in which something is said relatively because of the relation of another to it, as, for example, right and left in a column....A column is said to be on the right, because a man is to the left of it" (no. 1027).

(2) **Relation according to accident.** In this respect, things may be said to be relative because something they are connected with is so. Thus medicine might be called relative, because its genus, science, is relative. Equality and likeness in the abstract may be called relative, because in the concrete something is equal or alike. A subject may be called relative, because an accident is—as one man might be said to be twice another man.

C. Passions or Properties of Subject of This Science
1. Things Pertaining to Perfection of Being
a. Perfect

1) The perfect itself.
a) <u>According to itself.</u> Things are said to be perfect according to themselves in three ways:

1. <u>as that which has no part lacking</u>. Thus a man may be called perfect if he lacks no part; a day may be called perfect when there is nothing lacking to it.
2. <u>as that which lacks nothing pertaining to its proper power</u>. Thus a doctor is perfect if he possesses his art as he should, and the same may be said of a flute player. (One speaks also of a perfect fool.) Just as that is called perfect in the first sense to which nothing is lacking of its proper dimensive quantity, so that is called perfect in the second sense to which nothing is lacking of its proper quantity of power intended for it by nature. Both of these modes are considered according to interior perfection.
3. <u>as that which has attained its end.</u> Thus, when a man has attained his end which is beatitude or happiness, he is said to be perfect. Here perfection is considered in relation to something exterior. This end is not only last, but also that for the sake of which something is done. Thus, to reach that last thing which is death is not to attain an end in this sense.

A thing may be perfect in every way, surpassed by nothing in goodness, lacking nothing—and this is true of the first principle, namely, God. Or else a thing may be perfect in its own genus of being—as man is perfect when he has attained to beatitude, a body is perfect when it has three dimensions, the universe is perfect because there is nothing outside it.

b) With respect to something else. In this way that is perfect which contributes to the perfection of something else (as medicine is perfect which contributes to perfect health); or because it has something perfect (as a man is said to be perfect because he has perfect knowledge); or as representing something perfectly (as the likeness of a portrait may be said to be perfect); or, in general, any other ways in which something is referred to those things called perfect in the prime ways.

2) Conditions for the perfect. That which is perfect, as stated above, is terminated and absolute, not depending upon another, and not deprived of anything, but having those things which belong to it according to its genus. Hence one has the following terms signifying conditions needed for perfection:

a) Terminus. That which is ultimate for any thing, in such a way that nothing is outside that which is terminated, and everything that belongs to it is within it. Such is the definition of terminus. Of course, that which may be the terminus of one thing, may also serve as the principle of another—as the end of today is the beginning of tomorrow. Terminus is said in four ways:

1. as the end in any species of magnitude, or of something having magnitude—as point is the terminus of line, and surface of body.
2. similarly, as the extreme towards which of motion or action—although by extension it may be also used of the point from which the motion originates.
3. as the cause for the sake of which something is done—as last in one's intention, in contrast to the terminus which is last in motion or operation.
4. as the substance of a thing, i.e., the essence and definition signifying what the thing is. Indeed, it is the terminus or term of knowledge: "For the knowledge of a thing begins from certain exterior signs by which one arrives at knowing the definition of a thing; when one has arrived at which, there is had perfect knowledge of the thing" (no. 1048). The terminus in knowledge parallels the terminus in the thing, and the wholeness of the former involves having everything contained in the latter.

Terminus is said of principle, but not conversely, in that while every principle is a terminus of that which begins from it, that at which motion ends is a terminus but in no way a principle.

b) Per se.

(1) Secundum quod (that according to which). Since this is said more extensively than per se, its four meanings must be considered first:

1. as the species (i.e., the form) and the substance (i.e., the essence) of a thing are that according to which it is said to be.
2. as the subject in which something is disposed to be produced first is that according to which—as a body is said to be colored according to surface. Whereas the first mode pertains to form, this mode pertains to matter.
3. as universally any cause is according to which. Thus it is the same to inquire according to what something happened, and why it happened.
4. as position and place are signified, in the sense of *according to* meaning nearby or along with—for example, *He stood alongside him*, denoting according to what place someone stood. (This is clearer in the Greek.)

(2) Per se (according to itself). The four senses of per se are derived from a comparison to *secundum quod* (that according to which).

The first of these is found when the definition signifying what the being of each thing is, is said to be in it according to itself. Thus the *what it was for Socrates to be* (*quod quid erat Socrati esse*), i.e., his definition, is said of Socrates per se. Not only the definition but the parts of the definition, the genus and specific difference, are thus predicated per se. (This is also the first way of being per se set down in the *Posterior Analytics*.)

Per se is used in a second sense when something is in a first subject, when it is in it of itself. This may be true either because something is in the whole of the first subject, as color is thus said to be per se in surface (and thus per accidens in body through surface), or because something is in a part of the first subject—as man is said to be living per se, because a part of him, namely, the soul, is the first subject of life. (This is the second way of being per se set down in the *Posterior Analytics*, namely, when the subject is placed in the definition of the predicate. For the first and proper subject is placed in the definition of the proper accident.)

Per se is used in a third sense when something is said to be per se of which there is no other cause—as is the case with all immediate propositions, which, namely, are not proved through any middle. "Whence, although man has many causes, such as animal and two-footed, which are formal causes of himself, nevertheless, of this proposition *Man is man*, since it is immediate, there is no cause—and because of this, man is man according to himself" (no. 1056). (This is the fourth way of being per se set down in the *Posterior Analytics*, namely, when the effect is predicated of the cause—as when it is said that something killed, died because of being killed; that something cold, became cold because of being made cold.)

Per se is used in a fourth sense inasmuch as that is said to be per se which is by itself, i.e., alone. In this sense a man in the desert would be said to be per se, meaning solitary. In general, that would be per se in this sense which is in some thing, understood as being in that thing alone. It is true that the definition is in the defined alone, but there, when the definition is said to be per se in the defined, the meaning is primarily in the sense of being a statement of the essence. (This is the third way of saying per se set down in the *Posterior Analytics*.)

(3) Disposition. Since one meaning of according to which implies position, a discussion of disposition is appropriate. In general, disposition is nothing other than the order of parts in that which has parts. This may be in three ways:

1. according to the order of parts in place—and thus disposition is in the predicament of *situs* or position.
2. accordingly as the order of parts is considered according to potency or power—and thus disposition falls under the first species of quality in the *Predicaments*, as something is said to be disposed toward sickness or health accordingly as its parts are ordered in the active or passive power of the thing.
3. accordingly as the order of the parts is considered according to the outline and figure of the whole. Thus disposition or *situs* is posited as a difference in the genus of quantity—one species having position, such as line, surface, body, and place; another not, such as number and time. Time, as the numbering of motion, does not have position.

It is clear that disposition implies order, since its derivation implies position, and order is involved in the notion of position.

c) Having or habit.

(1) Twofold sense of having or habit. First, having designates a medium between the one having and that which is had. Although it is not an action, having in this sense is considered after the manner of an action, just as heating is a middle between that which heats and that which is heated—either actively, as the act emanating from the agent; or passively, as the motion undergone by the patient. When one thing makes, and the other is made, the middle is making. Thus, in regard to having, as when it is said that a man has a suit on, the having is a middle between the man and the suit, and is one of the predicaments, namely, having or *habitus*.

Secondly, having means the disposition according to which something is disposed well or ill. In this respect, health or sickness are habits.

The disposition may be either as the thing is disposed in itself, as in the case of health; or in relation to something, as one is called robust who is well disposed in doing something.

This may be likewise a disposition either of the whole or of a part. Thus the virtues of the parts of the soul are certain habits: temperance in the concupiscible, fortitude in the irascible, prudence in the rational part.

(2) Things consequent upon having or habit.

(a) After the manner of opposition.

1* Passion: as imperfect to perfect. Passion is said in the following four ways:

1. as the quality according to which alteration takes place, e.g., the redness of an apple. This is the third species of quality in the *Predicaments*, in which alone there can be alteration (as proved in *Physics* VII).
2. as passion is said with respect to the actions of quality and alteration. And in this sense, passion is one of the ten predicaments, as in the case of being heated, or being cooled, or of an apple being reddened.
3. as passion is taken for those alterations in particular which terminate at something evil, lamentable or sad. (For passion in the

sense of an alteration toward a good state has more the sense of a perfecting.)

4. as passion refers not to any harmful change at all, but to one of great harm. Thus one might refer to an ultimate torment as a passion.

(It should be noted here that terms such as *disposition, habit, passion*, because they are each susceptible of referring to different predicaments, are therefore not placed here exclusively under some specific predicament, such as quality, quantity, or relation.)

2* Privation: as direct opposition. Privation includes in its notion both negation and aptitude of subject; that is, it is not simply an absence, but an absence where there should be presence. For example, blindness is not simply absence of sight, but an absence where sight should be present. Therefore the modes of privation are distinguished according to both negation and aptitude of subject.

a* Aptitude of subject.

1. On the part of the thing which is deprived. In this respect, a plant may be said to lack or be deprived of sight, not that it is apt for sight, but rather because sight is something apt to be had by something. This excludes things which are not apt to be had by anything.

2. On the part of the subject. In this respect, that is said to be lacking which the subject is apt for having, but does not have, whether specifically or generically. Thus blindness is privation for man according to species, but of mole according to genus, insofar as it belongs to the genus, animal, to have sight. Therefore things may be impeded from having some characteristic not because of their genus, but because of their specific difference—as man is impeded from having wings.

3. According to circumstances. In this respect, even in an apt subject, not any lack at all is called privation. For example, a puppy is not called blind if it does not see at the moment of birth, but only when it should; darkness is not called night, the privation of day, anywhere there is no light, as in a cave, but only where light should be in daytime; a man is not stunted if he is not so tall as a mountain, or slow if he does not run like an antelope, or ignorant if he does not have knowledge as God does.

4. According to violent removal. Thus one is said to be deprived of his life by a bandit.

b* Negation.

1. As signified by various prefixes and suffixes. Thus unequal is the privation of that which could be equal; invisible of that which could be visible; armless of that which could have arms.
2. As signified not by total lack, but by having ill. Thus, something which has a sickly color is said to have no color; a radiator which has little heat is said to have no heat.
3. As having slightly. This is contained under the previous number in the sense that to have little of something is equivalent to having it badly.
4. As being not easy. Thus a pen might be called unusable, because it is not easy to use.
5. As being wholly lacking. Thus a man deprived of one eye is not said to be blind, but only a man deprived of both.

Corollary: From the above, there are plainly middles between being in a good state and being in the opposite extreme. A thing does not become bad by the defect of just any goodness at all. Thus a man is not reprehended if he recedes only slightly from the middle of virtue.

(b) After the manner of an effect. First, that is said to have which leads something according to its own nature, in natural things; or according to its will, in voluntary things. Thus a fever is said to have or possess a man, when he follows the nature of fever; a tyrant is said to have or hold a city which he rules according to his own good pleasure. Thus, too, one who is clothed has his clothes on, and a rich man has his possessions—since the clothes take the shape of the wearer, and the rich man uses his possessions as he wills.

Secondly, that is said to have in which a thing exists as in a proper subject. Thus the statue is said to have a certain shape; a man is said to have science; and in general, a thing is said to have quantity, or any accident, or any form.

Thirdly, the container is said to have the contents, and the contents to be had by that which contains. Thus a bottle has wine, and a city has inhabitants, and the whole has parts. (The whole, incidentally, differs from place as a container, since the whole is not separated from the parts—but the containing place is.)

Fourthly, that is said to have which prevents something from its natural inclination. Thus a column is said to have a stone on top of it—which it prevents from falling. As the first type was that of a violent motion—for example, a tyrant having a city in the palm of his hand and ruling it according to his pleasure—this type is that of a violent rest. To this also is reduced the third type, by which the containing has the contained—since otherwise the contents, unprevented, would, as in the case of the wine in a bottle, go their own way.

"Aristotle states in conclusion that the phrase *to be in something* is said in the same way as *to have*, and the manners of *being in* something follow upon the manners of *having*.

"Now there are eight ways of being in something laid down in *Physics* IV. Two of these, namely, as the integral whole is in the parts, and conversely; and two others, namely, as the universal whole is in the parts, and conversely; and another way, accordingly as the located is in place—all these follow upon the third manner of having: accordingly as the whole has parts, and place that which is located in the place.

"But the way in which something is said to be in something as in the efficient or moving cause—as the things of the kingdom are in the king—follows upon the first way of having set down here. But the manner of being in according to which the form is in the matter, is related to the second way of having set down here. But the way in which something is in the end is reduced to the fourth way of having set down here, or also to the first—since it is according to the end that the things move and rest which are for the end" (no. 1084).

b. Whole

Perfect and whole mean nearly the same, as is stated in *Physics* III. Here there first comes a discussion of part, then of whole. Concerning part, since parts are that out of which the whole is constituted, first there is a discussion of the ways in which something is out of or from something; then of the ways in which part is said.

1) Meaning of from.

a) To be made from something properly and primely.

1. <u>as from matter</u>—either in the common sense, as swords are made from metal, or in the specific sense, as swords are made from steel.

2. as from a first moving principle—as a battle arises out of an insult, and a house is from a builder, and health from medicine.
3. as, in the way of resolution, parts from the whole—as one can go from a house to the stones that compose it, from a poem to the verses out of which it is composed. In this case, instead of beginning from the material principle and working toward the form, one begins from the form, which is the end of generation, and works toward the matter.
4. as a species from the parts of the species—as, according to reason, the definition is composed out of its specific parts, e.g., animal and rational in the case of man; or according to the thing itself, as letter in the case of syllable. This is different from the first way, where the parts are on the part of matter: these are parts that enter into the species, as do body and soul in the case of animal; and angle in the case of triangle.

Material parts are, so to speak, accidental: thus it is accidental to a circle to be divided into two semicircles, or to a right angle to contain an acute angle. Such parts do not enter into the definition, but rather the converse is true.

b) To be made from something according to part. This occurs when what is true of a part is said of the whole, as a child is said to be from his father, although he is from a part of his father, namely, the sperm, and from a part of his mother, namely, the ovum.

c) To be made from something because of order alone. This occurs where something is said to come from something when it comes after it. It may be in two ways: either according to time and motion—as day comes out of night, and summer out of winter according to the motion of the earth and sun; or according to time only, as when one says, "From May on, it is time to go swimming."

2) Meaning of part. Something is said to be a part in the four following ways:

1. as that into which something is divided according to quantity, and this in two ways: either as any minor quantity into which the greater one is divided is so called (for example, as 2 is part of 3); or solely that lesser part which is a measure of the greater (thus 2 would not be a part of 3, but would be a part of 4).

2. as that into which something is divided without quantity—as the species are thus said to be the parts of the genus. In this case, the whole which is the genus is in each of the parts, i.e., the species.

3. as that into which some whole is divided, or out of which it is composed, whether it is a species, or has a species, as in the case of an individual. Thus angle is a part of triangle in the former sense; and bronze in the case of bronze sphere in the latter sense, where the parts are those of matter, into which, in the individual, the species are received.

4. as that which is set down in the definition of any thing, and these are parts of reason, as animal and rational in the case of man. In this respect, genus is a part of the species, whereas in the second way, species is a part of genus.

"From this it is evident that genus in the fourth way is a part of species, while in another way, namely, the second way, species is a part of genus. For in the second way, part is taken as the subjective part of the universal whole; but in the other three as an integral part.

"But it is taken in the first way for a part of quantity, while in the other two for a part of substance; nevertheless, in such a way that part according to the third way is a part of the thing, whether it be a part of the species or of the individual; while in the fourth way it is a part of reason" (no. 1097).

3) Meaning of whole.

a) Whole in common.

(1) Whole, in comparison to the defective. The common notion of whole consists in two things: first, that no one of the constitutive parts be lacking; secondly, that the parts be united in the whole. This is true both of the universal whole, in which the part is one with the whole, the species with the genus, and the whole is predicated of it; or of the integral whole, in which each part is not the whole, nor is the whole predicated of it, as syllable is not predicated of letter.

(a) Universal whole. The universal whole is considered as a whole in the sense that the many, of each of which it is predicated, may be considered its parts. Thus animal contains both man and horse. All of these are one in the whole, in the sense that each *is* the one whole.

(b)Integral whole. Its common notion, especially of that divisible into quantitative parts, is to be continuous and finite—finite in contrast to the infinite or unfinished; continuous in the sense of having parts not

separated and in act, but continuous and in potency (although the latter is not indispensable).

With respect to continuity, two differences should be noted:

1. That which is continuous by nature is more so than that which is continuous by art; for example, the continuity of the layers of skin than the continuity of two pieces of metal welded together.
2. "Since it is so that in quantity there is an order of parts—there being in quantity a beginning, middle, and end, in which the notion of position consists—necessarily all such continuous wholes must have position in their parts" (no. 1105).

A continuous whole is related to the position of its parts in one of three ways:

1. The diverse position of the parts makes no difference, as in the case of water and other liquids. Of these we say preferably *all the water* rather than *the whole water*.
2. The position does make a difference, as in the case of the parts of man or of any animal. Of these we say preferably *the whole animal* rather than *all the animal*.
3. The position may and may not make a difference, as in the case of clay or wax with a certain shape; position is indifferent in the matter, but not indifferent as to the form. In such cases, one uses both *whole* and *all*. Thus, of a clay statue one might say, *All the clay is of good quality, and the whole statue is beautiful.*

The reason why *all* is said of things in which the position of parts makes no difference, is because *all* is distributive: things in which position makes no difference, such as water, may be broken down into similar parts which are, so to speak, multiplications of the whole; whereas in things in which position of parts does make a difference, the perfection of the whole does not belong to any of the parts.

"Now whole signifies the collection of parts in some one thing: and therefore in those things, whole is properly said in which, from all the parts taken together, there is made one perfect thing, whose perfection belongs to none of the parts—as in the case of a house and an animal. Whence *all animal* is not said of one animal, but of several" (no. 1108).

Likewise, in cases where the parts are all alike, one may say *all* either in the singular or the plural—for example, *All water is wet* or *All animals have sense knowledge*; but of the integral diversified whole, one says, *The whole man is living.*

(2) Defective, as opposed to whole. In order that some whole be termed defective, seven conditions are required on the part of the whole, namely:

1. It must be a quantitative whole, having parts divisible according to quantity. A genus or universal whole cannot be called defective if one of its species is removed.
2. It must be a whole integrated out of parts. Thus the ultimate parts may not be called defective.
3. A remaining part of something having two parts cannot be called defective, since the residue must be greater than that which is removed.
4. No number may be defective, no matter how many parts it has, since if any part of a number be removed, it does not remain the same. "For example, if a cup is truncated, it still remains a cup; but number does not remain the same, any part of it having been removed. For any unity added or subtracted varies the species of number" (no. 1113).
5. It must have dissimilar parts, since otherwise the notion of the whole remains in each part, as in the case of the parts of water.
6. Nothing can be called defective in which position makes no difference, as in the case of water or fire.
7. It must be a continuous thing. Thus a musical harmony is not defective if a note is removed, even though the notes occupy determinate positions.

Likewise, on the part of that which is removed, there are three conditions:

1. That which is removed cannot be a principal part of the substance, without which the substance could not be—as in the case of the head of a man.
2. It must not be any part at all, but in an extremity. Thus a man would be called defective if he lost a hand, but not if he lost his tonsils.

3. It must be, furthermore, a part which does not regenerate. Thus, the loss of hair or nails does not constitute a man defective.

b) That whole which is genus.

(1) Ways in which genus is said. First, genus means the continuous generation of certain things having the same species. In this sense one speaks of the human genus (or kind). Such a genus is, according to Porphyry, a multitude of things having a relation to each other and to one principle.

Secondly, genus means the things which proceed from some first mover into being. Thus the genus is named after its progenitor, as Greeks are called Hellenes by kind from the name of their first progenitor (Hellen). This is the second way laid down by Porphyry (in his *Isagoge*, an Introduction to the *Predicaments*).

Thirdly, genus is used when surface is called the genus of superficial figures, and solid that of corporeal figures. Genus in this sense does not signify the essence, but rather the proper subject. Just as the genus is mentioned in the definition of the species, so the proper subject is mentioned in the definition of an accident. Thus odd and even are defined as passions of number.

Fourthly, genus means that which is set first in the definition and is predicated as *what* and the differences are its qualities. Thus animal is the genus of man, and rational is predicated as a certain substantial quality.

"For the genus is related to the difference as subject to quality. And therefore it is evident that predicable-genus and genus-subject are grouped, so to speak, under one mode, and both are after the manner of matter. For although predicable-genus is not matter, nevertheless it is taken from matter, as difference is from form. For something is said to be animal because it has sensitive nature. But it is called rational because it has a rational nature, which is related to sensitive as form to matter" (no. 1123).

(2) Ways something is said to be of diverse genus. In the first way (omitting the first two ways of stating genus, which do not pertain particularly to philosophy, and beginning with the third way), things are said to be of diverse genus whose prime subject is diverse. Thus, since the first subject of color is surface, and the first subject of taste is moisture, color and taste are of diverse genus. These subjects must not be able to resolve into one another, as solid into surface, nor into some

same thing. Thus species and matter are of diverse genus, since they have nothing in common, speaking essentially.

In another way, those things which are said according to a different figure of the predicaments (i.e., according to a different category—such as substance, quality, and so forth) are said to be of diverse genus. In effect, one category is not contained under the other, nor is there one common genus of all the predicaments.

As a consequence of the above, some things, such as color and taste, will be of diverse genus as to the first way, i.e., as to proper subject, and of the same genus as to the second way, i.e., as to the particular predicament, namely, quality.

"The first type of diversity of genus is more the field of the natural scientist and also of the [first] philosopher, since it is more real. But the second way is considered by the logician, since it is of reason" (no. 1127).

2. Things Pertaining to the Defect of Being
a. False

1) How said in things. There are two ways in which a statement signifying a reality is not properly composed.

The first way happens when that is composed which either should not, or cannot, be composed. Thus the contingent statement *You are sitting* is false when you are standing; the impossible statement *The diameter of the square is commensurable with the side* is always false.

The second way happens when something existing appears to be what it is not. Thus the things in dreams are, as dreams, real, but not as realities outside of dreams. Something may appear to be gold which is not—but it *is* something.

Thus, that is false in things which either is not at all, as in the first way, or is something, but not what it appears to be.

2) How said in definitions.

1. when a true definition is applied to that to which it does not belong—as the definition of circle to triangle.
2. when the elements of the definition itself are incompatible—as if one were to call something an inanimate animal. The latter type of definition is obviously a definition of nothing.

3) How said of human beings.

1. when a man is prompt and joyful in such false accounts, i.e., who loves such falsehood for its own sake, not, for example, for the sake of gain.
2. when a man states false accounts, which therefore are of nonbeing.

"He who voluntarily states a falsehood [the first case], although he is worse according to morals, nevertheless is more intelligent than he who believes himself to state the truth, although he is involuntarily speaking falsehood [the second case]" (no. 1138).

b. Accident

There are two senses in which the term *accident* is used. First, an accident means that which is in something and may be truly affirmed of it, nevertheless, not of necessity, nor for the most part, but in the lesser part.

This is true, for example, of the accident of finding a treasure when digging for fishing worms. In the same sense, a white musician is an accident, since it need not be, either of necessity, nor for the most part.

In a word, anything is in anything else accidentally when it is not in it according to itself (per se) or by nature. Thus, cold weather in summer is accidental, since it does not belong to summer as such, or by nature. Of such accidents there is no determinate cause, but rather they may be caused by various accidental causes—as the man finding the treasure may be digging for worms, or to lay a sewer.

Secondly, an accident means that which is in something according to itself, and nevertheless is not of its substance. This meaning is contrasted with the second way of saying per se, as for a triangle to have three interior angles equal to two right angles.

"Accident, therefore, according to the first way, is opposed to according to itself (per se). But accident in the second way is opposed to substantially" (no. 1143).

Chapter 9

How Metaphysics Treats of Being
(*Metaphysics*, VI)

A. The different mode of treating being in first philosophy
    1. It treats the principles of being as being
        a. How it agrees with other sciences
        b. How it differs from other sciences
    2. How it differs from other sciences in its treatment of being
        a. Natural science differs from practical science
        b. Natural science differs from other speculative sciences
            1) Natural sciences
            2) Mathematics
            3) First philosophy or metaphysics
B. Certain modes of being excluded from first philosophy
    1. Exclusion of being per accidens
        a. No science of accidental being
            1) By a sign
            2) By an argument
        b. What determined about accidental being
            1) What may be determined
                a) Its cause
                b) Its nature
                c) No science of being per accidens
            2) Exclusion of opinion denying being per accidens
                a) Exclusion of the opinion
                b) A conclusion
                c) How reconcile accident and infallible divine providence
                    (1) Area of contingency in universal causes

How Metaphysics Treats of Being
(*Metaphysics*, VI)

A. The different mode of treating being in first philosophy
    1. It treats the principles of being as being
    2. How it differs from other sciences in its treatment of being
B. Certain modes of being excluded from first philosophy
    1. Exclusion of being per accidens
    2. Exclusion of being as truth

The subject of first philosophy, namely, being and unity, and those things which follow being as such, has already been outlined (in Chapter 6).

Likewise the multiple ways in which all these things are stated have been surveyed (in Chapter 8).

It now remains to treat of being and its properties. As a first step in this, it is necessary to determine the way of treating being which is appropriate to this science. As has been seen, in addition to general logic, there is also a logic or method proper to each science. At this point, therefore, one must determine the method proper to first philosophy.

A. The Different Mode of Treating Being in First Philosophy
1. It Treats the Principles of Being As Being
a. How It Agrees with Other Sciences

Every science seeks the principles and causes of its subject. Thus medicine seeks the causes of health; mathematics seeks the principles which open up a knowledge of mathematical properties, such as those of the triangle; practical science seeks the universal principles from which it can proceed to particular operations.

These principles are either more certain to us, because they are closer to the senses, as in the case of natural things; or they are more simple and prior according to nature, as in the case of mathematics.

"But knowledge which is sensitive only, is not through principles and causes; rather, it arises from the fact of the sensible object being presented to the sense. For to discourse from causes to the caused, or conversely, does not belong to sense, but is of intellect alone" (no. 1146).

b. How It Differs from Other Sciences

"All these particular sciences mentioned above are concerned with some one particular genus of being, such as, for example, number, or magnitude, or something similar. And each treats circumscriptively of its 'subject genus,' i.e., of that genus and not of another—as the science which treats of number does not treat of magnitude. For none of them treats of 'being absolutely speaking,' i.e., of being in common, nor of any particular being as it is being. Thus arithmetic does not determine concerning number as it is being, but as it is number. For to consider any being insofar as it is being, is proper to the metaphysician" (no. 1147).

Since everything has being through its essence, just as the particular sciences do not treat of being as such, neither do they treat of definition.

"Now the *what something is* of its subject is made plain by some sciences through sense, as the science which is of animals takes what is animal through that which 'appears to sense,' i.e., through sense and motion, by which animal is discerned from nonanimal. Other sciences derive the *what something is* of their subject by supposition from some other science, as geometry derives what magnitude is from the first philosopher.

"And thus, from the *what something is* which is known through sense or supposition, the sciences demonstrate the proper passions which are according to themselves in the subject-genus concerning which they are. For the definition is the middle term in demonstrations which are *because of which* [*propter quid*, i.e., giving the proper cause because of which something is].

"But the mode of demonstration is diverse, since some demonstrations are necessary, as with the mathematical sciences; some are 'weaker,' i.e., not with necessity, as in the natural sciences, in which many demonstrations are taken from those things which do not inhere always, but frequently" (no. 1149).

"And just as no particular science determines *what something is* [i.e., definition, since definition, as such, is common to all the sciences], so also none of them states of the genus-subject, about which it is, that it is or is not. And this comes about reasonably, since it belongs to the same science to determine the question, whether something is, and to manifest what something is. For what something is must be taken as a middle to show whether something is. And both belong to the consideration of the [first] philosopher, who considers being as being. And therefore each and every particular science supposes of its subject both *that* it is and *what* it is, as is stated in *Posterior Analytics* I" (no. 1151).

2. How It Differs from Other Sciences in Its Treatment of Being
a. Natural Science Differs from Practical Science

"Natural science is not about being absolutely speaking, but about a certain genus of being, namely, about natural substance, which has within it the principle of motion and rest. From this it appears that it is neither active nor factive. For to act and to make differ. Acting, indeed, is according to an operation which remains in the agent, as in the case of choosing, understanding, and so forth—whence the active sciences are called moral sciences. Making, however, is according to an operation which goes outside to the transmutation of matter, as in the case of sawing, burning, and the like—whence the factive sciences are called the mechanical arts.

"That natural science is not factive is evident, since the principle of the factive science is in the one making, not in the product, which is the artifact. But the principle of motion in natural things is in the natural things themselves. Now the principles of things makable by art, which is in the maker, are, first of all, the intellect, which first finds the art; and secondly, the art, which is a habit of the intellect; and thirdly, some power which carries out, as in the case of the motive power through which the artisan carries out the conception of art. Whence it is evident that natural science is not factive.

"And for the same reason it is evident that it is not active. For the principle of the active science is in the agent, not in the action or the *mores*. This principle is...election [choice]. For the same thing is able to be done and able to be elected [or chosen]. Thus, therefore, it is evident that natural science is neither active nor factive.

"If, therefore, every science is either active, or factive, or theoretical [i.e., speculative], it follows that natural science is theoretical. Nevertheless it is 'theoretical,' i.e., speculative, as about a determinate genus of being, that which, namely, is able to be moved. For mobile being is the subject of natural philosophy. And it is solely about 'such a substance,' i.e., the quiddity and essence of a thing which according to its notion is not separable from matter, for the most part—and he [Aristotle] says this because of the intellect, which falls in a certain way under the consideration of the natural philosopher, and yet its substance is separable. Thus it is evident that natural science is about a determinate subject, which is mobile being; and that it has a determinate mode of defining, namely, with matter" (nos. 1152-55).

b. Natural Science Differs from Other Speculative Sciences

This difference will be ascertained by studying the proper mode of defining of each of the speculative sciences.

"Since definition is the middle of demonstration, and consequently a principle of scientific knowledge, it is necessary that diversity in the speculative sciences should be consequent upon a diverse mode of defining" (no. 1156).

1) Natural sciences. Certain things are defined after the manner of the definition of snub-nosed, a definition which clearly requires the inclusion of matter. Thus, a snub-nosed person might be defined as a person with a nose having a concavity in the middle.

Other things are defined after the manner of concave, in a way that leaves matter aside. Thus concave could be defined as that whose middle recedes from the extremities.

The definitions of all natural things, of animal, nose, bone, flesh, and so forth, are like that of snub-nosed.

"For of none of the aforesaid can the definition be assigned without motion. Rather, each and everyone of them has sensible matter in its definition, and consequently, motion. For to every sensible matter there corresponds a proper motion....And because of this, the natural philosopher considers certain things even of the soul, namely, those which are not defined without sensible matter. For it is stated in *De Anima* II that the soul is the first act of a physical organic body having the power of life.

"But the soul accordingly as it is not the act of such a body does not pertain to the consideration of the natural philosopher, if as soul it is able to be separated from the body" (nos. 1158-59).

2) Mathematics. In contrast to natural science, mathematics defines its subject matter without sensible motion and matter. As considering its subject without motion, it plainly cannot be an active or a factive science, since neither doing nor making can be without motion. However, whether the fact of treating mathematical things without motion constitutes them as existing separately from the mobile world, as Plato thought, is another question, to be solved later.

"Nevertheless, this is plain: that mathematical science speculates concerning certain things insofar as they are immobile and insofar as they are separated from sensible matter, although according to being they may not be immobile or separable. For their definition is without sensible matter, as, for example, the definition of concave or curved.

"In this, therefore, mathematics differs from physics [i.e., natural philosophy or natural science], since physics considers those things whose definitions are with sensible matter. And therefore it considers nonseparated things insofar as they are nonseparated. But mathematics considers those things whose definitions are without sensible matter. And therefore, even if those things are not separated which it considers, nevertheless it considers them insofar as they are separated" (no. 1161).

3) First philosophy or metaphysics. If there is some being which is actually immobile according to being, and consequently eternal and separable from matter according to being, such a being will transcend the consideration of physics, which deals with mobile being, and mathematics, which deals with being separable from matter according to reason only. (Certain mathematical sciences are, however, applied to mobile things, as in the case of astronomy.) These immaterial and immobile beings are the causes of the sensible things manifest to us. As being the chief beings, they are the causes of other, participated being; as causes of generation, they must themselves be ungenerated.

"Hence it is evident that the science which treats of such beings is the first of all, and considers the common causes of all beings. Whence it is the causes of beings accordingly as they are beings, which are sought in first philosophy as he [Aristotle] proposed in Book I. From this there also appears the falsity of the opinion of those who set down that Aristotle thought that God was not the cause of the substance of the heavens, but of its motion only.

"One should also note that although there pertains to the consideration of first philosophy those things which are separated according to being and definition from matter and motion, that nevertheless the [first] philosopher scrutinizes not only those but also sensible things insofar as they are being" (nos. 1164-65).

Since, if there is a divine being, such a being will be among the immobile and immaterial beings which are the object of this science, it is rightly called theology. The subject matter of this science will therefore be both universally of being in common, and determinately of separable and immobile beings.

"If there is no other substance besides those which exist according to nature, of which is physics, physics will be the first science. But if there is some immobile substance, this substance will be prior to natural substance, and consequently, the philosophy concerning such a substance will be first philosophy. And since it is first, it will therefore be universal, and it will belong to it to speculate concerning being as it is being, and of *what something is* [i.e., of essence, and the definition stating it], and of those things which belong to being insofar as it is being. For it is the same science which is of the first being, and of being in common, as was had in the beginning of Book IV" (no. 1170).

B. Certain Modes of Being Excluded from First Philosophy
1. Exclusion of Being per Accidens

There are four ways in which being universally speaking may be said:

1. according to accident or per accidens;
2. as signifying the truth of a proposition;
3. as containing under it the figures of the predicaments;
4. as divided into potency and act.

It is the intention of this science to exclude the first two modes. After establishing that there can be no science of accidental being, there is then determined whatever may be determined.

a. No Science of Accidental Being

1) By a sign. For example, in the practical sciences, such as house-building, the builder is responsible for the house, but cannot control the accidental effects, for example, whether the house may prove a blessing to some, a curse to others. Likewise in speculative science, geometry is concerned with the properties of triangle such as its having its interior angles equal to two right angles, but whether a triangle be of wood or metal is of no concern to the science, being accidental to the nature of triangle.

2) By an argument. Accidental being is being, so to speak, in name only. Thus, white musician has only accidental unity and consequently only accidental being. It is not really one thing; it arises out of one being predicated of the other accidentally. This accidental being, such as white musician, is the principal tool of sophistry: thus, by neglecting to distinguish between being per se and being per accidens, one may argue, *John is different from John the musician; but John is John the musician; therefore John is different from himself.* Another further indication of the near nonbeing of being per accidens is the fact that beings which are not per accidens are generated and corrupted, but not so being per accidens: in order to produce grammatical musician one process does not suffice, but rather a separate one is required for each aspect; but two-footed animal or risible man is generated in a single process.

b. What Determined about Accidental Being

1) What may be determined.
a) Its cause. The cause of accidental being is that which occurs for the most part.

"In beings certain things are always the same from necessity—not, indeed, accordingly as necessity means violence, but as necessity is said to be that which may not be otherwise, as for man to be animal; while certain are not from necessity, nor always, but are according to more, i.e., for the most part. 'This,' namely, being for the most part, is the cause and principle that something is per accidens. For in things which are always there cannot be anything per accidens, since only that which is per se can be necessary and eternal, as was had in Book V. Whence it remains that only in contingent things can there be being per accidens.

"But that which is contingent to either side cannot be the cause of anything as such. For accordingly as it is to either side, it has the disposition of matter, which is in potency to two opposites—and nothing acts accordingly as it is potency. Whence it is necessary that the cause which is toward either side, as, for example, the will, in order to act, be inclined more to one part, by being moved by the desirable, and thus be a cause for the most part. Now that which is contingent in the lesser part is the being per accidens whose cause is sought. Whence it remains that the cause of being per accidens is the contingent for the most part, since its defect is in the lesser part. And this is being per accidens" (nos. 1182-83).

b) Its nature. A cook intending by his art to make a tasty dish, may also make a nourishing one; a builder building a home, may also build a happy home—but this is not a sure result of his art like a waterproof roof.

"What is outside the intent of the art, is not produced by the art, speaking absolutely. And therefore the accidental being which is outside the intent of the art, is not produced by the art. For of other things which are per se, there are sometimes determinate factive powers, but of being per accidens, no art or determinate power is productive. This is because, of those things which are, or are produced, by accident, there must be a cause according to accident and not determined. For effect and cause are proportionate to each other; and therefore, an effect per accidens has a cause per accidens, just as an effect per se has a cause per se" (no. 1185).

Obviously, then, the source of that which happens accidentally, for the lesser part, is that which happens for the most part. If such things did not happen sometimes, everything would be necessary.

"For if there were not produced sometimes that which is for the lesser part, then that which is for the most part would never fail, but would be always and of necessity. Thus all things would be eternal and necessary, which is false. And since the defect of that which is for the most part is because of matter which is not perfectly subject to the power acting for the most part, therefore matter is the cause of that which happens otherwise than 'for the most part,' namely of that which happens in the lesser part—a cause, indeed, which is not necessary but contingent" (no. 1186).

Obviously, too, everything cannot be accidental, just as everything cannot be necessary; because the accidental, in order to be for the lesser part, presupposes the existence of that which is seen to be for the most part. But although everything is not necessary, just as everything is not accidental, nevertheless some being will be shown to be absolutely necessary, in the end of this science.

c) **No science of being per accidens.** This is clear from the fact that all science is either of that which is always, or of that which is for the most part. In effect, one can teach or be taught only that which is always or for the most part. Since being per accidens is for the lesser part, it cannot be the object of science.

2) Exclusion of opinion denying being per accidens.

a) **Exclusion of the opinion.** There are those who hold that there is no such thing as accidental being, no such thing as an accident. Everything has a determined proper cause, and once this cause is laid down, the effect inevitably follows. Thus, if the unpredictable happens, it is not because of any accident in nature, but simply because of a lack of thorough knowledge of all the causes involved, on our part. This is the determinism which appears to have motivated Newtonian physics as developed by Laplace, and in which what we call chance, is reduced to human ignorance. (Today that outlook tends to be replaced by the new outlook of indeterminism whereby now, again from the viewpoint of the observing subject, nothing can be objectively determined—if only because the light rays involved in knowing something displace the thing observed and prevent any purely objective observation. One will note that this does not affect the idea of determinism in itself, which continues to hold that an object or particle is at a certain place at a certain instant even if immeasurably so.)

What are some of the consequences of this determinism which excludes accidents? It will introduce an untenable necessity into events. Thus, suppose that a man is struck by lightning and killed, while standing under a tree in Central Park; and that he is in Central Park because he took a short cut to the grocery store, and that he took a short cut to the grocery store to buy some cat food. According to determinism, from the moment he decides to go out and buy some cat food for his cat, he is bringing about his own death as surely as if he pointed a gun at his head and shot himself.

Why is this so? It is so because all effects follow from causes in the same determinate way. Since his being struck by lightning is caused from his deciding to buy cat food, when he made that decision he signed his death warrant.

One will object that at any moment his free will could have broken the chain of events, that he could have said, "Let the cat eat sardines;

and perish the thought of going out to buy cat food!" But thorough-going determinism does not admit of any nonmaterial factor entering into the sequence of events: a man's decisions are as physically determined as the phototropic motions of the plants.

Thus free will is the same type of illusion as that of the attributing of things to chance or accident. (It is the refusal to admit of any real accident that led Freud, an absolute materialistic determinist, to assume that so-called slips of the tongue could not be accidents, but must represent interior feelings which the speaker refuses to admit to himself and tries to submerge. Thus, if a man should say to another, "I should be glad to hinder—I mean, handle—your case," this could not be an accident, but must reveal some submerged, usually iniquitous, design.)

b) A conclusion. It is plain that, no matter what they may say, human beings do not accept as a fact the absolutely physically determined sequence of events. And if this cannot be so, neither can the suppositions be accepted from which it follows, namely, that every effect has a per se cause, and that once the cause is laid down the effect must follow. Thus there must be events in reality which fail to have any proper cause in which they may be foreseen. Likewise, even if a cause is already in motion, its effect need not always necessarily follow.

c) How reconcile accident and infallible divine providence. The exclusion of the opinion that there can be no accidents seems to exclude not only fatalism and determinism, but also divine providence. The former opinion is expressed as follows:

"Now those who posit fate, say that the contingent things which are done here, and which appear to be accidental, are reducible to some power of a heavenly body, through whose action those things which, considered in themselves, appear to come about by accident, are produced with a certain order" (no. 1203).

This outlook of fate does not differ from that of determinism, which, if it does not attribute the necessary sequence of apparently accidental events to some planet, nevertheless does attribute it to a physically determined sequence circumscribed in the physical universe.

Indeterminism does not deny this so much as it questions one's ability ever to measure objectively the determinism whose existence, nevertheless, is not challenged.

Insofar as the results are concerned, the acceptance of divine providence likewise excludes the possibility of any intrinsically undetermined event—since all things are under the deliberate divine control.

How may the acceptance of chance events be reconciled with the infallible fulfillment of providence—both of which must be held by the Christian?

(1) Area of contingency in universal causes. "In order clearly to see these things, one must consider that the higher a cause is, by so much the more does its causality extend itself to more things. For the higher cause has a proper effect which is higher, which is more common and found in more. For example, in artificial things, it is evident that the political art, which is over the military art, extends itself to the whole status of the community. But the military art extends only to those who are contained within the military order. For the ordination which is in effects from some cause extends only so far as extends the causality of that cause. For every per se cause has determined effects which it produces according to a certain order. It is plain, therefore, that the effects, related to some lower cause, appear to have no order but fall in with each other accidentally, which effects, if they be referred to a superior common cause, are found to be ordered, and not accidentally conjoined, but to be produced simultaneously by one per se cause" (no. 1205).

"For example, the flowering of this or that plant, if it be referred to the particular power which is in this or that plant, appears to have no order—rather, it appears to be accidental—insofar as when this plant flowers, another should flower. And this is because the cause of the power of this plant extends to its flowering, and not to the flowering of another: whence it is indeed the cause that this plant should flower, but not that it should flower simultaneously with another. But if it be referred to the power of the heavenly body, which is the common cause, this is found to be not per accidens, that when this plant flowers, the other should flower, but to be ordered by some first cause ordering this, which simultaneously moves both plants to flower.

"For there is found in things a threefold gradation of causes:

1. There is first an incorruptible and immutable cause, namely, the divine.
2. Under this there is secondly a cause which is incorruptible, but mutable, namely, the heavenly body.
3. Under this there are thirdly the corruptible and mutable causes. These causes, therefore, in the third degree are particular, and determined to their proper effects according to the species of

each. For example, fire generates fire; and man generates man; and plant, a plant" (nos. 1206-7).

"But the cause of the first degree is absolutely universal: for its proper effect is being. Whence, whatever is, and in whatever way it is, is properly contained under the causality and ordination of this cause.

"If therefore we should reduce the things which are here contingent to particular proximate causes only, many things are found to come about by accident, both because of the *concursus of two causes*, of which one is not contained under the other, as when outside my intention thieves come upon me—for this concursus is caused by a twofold motive power, mine, namely, and the thieves'—and because of the *defect of the agent*, to whom there occurs a weakness such that it is not able to arrive at the end intended, as when someone falls on the way because of tiredness; and also because of the *indisposition of the matter*, which does not receive the form intended by the agent, but one of another sort, as happens in the monstrous births of animals.

"But if these contingent things are further reduced to a heavenly cause, many of them are found to be not accidental; since the particular causes, even though they be not contained under each other, nevertheless are contained under one common heavenly cause, whence their concursus can have some one determinate celestial cause. Now since this power of the heavenly body is both incorruptible and impassible, no effect can go outside the order of its causality due to the defect or weakness of this power. But since it acts by moving, and every such agent requires determined and disposed matter, it can occur that in natural things the heavenly power does not attain its effect because of the indisposition of the matter—and this will be accidental....When some agent produces its effect for the most part, and not always, it follows that it fails in the lesser part—and this is per accidens" (nos. 1209-12).

"Likewise for another reason things may be found to be accidental after reduction to the heavenly body has been made. For in these lower things there are found certain agent causes which are able to act of themselves without the impression of the heavenly body, namely, *rational souls*, to which the power of the heavenly body does not attain (since they are forms not subject to bodies) unless accidentally, insofar, namely, as from the impression of the heavenly body there is made some change in the body, and accidentally in the powers of the soul, which are acts of certain parts of the body, from which the rational soul is inclined toward act, although no necessity is imposed, since it has free domain over the passions to be able to refuse assent to them" (no. 1213).

"But if these contingent things are reduced further to the highest divine cause, nothing may be found which escapes its order, since its causality extends to all things insofar as they are beings. Therefore its causality cannot be impeded through the indisposition of the matter, since both the matter itself and its dispositions do not escape the order of this agent, which is an agent after the manner of that which gives being, and not solely after the manner of that which moves and alters. For it cannot be averred that matter might be presupposed to being as it is presupposed to being moved, as the subject thereof; rather, it is a part of the essence of the thing. Just as, therefore, the power of that which alters and moves is not impeded by the essence of motion, or its terminus, but by the subject which is presupposed, so the power of that which gives being is not impeded by matter, or by anything whatever which might in any way occur to the being of the thing. From this it is also clear that there can be no agent cause in these lower things which is not subject to its order.

"It remains therefore that all things which occur here, insofar as they are referred to the first divine cause, are found to be ordered and not accidental, although by comparison to the other causes they may be found to be accidental. And because of this it is stated according to the Catholic faith that nothing is done by accident or fortuitously in the universe, and that all things are subordinated to divine providence....

(2) Contingency coordinated with infallible divine cause. "It remains now to see how the laying down of fate and providence does not remove contingency from things, as though all things were to happen from necessity. Concerning fate, indeed, this has been made plain from what has been said. For it was shown that although the heavenly bodies and their motions and actions as far as in themselves is concerned have necessity, nevertheless their effects in these lower things can fail, either because of the indisposition of the matter, or because of the rational soul, which has free choice as to following the inclinations which derive from the heavenly impression or not to following them. And so it remains that these effects do not come about with necessity, but contingently. For the laying down of a celestial cause is not the laying down of a cause such that the effect follows with necessity, as upon the composition of contraries there follows the death of an animal, as was touched upon in the letter [of the text of Aristotle].

"But there is a greater difficulty concerning providence. For divine providence cannot fail. These two things, indeed, are impossibly combined: namely, that something should be foreseen by God, and it not be done. And so it seems that since providence has been laid down, it must be necessary for its effect to follow.

"But one must understand that there depends from the same cause both the effect and all the things which are the per se accidents of this effect. For just as man is from nature, so are all his per se accidents, such as to be able to laugh, and to be receptive to training of the mind. But if some cause should not make man absolutely, but *such* a man, it will not belong to it to constitute those things which are the per se accidents of man, but to use them only. For the political scientist makes a man civic, but he does not, however, make him susceptible to training of the mind, but rather uses this property of man to the end of making him civic.

"As was said, being insofar as it is being has as its cause God himself. Whence, just as being itself is subjected to divine providence, so also all the accidents of being as being, among which are necessary and contingent. To divine providence it pertains, therefore, not only to make this being, but also to give it contingency or necessity. Accordingly as it has willed to give to each thing contingency or necessity, it has prepared for it mediate causes, from which it may follow with necessity or contingently. Every effect, therefore, accordingly as it is under the order of divine providence, is found to have necessity. From this it comes about that this conditional is true: 'If something is foreseen by God, it will be.'

"But accordingly as some effect is considered under the order of a proximate cause, thus not every effect is necessary, but one is necessary and the other contingent according to the analogy of their cause. For effects in their nature resemble the proximate causes, not the remote, to whose condition they are unable to attain.

"Thus, therefore, it is plain that when we speak of divine providence we should not say only that this thing is provided by God that it be, but that this thing is provided by God that it be contingently or that it be with necessity. Whence it does not follow according to the argument of Aristotle laid down here that from the fact of the laying down of divine providence all effects are necessary, but that it is necessary for the effect to be contingently or of necessity. This, indeed, is peculiar to this cause, namely, to divine providence. For the remaining causes do not constitute the law of necessity or contingency, but rather use it as constituted by the higher cause. Whence there is subjected to the causality of any other cause whatever only that its effect be. But that it should be necessarily or contingently depends on the higher cause, which is the cause of being insofar as it is being—from which the order of necessity and contingency in things derives" (nos. 1215-22).

2. Exclusion of Being As Truth
a. How This Being Is Said

A certain type of being means nothing other than that something *is* true. "For when we ask if man is animal, we answer that he *is*, by which is signified that the aforesaid proposition *is true*. And in the same way, nonbeing signifies, so to speak, falsity. For when one answers, 'He *is not*,' it is signified that the proposed statement *is false*" (no. 1223).

The being in question here is concerned with composition and division. Incomplex expressions such as *man, animal*, signify neither truth nor falsehood. It is only expressions made complex by the composition and division which constitute affirmation and negation (for example, *Man is animal, Man is not animal*), which have truth or falsity. And since expressions are signs of thoughts, the same is to be said of the conceptions of the intellect: the simple ones have neither truth nor falsehood, but only those made complex by affirmation or negation.

Since the composition and division of verbal expression is simply the expression of the composition and division of the intellect, the question arises of how the intellect considers the elements of composition and division, whether separately or conjointly. That is, in the statement *Man is animal*, does the intellect consider *man* and *animal* as separate things or as a unity? In knowing them first, the intellect considers them separately, conceiving what man is and what animal is without affirming or denying anything. Subsequently the intellect knows the two as constituting a certain unity, in which it considers the whole, not the parts, as the mind knows house as a whole, not as a sequence of knowing first foundation, then walls, and so forth—and this unity constitutes either affirmation or negation.

Where, then, do truth and falsehood lie? In things or in the mind? The truth or falsehood of our statement lies in the mind—not in the act of the mind which is the grasp of incomplex realities, but in the act of composing and dividing.

"Now the intellect has two operations, one of which is called the understanding of indivisibles, whereby the intellect forms simple conceptions of things by understanding the *what something is* of each thing. The other operation is that by which it composes and divides.

"But truth and falsity, even though they are in the mind, nevertheless are not connected with that operation of the mind whereby the intellect forms simple conceptions, and the *what something is* of things....Whence it remains, through the process of division, that since truth and falsity are not in things, nor in the mind concerned with simple things and *what something is*, that they are related to the composition and division of the mind first and principally, and secondarily to the expression which signifies the conception of the mind. And he [Aristotle] further concludes that whatever should be considered concerning being and nonbeing thus said, namely, as being signifies true, and nonbeing false, should be scrutinized 'later,' namely, at the end of Book IX, and also in the book *De Anima*, and in logic. For the whole of logic is seen to be of being and nonbeing thus stated.

"It should be known, however, that since any knowledge is perfected by the fact of the likeness of the thing known being in the knower, then just as the perfection of the thing known consists in its having such a form by which it is such a thing, so the perfection of knowledge consists in this, that it should have the likeness of the aforesaid form. Now from the fact that the thing known has the form which is due it, it is called good; and from the fact of having some defect, it is called bad. And in the same way, from the fact of the knower's having the likeness of the thing known, he is said to have true knowledge; from the fact of failing in such a likeness, he is said to have false knowledge. Therefore, just as good and bad designate the perfections which are in things, so true and false designate the perfections of knowledge.

"But although there may be in sensitive knowledge the likeness of the thing known, nevertheless it does not pertain to sense to know the notion of this likeness, but solely to the intellect. And therefore, although sense may be true of the sensible thing, nevertheless sense does not know truth, but solely the intellect. And because of this it is stated that true and false are in the mind.

"Now the intellect has in itself the likeness of the thing understood accordingly as it conceives the notions of incomplex things. Nevertheless it does not because of this judge the likeness, but solely when it composes or divides. For when the intellect conceives that which is mortal rational animal, it has in itself the likeness of man. But it does not because of this know itself to have this likeness, since it does not judge man to be rational animal and mortal. And therefore in this sole second operation of the intellect is there truth and falsehood, accordingly as the intellect not only has the likeness of the thing understood, but also reflects on that likeness, knowing and judging it. From this, therefore, it is evident that truth is not in things, but solely in the mind, and also in composition and division.

"And if a thing be sometimes said to be false, or also a definition, this will be in reference to affirmation and negation. For a thing is said to be false, as was had in the end of Book V, either because it wholly is not, as, for example, a diameter [diagonal] commensurate [with the side of a square]; or because it is, indeed, but is disposed to being seen other than it is. And in the same way a definition is called false—either because it is of no thing, or because it is assigned to something other than that of which it is the definition. For in all these ways it is clear that false in things or in definitions is said by reason of a false enunciation concerning them....

"It is also evident that nothing prevents the true from being a certain good, accordingly as the intellect knowing is taken as a certain thing. For just as any thing is called good by reason of its perfection, so too the intellect knowing, by its truth.

"It also appears from all of this which is said that true and false, which are the objects of knowledge, are in the mind. But good and evil, which are the objects of appetite, are in things. Likewise just as knowledge is perfected by the things known being in the knower, so any appetite is perfected by the order of the one desiring to the things able to be desired" (nos. 1232-40).

b. Exclusion of Being As Truth, and Accidental Being

"He [Aristotle] excludes being as true and being per accidens from the principal consideration of this doctrine, saying that the composition and division in which there is true and false are in the mind and not in things. There is found, indeed, a certain composition in things, but such a composition makes one thing, which the intellect receives as one by simple conception.

"But the composition or division by which the intellect conjoins or divides its concepts, is only in the intellect, not in things. For it consists in a certain comparison of two concepts—whether these two are the same in reality or diverse. For the intellect sometimes uses one as two in forming a composition—as one says, "Man is man"—from which it is evident that such a composition is only in the intellect, not in things. And therefore, whatever is a being in the sense of the true and exists in such a composition, is other than those things which properly are beings, which are the things outside the soul, each of which is either 'what something is,' i.e., substance, or quality, or quantity, or something [else] incomplex, which the mind conjoins or divides.

"And therefore both are to be passed over, namely, both being per accidens and the being which signifies true—since of the former, namely, being per accidens, the cause is indeterminate, and therefore it does not fall under art, as was shown; while of the latter, namely, being as true, the cause is 'some passion of the mind,' i.e., of the intellect composing and dividing. And therefore it pertains to the science of the intellect [i.e., psychology and logic].

"And another reason is because both, i.e., both being as true and being per accidens, are concerned with a certain genus of being, not with the being absolutely speaking per se which is in things; nor do they show forth any other nature of being existing outside per se being. For it is evident that being per accidens is from the accidental concourse of beings outside the mind, both of which are per se. For example, although musical grammarian is per accidens, nevertheless both grammarian and musical are being per se, since both, taken per se have a determinate cause. And likewise the intellect makes composition and division concerning those things which are contained under the predicaments.

"Whence, if one should sufficiently determine that genus of being which is contained under the predicaments, it will be manifest concerning being per accidens and being as true. And because of this such beings are passed over. But rather one must scrutinize the causes and principles of being said per se, insofar as it is being" (nos. 1241-44).

Chapter 10

Substance, the Principal Subject of Metaphysics

(*Metaphysics*, VII-VIII)

A. Sole treatment of substance is sufficient
B. Treatment of substance
  1. Manner and order of treatment
    a. Manner: according to form
    b. Order: from sensible substances to intelligible substances
  2. The treatment
    a. According to logical and common notions
      1) Definition properly only of substance
      2) Definition of accidents
      3) Definition stands for substance, not excluding accidents
      4) Essence is a principle both speculatively and practically
      5) Parts of definition are not parts of thing
      6) Study of sensible substances to reach immaterial substances
      7) In material things, essence is defined without individual matter
      8) Definition is one of a substance that is one
      9) Definition is properly through intrinsic causes of substance
      10) Definition seeks something of something
      11) Sensible substances used as effects to reach immaterial substances as causes
    b. According to proper principles of sensible substance
      1) Recapitulation of principal intent of science

2) Principles of sensible substance
   a) Matter
   b) Form
   c) The composite

Substance, the Principal Subject of Metaphysics
(*Metaphysics*, VII-VIII)

A. Sole treatment of substance is sufficient
B. Treatment of substance
    1. Manner and order of treatment
      a. Manner: according to form
      b. Order: from sensible substances to intelligible substances
    2. The treatment
      a. According to logical and common notions
      b. According to proper principles of sensible substance

The aim of every science is to arrive at a knowledge of the principles and causes of its subject. In the case of metaphysics, this means arriving at a knowledge of the principles and causes of being in common.

In the present chapter, the intent is to show that the treatment of being in common is adequately handled by the treatment of substance; and that this treatment of substance proceeds from sensible substance to immaterial or separated substance.

Before this, however, it is appropriate to give the plan of what remains to be treated in this summary of metaphysics. This involves a treatment of:

    1. being as being
      a. as being
        1) as divided into the ten predicaments, principally substance (chapter 10)
        2) as divided into potency and act (chapter 11)

b. as one (chapter 12)
2. first principles of being (chapter 13)

A. Sole Treatment of Substance Is Sufficient

It will be sufficient, in order to treat of being in common, to treat of substance, and initially, of sensible substance. This is because substance is that which truly is, while the remaining type of being, namely, accident, depends upon substance for existence.

This may be seen from the fact that when we ask what something is, we state, not an accident, but the substance of the thing. Thus, when we ask what man is, we do not answer that he is something short, or something heavy, or something moving. That is, we do not state his being in terms of accidents, but answer rather in terms of his substance, saying that he is, for example, man, or rational animal.

Likewise, what comes into being properly speaking is substance, not accident. Thus, when a man begins to be, he begins to be as a substance. When he begins to be in any subsequent way (for example, when he begins to be hot), this is not an absolute beginning, since he already exists as a substance.

"In three ways substance is first among all beings, namely, according to knowledge, and according to definition, and according to time.

"And that it is first according to *time* is proved from the fact that none of the other predicaments is separable from substance; for no accident is found without substance, but some substance is found without accident [namely, God]. And thus it is evident that, while substance is not necessarily accompanied by accident, the converse, however, is true.

"And that it is also first according to *definition*, is evident from the fact that in the definition of any accident it is necessary to place the definition of the substance. For just as in the definition of snub-nosed there is placed nose, so in the definition of any accident its proper subject is placed. And therefore, just as animal is prior in definition to man—since the definition of animal is placed in the definition of man—for the same reason substance is prior in definition to accidents.

"That it is also prior in the order of *knowledge* is plain. For that is first according to knowledge which is more known and manifests the thing more. But each thing is more known when its substance is known than when its quantity or quality is known. For it is then that we most believe ourselves to know each thing, when we know what a man is, or fire is, more than when we know how it is qualitatively, or how much quantitatively, or where it is, or know it according to some other predicament. For the same reason, even concerning those things which are in the predicaments of the accidents, we then know each thing when we know what it is. For example, when we know what qualitative being is, we know quality, and when we know what quantitative being is, we know quantity. For just as the other predicaments do not have being except from the fact of inhering in substance, so they do not have knowability except insofar as they participate in something of the mode of knowing of substance, which is to know what something is" (nos. 1257-59).

The fact of substance's being the basic type of being is further brought out from the fact that when the ancient philosophers sought an answer to the question "What is being?" they were seeking simply to know what is the *substance* of things. Some made this substance of things one and motionless, as did Parmenides and Melissus; others, some one mobile thing, as did the natural philosophers, who laid down one sole material principle of things. Still others laid down several material substances, either in finite number, as in the case of Empedocles with four elements; or in infinite number, as in the case of Anaxagoras, with his infinite similar parts, and Democritus with his infinite indivisible bodies.

B. Treatment of Substance
1. Manner and Order of Treatment
a. Manner: According to Form

In treating of substance one will naturally begin with that substance acknowledged by all, namely, sensible substance. All indeed recognize the existence of such sensible substances as animals, plants, chemical elements and compounds, sun, moon, stars, and the like. (Whether these sensible substances are the only substances is a further question, to be investigated after the examination of sensible substances.)

The sensible substance to be determined is first substance, i.e., the singular, existing substance, called such in contrast to second substance, which is the universal concept of substance in terms of genus or species. Thus, this individual man, Peter, is first substance, while the universal idea, man, is second substance (see *Predicaments*, c.5).

This first substance, the actually existing individual substance may be divided in terms of matter, form, composite. Of these three, matter is least act, and is being in potency; form is its actualization, and is even more actual than, and therefore prior by nature to, the composite of both—since in the composite there is something of matter.

This dividing of the composite in terms of matter and form was not, of course, made from the start. Rather, what we call the composite of matter and form (for example, water, air, and so forth), the first philosophers called the matter of things. What we call accidents, they called forms of things, for example, the shape of things, the color of things, and other quantitative and qualitative aspects. They did not, therefore, recognize substantial change, but only accidental change in the permanently remaining matter of things, i.e., in the permanent water, air, and so forth. For us, the basic matter is prime matter, which of itself has no form, and is constituted into a composite substance by its combination with substantial form, the form that makes it water, air, and so forth. One substantial form may be supplanted by another substantial form in substantial change, giving rise to a new substance.

Thus, prime matter can neither exist, nor be known, by itself, since it has by itself no actuality, no form. The composite of matter and form is that which strikes the senses, and it is through the perception of radical substantial changes in the composite that one arrives at the realization that there must be a subject matter for such radical changes, itself devoid of all form, namely, prime matter. Because matter has no form of its own, and because it is through form that one knows, therefore, in dealing with composites of matter and form, to know the substance it is sufficient to know the form.

The first step will be, then, to know the form of material things. This is equivalent to knowing their essence or quiddity or nature or whatness. For although the essence, as the universal nature abstracting from singular characteristics, involves both the form and the matter, nevertheless, to know the form is sufficient, since the form is known as a form which requires a certain matter. Thus the idea of man, while being of a certain form, is of a form understood as in matter.

b. Order: from Sensible Substances to Intelligible Substances

Through the knowledge of sensible substances one arrives at the knowledge of intelligible or immaterial substances, which are the principal object of this science.

"[This study of the essence of sensible substances] is, so to speak, preparatory and necessary for the task, in order that from these sensible substances, which are more manifest to us, we may pass to that which is 'better known absolutely and by nature,' i.e., to the intelligible substances which are our principal object. For thus is teaching done in all things or for all men: by proceeding from those things which are less known according to nature to those things which are more known according to nature.

"For since every discipline is brought about through those things which are better known to the one learning, who must have previous knowledge of certain things in order to learn, our learning must proceed from those things which are better known to us, which are often less known according to nature, to those things which are more known according to nature, but less known to us.

"For to us whose knowledge begins from the senses, those things are better known which are closer to sense. But those things are better known according to nature, which by their very nature are more knowable. And such are those things which are more being, and more actualized. Such, indeed, are remote from sense. But sensible forms are forms in matter....

"...Accordingly as anything is being, so also it is knowable. It is, for example, plain that accidents and motions and privations have little or nothing of being, yet these are more known to us than the substances of things, because they are closer to sense, since they, by their very nature, fall upon sense as proper or common sensibles. But substantial forms do so per accidens.

"...Sometimes the same things are better known both by nature and as to us, as in mathematics, which abstracts from sensible matter. And therefore, in such cases, one always proceeds from things better known according to nature. And even though those things which are better known to us, are weakly known as to nature, nevertheless, from such ill-known things according to nature, which, however, are more knowable to the one knowing, we must try to know those things which are 'wholly,' i.e., universally and perfectly, knowable, proceeding to the knowledge of them through those things which are weakly known in themselves, as was already stated" (nos. 1300-1305).

2. The Treatment
a. According to Logical and Common Notions

The intent here is a study of the essence, or quiddity, or nature, of sensible substances primarily from the logical viewpoint, i.e., from the viewpoint of certain considerations which the mind makes, such as the division of the nature of a thing into genus and specific difference, constituting together the species, and of which the definition is the expression.

That will pertain to the essence of a sensible substance, in whose definition the subject is not placed. Thus the essence or nature of man is expressed as rational animal—neither of which elements requires man in its definition. Rather, it is they which constitute man. Accidents, on the other hand, even when they are properties, presuppose the subject, and the subject must be included in their definition. Thus to be a musician, or something having the power to laugh, does not state the essence of man, since they do not make man a man.

"To be a musician is not your being, since those things which pertain to the quiddity of musician are outside your quiddity, although musician is predicated of you....

"That therefore pertains to the what-it-is of you, which is what you are 'according to yourself,' i.e., because it is predicated of you per se and not per accidens. Thus there is predicated of you per se, man, animal, substance, rational, sensible, and other such, all of which pertain to the what-it-is of you" (no. 1310).

1) Definition properly only of substance. A definition is constituted out of genus and specific difference, both of which express an aspect of the essence or quiddity of the thing, and together constitute the species. A definition is properly given only of a substance, which exists per se. Thus it is not properly given of accidents, such as qualities or quantities, although these of course do have definitions in their own way, in which the subject must be mentioned after the manner of a genus—snub-nosed is having a curvature of the nose. Nor is it properly given of a composite of substance and accident, such as a musical man, since this unity does not exist per se, but per accidens only.

Many definitions are simply clarifications of a word, as in the case of lover of wisdom given as the definition of philosopher. Such definitions are called nominal definitions, i.e., definitions or clarifications of a word by other words more known to the listener. A definition in the strict sense, however, as here taken, must be of the nature or quiddity of a substance, in terms of genus and specific difference. Such are real definitions, definitions of a thing (*res*), and specifically of a thing which exists per se and not in something else, namely, a substance.

2) Definition of accidents. Although definition belongs properly to substance as that which truly is, nevertheless, to the extent that an accident has being, it also has a definition. Thus it has a definition analogically.

"To be *subject to medicine* [or *medicable*] is said of different things with respect to one and the same thing. Nevertheless it does not signify one and the same of all the things of which it is said, nor yet is it said equivocally. For a body is said to be subject to medicine, because it is the subject of medicine; and a work is called subject to medicine, because it is exercised by medicine, as in the case of purgation; and a container is subject to medicine, because medicine uses it, as a clyster. And thus it is evident that *subject to medicine* is not stated wholly equivocally of these three, since in equivocal things there is not had respect to some one thing.

"Nor yet is it stated univocally according to one notion. For it is not the same notion according to which that is called subject to medicine which medicine uses, and which medicine produces. But it is said analogically through respect to one thing, namely, to medicine. And likewise *that which something is*, and definition, are said neither equivocally nor univocally of substance and accident, but through respect to one thing. For it is said of accident through respect to substance....

"...Substance, which has an absolute quiddity [or whatness], does not depend in its quiddity upon another. But accident depends upon the subject, although the subject may not be of the essence of the accident—as the creature depends upon the creator, and yet the creator is not of the essence of the creature, in such a way for it to be necessary to place that external essence in its definition. Now accidents do not have their being except by the fact of inhering in a subject; and therefore their quiddity depends upon the subject, and because of this it is necessary for the subject to be placed in the definition of the accident, sometimes in direct line, sometimes, indeed, obliquely.

"It is placed there in direct line when the accident is signified as concretely in the subject, as when I say, "A snub-nose is a concave nose." For then nose is placed in the definition of snub-nose as though it were its genus, in order to designate that accidents do not have subsistence, except from the subject. But when an accident is signified after the manner of a substance in the abstract, then the subject is placed in its definition obliquely, as a difference, as when it is said that snub-nosedness is concavity of the nose" (nos. 1337, 1352-53).

3) Definition stands for substance, not excluding accidents. What does the definition stand for? Is it identical with the substance, or does it stand solely for the essential principles of the substance? In other words, is man *rational animal*, or is man *humanity*?

"It should be known...that it is the *that which something is* [*quod quid est esse*] which the definition signifies. Whence, since the definition is predicated of the defined, it is necessary that the *that which something is* be predicated of the defined. Therefore the *that which something is* of man is not humanity, which is not predicated of man, but mortal rational animal. For humanity is not the answer to the question, "What is man?" but rather rational and mortal animal are. But nevertheless humanity is taken as the formal principle of that which is the *that which is the being*—as animality is taken as the principle of the genus and is not the genus; rationality as the principle of the difference and is not the difference.

"Now humanity is not as such entirely the same as man, since it implies only the essential principles of man, and the exclusion of all accidents. For humanity is that by which man is man—but none of the accidents is that by which man is man. Whence all the accidents of man are excluded from the meaning of humanity. But that which is man is that which has essential principles, and to which accidents can inhere. Whence, although in the meaning of man there are not included his accidents, nevertheless man does not signify something separated from the accidents. Therefore man signifies as a whole; humanity signifies as a part.

"But if there is some thing in which there is not any accident, there it is necessary that the abstract differ in nothing from the concrete. This is most evident of God" (nos. 1378-80).

4) Essence is a principle both speculatively and practically. The essence or quiddity of a thing is a principle both in speculative and practical matters. Thus, the definition is a principle in demonstration; and the notion or essence of that which one wishes to produce, in the mind of the one producing, is the principle in production.

"Demonstrative syllogisms are from the *what something is*, since in demonstrations the middle is a definition,...and in operative things, generations are from *what something is*. For, just as the speculative intellect proceeds to demonstrating passions of subjects from the consideration of the *what something is*, so the intellect proceeds to doing something from the species of the artifact [in the mind], which is its *what something is*" (no. 1450).

5) Parts of definition are not parts of thing. What of the parts of the definition? Are they the same as the parts of the thing? Plainly this is not the case, since the parts of the definition are predicated of the defined, but not the parts of the thing. Thus, of man there is predicated, not only rational animal, but likewise rational or animal separately. But there are not predicated of man the integral parts of man such as body or soul or head or arm. However, it may be said that the parts of the definition are in a certain sense taken from the parts of the thing, i.e., from the essential parts, not the integral or material parts.

"It should be stated that the parts of the definition signify the parts of the thing, insofar as from the parts of the thing, the parts of the definition are taken, but not in such a way that the parts of the definition are the parts of the thing. For animal is not a part of man, nor is rational; but animal is taken from one part, and rational from another. For animal is that which has sensitive nature, while rational is that which has reason. Whence it is that the genus is taken from matter, the difference from form, the species from matter and form together. For man is that which has reason in sensitive nature" (no. 1463).

Although the parts of the definition, such as rational and animal in regard to man, are derived from that which is formal in man, since matter, as such, is unknowable, nevertheless the definition of natural, i.e., sensible, material things, involves the setting forth of those forms as forms in matter, in such a way that matter is known as part of the essence. "It remains that sensible matter is a part of the essence of natural substances, not only as to individuals, but also as to the species themselves" (no. 1468). Thus, while matter does not enter into the form, it does enter into the definition of the composite which actually exists.

"Although matter is not a part of the form, nevertheless the matter without which the intellect cannot conceive the form must be placed in the definition of the form—as organic body is placed in the definition of soul [defined as the first act of a physical organic body having the power of life]. For just as accidents do not have perfect being except as they are in a subject, so neither do forms except as they are in their proper matters" (no. 1477).

6) Study of sensible substances to reach immaterial substances. What of other substances beyond material substances? It is proper to this science to determine concerning such substances also.

"For in this science we endeavor to determine concerning sensible substances 'for the sake of this,' i.e., because of immaterial substances, since speculation concerning sensible and material substances belongs in a certain way to physics, which is not first philosophy, but second, as was stated in Book IV. For first philosophy is of first substances, which are the immaterial substances, concerning which one speculates, not only insofar as they are substances, but also insofar as they are such substances, namely, immaterial substances. Concerning sensible substances, however, one is not speculating insofar as they are such substances, but insofar as they are substances, or even beings, or insofar as through them we are led to a knowledge of immaterial substances. But conversely, the physicist determines concerning material substances, not insofar as they are substances, but insofar as they are material and have within themselves the principle of motion" (no. 1526).

7) In material things, essence is defined without individual matter. In the case of immaterial things which are form only, the definition is identical with the individual; but in the case of material things, individuated by matter, with one specific form, the definition is identical, not with the individual, but with the species.

"Now definition is not assigned to [material] individuals, but to species; and therefore individual matter, which is the principle of individuation, is outside of that which is the *that which something is* [*quod quid erat esse*]. It is impossible, however, for the species to exist in real nature except in this individual. Whence it is necessary that any real thing, if it has matter which is part of the species, pertaining to the *that which something is*, also have individual matter, which does not pertain to the *what something is*. Whence no thing of nature, if it has matter, is the *what something is* itself, but has it. Thus Socrates is not humanity, but has humanity....Although man outside of singular things does not exist in real nature, he exists nevertheless in reason, which pertains to logical consideration....For man in common is identical with his *what something is* logically speaking" (nos. 1535-36).

8) Definition is one of a substance that is one. Although the definition contains a plurality of parts, namely, a genus and at least one difference, how is it nevertheless one of one thing?

"Definition is a certain notion having its unity from the differences, in such a way that the whole essence of the definition is comprehended in a certain way in the difference. For the reason why animal, which is a genus, cannot be without species, is because the forms of the species which are the differences are not other forms from the form of the genus, but are the forms of the genus with determination. Thus it is plain that animal is that which has a sensitive soul. But man is that which has such a sensitive soul, namely, one with reason....Whence, when the difference is added to the genus, it is not added as though it were a different essence from the genus, but as though implicitly contained in the genus, as the determined is contained in the indeterminate, as white in colored....[Thus] nothing prevents the same genus from containing within itself diverse differences, as the indeterminate contains within itself diverse determinate things....In definitions in which there are many differences, it is necessary to divide the genus not only into its differences, but also to divide the first difference into the second difference....Sometimes necessity requires that we use, in place of per se differences, per accidens differences [e.g., winged or nonwinged, in the case of footed animals], insofar as they are certain signs of the essential differences which are unknown to us. [Essential differences here would be cloven and noncloven in respect to footed.]...

"It is evident, then, that the many parts of a definition do not signify many parts of the essence, out of which the essence is constituted as though from different parts; but all signify one thing which is determined by the ultimate difference. It is also evident from this that of any species there is only one substantial form—as of lion there is one form by which it is substance, and body, and animated body, and animal, and lion. For if there were several forms according to all the aforesaid, they would not all be able to be comprehended by one difference, nor would one thing be constituted from them" (nos. 1549-52, 1564).

9) Definition is properly through intrinsic causes of substance. As has been said, in seeking the nature or essence of things, which the definition expresses, it is a question of stating a form in matter, i.e., the formal and material causes. These are the causes which state what something is. The efficient and final causes, as extrinsic to the thing, do not properly state what the thing is, although, logically speaking, any answer to the question "What is something?" i.e., any of the causes, may be given as a statement of what something is.

"For the logician considers the mode of predication, and not the existence of a thing. Whence, whatever is answered to the question, 'What is something?' he states as pertaining to the *that which some-*

thing is—whether it be intrinsic, as are matter and form, or extrinsic, as are the agent and the end. But the philosopher, who seeks the existence of things, does not include the end or agent—since they are extrinsic—under the *that which something is*. Whence, if we should say that a house is something protecting from the cold and heat, logically speaking this states the *that which something is*, but not, however, according to the consideration of the philosopher. Whence he [Aristotle] states that that which is sought as the cause of the form in the matter is the *that which something is*, logically speaking—which nevertheless, according to the truth of things and physical consideration, is in certain things 'that for the sake of which,' i.e., the end, as in the case of a house or a bed" (no. 1658).

10) Definition seeks something of something. In all questions we ask something other of something, for example, why stone and wood are a house, why an organic body is man; and not the same thing of itself, for example, why man is man. "[The reason is that] to seek something of itself is nothing; but to seek something other of something is to seek something" (no. 1664).

"In all questions something is sought of something, such as the cause of matter, which is the formal cause; or the cause of the form in the matter, as are the end and the agent. It is plain that in simple substances, which are not composed of matter and form, there is no question. For in every question, as was stated, it is necessary for something to be known, and something to be sought which we ignore [for existence is presupposed to seeking what something is; that it is so, is presupposed to seeking why it is so]. But such substances are either known as wholes, or ignored as wholes, as will be stated in Book IX. Whence there is no question in them" (no. 1669).

11) Sensible substances used as effects to reach immaterial substances as causes. "Because of this [i.e., lack of composition of matter and form], there cannot be any doctrine of them [simple or immaterial substances], as in the speculative sciences. For doctrine is the generation of science, but science is produced in us by the fact that we know the reason for which. For of the demonstrative syllogism producing science, the middle is *that because of which* [*propter quid*].

"But lest the consideration of such substances appear wholly foreign to physical doctrine, he [Aristotle] therefore adds that the way of asking concerning such substances is other. For we do not arrive at the knowledge of these substances except from sensible substances, of which the simple substances are in a certain way the causes. And therefore we use sensible substances as known, and through them we seek the simple substances. Thus the philosopher investigates the immaterial moving substances, through motion. And therefore, in the doctrines and questions concerning such, we use effects as the middle to investigate simple substances, whose quiddities we ignore. And likewise it is evident that those substances are compared to the former in the way of doctrine, as forms and the other causes to matter. For just as we seek in material substances the form, end, and agent, as causes of the matter, so we seek the simple substances as the cause of material substances" (nos. 1670-71).

b. According to Proper Principles of Sensible Substance

In what has gone before, substance has been treated from a logical viewpoint, i.e., considering the mode of predication of definition to substance, of the parts of the definition to the parts of the substance, and so forth. Here it is intended to treat of the proper principles of sensible substance, namely, matter and form, and the composite.

1) Recapitulation of principal intent of science. "Since this science considers being in common as its proper subject, which, indeed, is divided into substance and the nine genera of accidents, and the knowledge of accidents depends upon that of substance, as was proved in Book VII, it remains that the principal intent of such a science is concerning substances. And since to know each thing does not occur except by knowing its principles and causes, it follows that it pertains to this science to seek the principles, and causes, and elements, of substances" (no. 1682).

The method of doing this consists in going from sensible substance towards immaterial substance. "It is now immediately necessary to treat concerning those substances which all admit to be, namely, of sensible substances, in order that one may proceed from things which are manifest to things which are not" (no. 1685).

2) Principles of sensible substance.

a) Matter. "All sensible substances have matter. This is so because all are in motion—and motion is not without matter" (no. 1687). Matter, form and composite are all differently related to sensible substance. Matter is said to be substance, not as something existing in act of itself, but as though in potency to being something in act. Form, also called the notion of a thing, since from it is taken the notion of the species, is called substance as being in act, and as being separable, in reason, from matter, although not in the nature of things. The composite of both is called substance as absolutely separable, i.e., as able to have existence of itself in the nature of things. It alone undergoes generation and corruption. While form is separable by reason, i.e., can be understood without individuating sensible matter (though not without matter in common), matter cannot be understood without including form, since it is grasped only as being in potency to form.

How does one arrive at the need for positing matter as an underlying substance and subject?

"In every change it is necessary that there be a subject common to the terms of the change in contrary changes—just as in change according to place there is some common subject, which is now here, and subsequently there. And in growth, there is a common subject which now has such-and-such a quantity, and later a lesser, as to decrease; and a greater, as to increase. And in alteration [qualitative change] there is a certain subject which now is healthy, now sick. Since, therefore, there is a certain change according to substance, namely, generation and corruption, it is necessary that there be some common subject which is the subject of the contrary changes according to generation and corruption; and this after one has laid down the terms, which are form and privation, in such a way, namely, as for it to be at one time in act through form, at one time the subject of the privation of that form.

"Now from this reasoning of Aristotle it appears that substantial generation and corruption are the principle of arriving at the knowledge of prime matter. For if prime matter had of itself any proper form, it would be something in act through it. And thus, when another form would be added, matter would not *be absolutely* through it, but would be made *this* or *that* being. And thus there would be generation in a certain respect and not absolutely. Whence all those who laid down the first subject to be some body, such as air and water, laid down generation to be the same as alteration. It is also plain from this reasoning how the understanding of prime matter is to be taken—since it is to all forms and privations as the alterable subject is to contrary qualities" (nos. 1688-89).

b) Form. Form is related to matter as act to potency. In this respect, too, the specific difference which gives determination to the genus and constitutes the species, is taken from that which is formal in the thing, while the genus is taken from that which is material. This is not to say, however, that the specific difference and the genus correspond to form and matter, since genus and specific difference combine to express that which is formal in the substance, i.e., they represent the form or species, with the matter implied.

"It is not to be understood that the difference is form, or the genus is the matter, since genus and difference are predicated of the species [e.g., animal and rational of man], but matter and form are not predicated of the composite [e.g., man is not his form or matter]; but this is said because the genus is taken from that which is material in the thing, while the difference is taken from that which is formal. Thus the genus of man is animal, since it means something having sensitive nature, which, indeed, is related materially to intellective nature, from which rational is taken, which is the difference of man. For rational signifies something having intellective nature. Whence it is that the genus has the differences virtually, and that genus and difference are proportionate to matter and form, as Porphyry says....

"...In the definition of house, stones and wood are the matter, and such-and-such a mode of composition is as the form. And in some cases the end is further added, from which the necessity of the form depends....Since in definition one thing is compared to the other as act to matter, certain ones, in defining things by matter alone, define insufficiently. Thus do those who define house by cement and stone and wood, which are the matter of the house—since such a definition does not express a house in act, but in potency. But those who say that a house is a covering for men and riches, state the form of a house, but not the matter. But those who say both, define the composite substance. And therefore their definition is a perfect notion. Now the notion which is taken from the difference, pertains to the form; while that which is taken from the intrinsic parts, pertains to the matter" (nos. 1697-1700).

Although definition involves both matter and form, it does not, however, involve individual matter. Thus definition defines the species, not the material individual as such.

"That which is the being of a thing [*quod quid erat esse*] is what the definition signifies. But the definition signifies the nature of the species. Now if there is some thing which is composed of matter and form, it is necessary that in that thing there be something in addition to the nature of the species. For since matter is the principle of individuation, it is necessary that in every composite of matter and form there be individuating principles which are outside the nature of the species. Whence such a thing is not only its quiddity [essence], but something beyond this. But if there be any thing which is form alone, it does not have any individuating principles beyond the nature of the species, since the form itself, existing by itself, is individuated through itself. And therefore the thing itself is nothing other than its own essence" (no. 1710).

In addition to prime matter, there is the proper matter of each thing, namely, the elements. That is, although everything comes ultimately from prime matter, nevertheless it follows a certain order. Thus, though water and salt are both made from prime matter, the immediately previous steps involve an elemental matter under forms that differ from each other—hydrogen and oxygen in one case, sodium and chlorine in the other. Because of this order, although one can go from one thing to another (for example, from vegetable food to flesh and blood), one cannot reverse this process and, starting from flesh and blood, reestablish the original food. Rather, the flesh and blood must return to prime matter before they can become the vegetable food again.

c) **The composite.** In addition to the prerequisite elemental matter for the production of a thing, there is also the action of the agent. It is the agent, acting for the end, that has the final word, uniting form to matter to constitute a unity of the composite of both. In effect, the reason in artificial things why the same wood may become either a bed or a table is ultimately the intent in the mind of the agent. So too it is in natural things, i.e., matter and form uniting as substance, under the action of the agent, acting for an end.

In stating the nature of a thing, since its ultimate form depends upon all the causes, it is in the interest of knowing the thing perfectly to state all four causes, and this not in a generic way only, but as proximately as possible. In defining substances, one states the form and matter. In defining accidents, one states the accidental form with the subject, or substance, serving as matter. Thus, while man is defined as rational animal, with genus and specific difference expressing the form and connoting the matter, calm (of the sea) would be defined as stillness of the sea. In mentioning the subject of an accident, one would mention the first subject. Thus color is subjected in surface, not immediately in body.

In material things, matter may be understood in two ways: as sensible, and, in mathematics, as intelligible:

"Sensible matter is that which is concerned with sensible qualities, hot and cold, rare and dense, and other such—with which matter, indeed, natural things are in concretion—but mathematics abstracts from them. Now intelligible matter is called that which is taken without sensible qualities or differences, as in the case of the continuum. And from this matter mathematics does not abstract.

"Whence, whether in sensible or in mathematical things, it is always necessary that in the definitions there be something as matter and something as form. Thus, in the definition of a mathematical circle *circle is a plane figure, plane* is as the matter, and *figure* as the form. For there is the same reason why the mathematical definition is one, and why the natural definition is (although in mathematical things there is not an agent, as in natural things), since in both cases one thing is as the matter, the other as the form" (nos. 1760-61).

In immaterial things, wholly separated from matter, there is immediate unity from the form, not the unity of form in matter:

"Whatever things do not have intelligible matter, as do mathematical things, nor sensible matter, as do natural things, as is the case of separated substances, immediately each of them is one certain thing. For in those things which have matter, each of them is not immediately one, but their unity is from the fact that unity comes to the matter. But if anything should be which is form alone, it is immediately one, since it is not a case of placing anything in it in any order whatever previous to its expecting unity from form.

"And he gives an example: Since the ten predicaments are not by addition to being (as the species are by addition of differences to the genera) but are themselves being, it is plain that being does not await something added in order to become this [being], namely, a substance, or a quantity, or a quality, but is immediately from the start a substance, a quantity, or a quality. And this is the reason why in definitions there is not laid down either one or being as a genus, since it would be necessary for one and being to be as matter to the differences through the addition of which being would be made either substance or quality.

"And likewise that which is wholly separated from matter, which is its own *what something is*, as stated above, is immediately one, just as it is immediately being. For there is not in it matter awaiting form from which it may have unity and being. And therefore, in such things there is no moving cause in order for them to be one. Certain of them have, nevertheless, a cause substituting [i.e., instituting by creation] substances without motion of their substances, and not as in generable things which are produced by motion. [In other words, the immaterial substances other than God do have a direct cause of their immaterial being, but not, as in material things produced from the potency of matter, a moving or efficient cause educing them from potency to act.]...

"...As was said, the ultimate matter, which, namely, is appropriate for the form, and the form itself, are the same. For one of them is as potency, the other as act. Whence, to seek what the cause of some thing is, and what the cause is of the thing's being one, is similar. For each thing, insofar as it is, is one, and potency and act are in a certain respect one. For what is in potency is made in act. And thus it is not necessary to unite them by some bond, as in the case of those things which are wholly diverse. Whence there is no cause making one those things which are composed of matter and form except that which moves the potency to act. But these things which absolutely do not have matter, are a certain one thing in themselves, as in the case of something that exists" (nos. 1762-64, 1767).

Chapter 11

Potency and Act
(*Metaphysics*, IX)

A. Potency
  1. Potency in itself
    a. Potency
      1) Equivocally and logically
      2) Analogically
    b. Impotency
  2. Potency in respect to that in which it is
    a. As it is in different things
    b. In the same subject
      1) Exclusion of errors
        a) Nothing possible except in act
          (1) Error excluded
          (2) Definition of to be in potency and to be in act
        b) Everything is possible even though not actual
          (1) Error excluded
          (2) Impossible consequence implies impossible
              antecedent
      2) Truth about potency and act in same subject
        a) How act precedes potency in same subject
        b) How potencies preceding act reduced to act
          (1) Irrational
          (2) Rational
B. Act
  1. Manifestation of act
  2. Diversity of act

3. When is something in potency and when not?
C. Relationship of potency and act
  1. According to priority and posteriority
    a. As to notion
    b. As to time
      1) In passive potencies
      2) In certain active potencies
    c. As to substance
      1) From things sometimes in potency, sometimes in act
        a) On the part of form
        b) On the part of the end
      2) Eternal things compared with mobile things in potency and act
  2. According to good and evil
  3. According to understanding of true and false
    a. From viewpoint of understanding itself
    b. From viewpoint of truth and falsehood
      1) Continuous substances
      2) Simple substances

Potency and Act

(*Metaphysics*, IX)

A. Potency
    1. Potency in itself
    2. Potency in respect to that in which it is
B. Act
    1. Manifestation of act
    2. Diversity of act
    3. When is something in potency and when not?
C. Relationship of potency and act
    1. According to priority and posteriority
    2. According to good and evil
    3. According to understanding of true and false

The first category of being, to which all the other predicaments of being are ordained, is substance. Thus quantity is considered insofar as it is the measure of substance; quality is considered insofar as it is a certain disposition of substance, and so forth. This is further evident from the fact that in the definition of every accident it is necessary to place the proper subject, which is ultimately substance.

But just as material being is divided into substance and the nine accidents, so too being is divided into potency and act, and this not only in the material realm, but in relation to being in common.

"It is not to our purpose here, however, to discuss the potency which is most properly so called. For potency and act are most commonly said of things which are in motion, since motion is the act of a being in potency. But the principal intent of this doctrine is not on potency and act accordingly as they are in mobile things only, but accordingly as they follow being in common. Whence, in immobile things there is found potency and act, as, for example, in intellectual beings.

"But when we shall have spoken on the subject of the potency which is in mobile things, and its corresponding act, we shall then be able to manifest potency and act as they are in intelligible things, which pertain to the separated substances, concerning which it will be questioned later.

"And this is the fitting order, since the sensible things which are in motion are more manifest to us. And therefore through them we arrive at the knowledge of the substances of immobile things" (nos. 1770-71).

A. Potency
1. Potency in Itself
a. Potency

Potency and the possible may be said in many ways, some of which are purely equivocal, some of which are analogical, i.e., able to be referred to a single basic meaning, namely, that of having some principle within themselves (see p. 141 above).

1) Equivocally and logically. Of the ways which are equivocal, one has, for example, the use of the word *potency*, or *power*, when speaking of geometrical things. Thus one speaks of the power of a line to be extended back upon itself, as in the case of the protraction of a straight line through four right angles to constitute a square. If the length of the original line is represented by 3 units, then the value of the square is 3 times 3, or 3 squared. This is also called 3 to the second power. The base of such squares, e.g., 3, is, so to speak, the matter which has the power to become squared.

Likewise in logical things, things are called possible or impossible, not because of any potency, but simply because they are in a certain way, or are not. Thus, things are called possible whose opposites may be true; impossible, whose opposites cannot be true. This difference is on the basis of the nonrepugnance or repugnance of the predicate to the subject.

2) Analogically. Potency taken analogically, however, is potency in the sense of a certain principle. Other meanings of potency are then referred to this as first. What sort of principle is taken as the prime analogate?

"It is the active principle which is the principle of change in another as other. And he [Aristotle] states this because it is possible that the active principle be simultaneously in the mobile thing or the thing which undergoes, as when something moves itself. And therefore it is stated that the principle which is called active potency, is the principle of change in another, as it is other; since even though it may happen that the active principle is in the same subject as that which undergoes, nevertheless, it is not there accordingly as it is the same, but as it is other.

"And that to that principle which is called active potency are reduced other potencies is plain. For in another way that is said to be passive potency which is a principle that something be moved by another as other. And he says this because even though the same thing should undergo something from itself, nevertheless it is not according to the same, but according to that which is other. Now this potency is reduced to the first active potency because passion [undergoing] is caused by an agent. And because of this, passive potency is also reduced to active potency.

"In another way potency denotes a certain state of impassibility...i.e., a certain disposition by virtue of which something is able not to undergo change for the worse....[Both of these ways, i.e., that of being able not to undergo change from another, and that of being able to undergo such change, clearly imply a primary concept of potency as that which is able to cause change in another.]

"In still another way potencies are spoken of not only in the order of doing and undergoing, but in the order of that which is well in both—as we say that someone is able to walk [or is an able walker], not because he is able to walk in any way whatever, but because he is able to walk well. Likewise we call wood combustible, because it can be easily burned. But green wood, which is not easily burned, we say to be incombustible. Whence it is plain that in the definition of those potencies which are spoken of in respect to acting or undergoing well, there are included the notions of the primary potencies which are spoken of as acting or undergoing absolutely: as in acting well there is included acting, and undergoing in undergoing well. Whence it is plain that all these modes of potencies are reduced to one first, namely, to active potency. And thus it is evident that this multiplicity is not according to equivocation, but according to analogy" (nos. 1776-80).

According to the aforesaid, passive potency is nothing other than a principle of undergoing something from another, in the order of matter—as, for example, to be burned is a certain undergoing made possible by combustible elements. Active potency, on the other hand, is in the agent, as heat is in that which heats, and the art of building is in the builder. In this respect, nothing undergoes anything from itself, i.e., to the extent that this would imply the identity of the agent and the patient. The doctor does indeed cure himself, but the one cured is cured, not as a doctor, but as a sick person.

b. Impotency

The different manners of potency are matched by proportionate manners of impotency, defined as the privation of potency. Privation may be said in several ways. For example, whatever does not have something in any way may be said to be deprived of it; and in this sense one would say that a stone was deprived of sight. In another more proper way, that is said to be deprived of something which does not have that which it normally should have. This may be either universally, or only at the time when it should have it. Thus a puppy which does not see at birth is not considered deprived of sight, but only if it does not see when it should, i.e., a few days later.

Likewise the qualifications of well may apply: thus we might call someone blind, not because he does not see at all, i.e., is deprived of sight, but because he does not see well.

Sometimes there is included in the notion of privation also the notion of violence: thus we often imply, when we say someone was deprived of something, that the loss occurred through violence, as if one should say that someone was deprived of his property by a tyrant.

2. Potency in Respect to That in Which It Is
a. As It Is in Different Things

In this respect, potency varies as it is in inanimate things and animate things (which have as a principle of acting and undergoing, not only a body but also a soul), especially animate things with reason.

"There are several types of soul [i.e., vegetative, sensitive, rational]: several of which do not differ much in acting and undergoing from inanimate things which act by the instinct of nature. For the parts of the nutritive and sensitive soul act by the impulse of nature. Solely the rational part of the soul is mistress of its act: in which it differs from inanimate things" (no. 1787).

What is the difference between potency in rational things and in others?

"The same rational potencies are disposed toward contraries: for example, the medical art, which is a certain potency [power, or principle of action on another]...is related to producing both sickness and health. But irrational potencies are not disposed to opposites, but one is ordained to one effect only, absolutely speaking" (no. 1789).

What is the cause of this difference? "Science, which is a rational potency [in the sense of an ability to produce change in another], is a certain notion of the thing known in the soul. But the same notion manifests the thing and its privation, although not in the same way—since it first manifests the existing thing, and then its privation....Whence it is necessary, if science is a certain notion of the thing known in the soul, that there be a same science of contraries. Of one of them, indeed, in a prior way, and according to itself; of the other subsequently. For example, medicine is in a prior way knowing and productive of health, but in a subsequent way of sickness....

"And since what the Philosopher said above of privation, he afterwards transferred to contrariety, he shows that there is the same notion of contrariety and privation. For just as privation is manifested through negation and removal, as, for example, the removal of sight manifests blindness, so also through negation and removal is the contrary manifested: since privation, which is nothing other than the removal of the other [opposite], is a certain first principle among contraries. For of all contraries, one is as that which is perfect, the other as imperfect and the privation of the other. For black is the privation of white, and cold is the privation of hot. Thus, therefore, it is plain that the same science is related to contraries.

"...It is plain that natural things operate through forms inhering in them. But there cannot be contrary forms in the same thing. Whence it is impossible that the same natural thing produce contrary things. But science is a certain potency of action, and a principle of motion, from the fact that someone has the notion of a thing to be made, and this principle of motion is in the soul....

"And therefore, just as a natural action proceeds to its effect, as though coupled to the form which is the principle of the action whose likeness is left in the effect, so the soul moves through its operation to both opposites 'from the same principle,' i.e., from the same faculty of reason" (nos. 1790-93).

b. In the Same Subject

1) Exclusion of errors.

a) <u>Nothing possible except in act.</u>

(1) Error excluded. What is the relation of potency and act in the same subject? To conceive of potency as different from act implies, of course, that things can be possible, not only when in act, but also before.

The opinion that a thing is possible only if in act would seem to derive from those who consider all things to come about with necessity. Consequently, whatever can be, must be; and if something is not, it is because it cannot be. This, of course, leads to impossible views.

First, it would mean the impossible supposition that when the builder is not building, he cannot build; and that when he does build, his building does not come from any previous art or learning, since it does not come from any potency.

"[This supposition that nothing is possible except what is in act] is shown to be impossible, supposing two things to be fact.

"One of these is that he who previously did not have some art, cannot possibly have it subsequently, unless he learn it, or receive it in some way, namely, by discovering it.

"The other is that if someone had a certain art, it is impossible for him afterwards not to have the same art, unless he reject it in some way, either by forgetting, or through some sickness, or through length of time in which one does not use a science. For this is the cause of forgetting. But it is not possible for someone to lose an art following the corruption of the thing [produced], as sometimes it is right that true knowledge is lost when the thing is changed—as, when someone truly opines Socrates to be seated, this true opinion thereof perishes when he stands up. But this cannot be said concerning art. For art is not the knowledge of that which is, but of that which is to be done. And thus, so long as the matter endures out of which art is able to make something, the being of art is always. Whence art cannot be lost by the corruption of the thing except in the aforesaid ways" (nos. 1797-98).

Secondly, this opinion, namely, that potency exists only when a thing is in act, also implies that inanimate things which strike the senses do not exist except when we are knowing them—in other words, that things are only as they appear.

"If, therefore, potency is not in the same thing except when it acts, it follows that nothing is hot or cold, sweet or bitter, and so forth, except when it is sensed as changing the sense. But that this is false is plain. For if this were true, it would follow that the opinion of Protagoras was true, which stated all properties and natures of things to consist solely in being sensed and opined. From which it followed that contradictories are true, since different people have contradictory opinions about the same thing. The Philosopher has disputed against this opinion in Book IV [see p. 91 above]. It is therefore false that potency does not exist without act" (no. 1800).

Thirdly, it would follow from this opinion that if one was not actually seeing, one would not have the power of sight, and would be, when not seeing, the same as a blind man. Thus one would be successively sightless and seeing many times in the same day.

Fourthly, since one cannot do that for which one has no potency, then he who stands, can never sit; and he who sits, can never stand. Nothing can ever become, and motion and generation are removed from reality. Obviously, such positions, in contradiction with experience, cannot be admitted.

(2) Definition of to be in potency and to be in act. What is it to be in potency? That is said to be in potency which, should it be supposed to be in act, nothing impossible follows. Thus, it is possible for someone to sit, supposing that, should he sit, nothing impossible follows:

What is it to be in act? The word *act*, imposed on things to signify actuality and perfection, as found in form, and other such things, comes, since the above are certain operations, principally from motion as to the origin of the word.

"For since names are the signs of intelligible concepts, we give names first to those things which we know first, although they may be posterior according to the order of nature. But among other acts, motion is most known and apparent to us, being sensibly seen by us. And therefore the name of *act* was first given to it, and from motion is extended to others.

"And because of this, to be moved is not attributed to nonexistent things, although certain other predicates are attributed to nonexistent things. For we say that nonbeings are intelligible, or opinable, or even desirable, but we do not say that they are moved. The reason for this is because, since to be moved signifies to be in act, it would follow that nonbeings in act would be in act, which is plainly false" (nos. 1805-6).

b) <u>Everything is possible even though not actual.</u>

(1) Error excluded. If it is a true definition of potency to say that it is that upon supposing which to be in act, there follows no impossibil-

ity, then plainly not everything that is not can be in potency: that whose supposed actuality would involve impossibility, cannot be in potency. Such a case would be the supposition of the commensurability of the diagonal of the square, if one should say that it is actually not measured, but is, as nonexistent, potentially commensurable. To suppose this to be, would be to suppose the impossible. Other statements, such as that Socrates is sitting when he is not, are false, but not impossible. To suppose the diagonal of the square to be commensurable, is considered to be both false and impossible.

(2) Impossible consequence implies impossible antecedent. Insofar as sequence is concerned, if a consequent is impossible, then the antecedent must be impossible. For example, if it is impossible for the diagonal of the square to be actually measured, then it must be impossible for it to be possible for it to be measured, as an antecedent. On the other hand, if the antecedent is impossible, the consequent need not be: for example, if man is an ass (impossible), he is an animal (actually true). Thus one can argue from impossible consequent to impossible antecedent, but not conversely.

2) Truth about potency and act in same subject.

a) How act precedes potency in same subject. "Some of the potencies are innate in the things to which they belong, as are the senses in the animals; some are acquired through practice, as the art of flute playing, and other such operative arts; others still are acquired through teaching or learning, as in the case of medicine and other such arts. Of the aforesaid potencies, those that are in us by habit and reason must be necessarily first carried out and preexercised in their acts before they are acquired. Thus, by playing the flute, one becomes a flute player; and by considering things of medicine, one becomes a doctor. But the other potencies, which are not acquired by usage, but are from nature and consist in undergoing, as is evident of the sensitive powers, do not proceed from their acts. For someone does not acquire the sense of sight by seeing, but since he has visual power, he is consequently made actually seeing" (no. 1817).

b) How potencies preceding act reduced to act. Before answering this, it is necessary to note that possibility involves possibility toward some determinate effect, at some determinate time, in some determinate way. Thus flowers which are able to grow, are not able to become just anything at all, at any time, in any place. Furthermore, rational potencies differ from others in being able to be productive of contraries.

(1) Irrational. "In irrational potencies [which include the nutritive and the augmentative in man] it is necessary that when the passive approaches the active, in that disposition in which the passive is able to undergo, and the active able to act, necessarily the one undergoes and the other acts—as is evident in the case when that which is combustible is applied to fire.

"But in rational potencies, it is not necessary: for it is not necessary for the builder to build, no matter how much the matter approaches him.

"...Irrational potencies are such that one is productive of one only; and therefore when the passive is present, it is necessary that it produce the one thing of which it is productive. But one and the same rational potency is productive of contraries....

(2) Rational. "...Since from a common cause there does not proceed a determinate effect, unless there be some proper thing which may determine the common cause more to this effect than to that, it follows that it is necessary, over and above the rational potency, which is common to two contraries, to lay down something which may approach it to doing one alternative [rather than the other], in order for it to go into act. This...is the choice of whatever it may be, i.e., the choice which pertains to reason.

"...Thus everything which has power according to reason, necessarily acts when it desires that of which it has the power, and in the way in which it has it" (nos. 1818-20).

B. Act

Possibility can lead to act even in things without motion. "For although the name *act* had its origin from motion, as was said above, nevertheless motion is not alone called act. Whence possible is not said solely in the line of motion" (no. 1824).

1. Manifestation of Act

Act exists when something *is*, yet nevertheless it is not as when it is in potency. "For we say the image of Mercury is in the wood in potency, and not in act; but if it be sculptured, then the image of Mercury is said to be in act in the wood" (no. 1825). The same may be said of a part in the continuum: "For the part, e.g., the half of it, is in potency insofar as it is possible for that part to be taken from the whole by the division of the whole; but once the whole is divided, that part will be already in act" (ibid.).

Why is there not a definition of act? "He [Aristotle] will answer that by induction in the area of singulars, through examples, we can manifest what we wish to state, namely, what act is; it is not necessary to seek a term, i.e., a definition of every thing. For the first simple things cannot be defined, since one cannot go to infinity in definitions. But act belongs to the first simple things. Whence it cannot be defined.

"But through the proportion of some two things to each other, it can be seen what act is. For example, one might take the proportion of one building to that which is buildable; and of the one awake to the one sleeping; and of him who sees, to him who has closed eyes while having visual power....But of any such different things, one part will be act, the other potency. And so proportionately, from particular examples, we are able to arrive at knowing what are act and potency" (nos. 1826-27).

2. Diversity of Act

Act may be either an act or an operation. Thus form is in matter as act; seeing is related to the visual power as an operation.

Certain things, such as the infinite and the void, are said to be act in ways different from other things:

"The infinite is not so said to be in potency as for it to be sometimes separate in act only. But act and potency are distinguished by notion and knowledge in the infinite. For example, in the infinite according to division, act is said to be simultaneously with potency, since the potency of dividing is never exhausted: for when it is divided in act, it is still further divisible in potency. But act is never separated from potency in such a way, namely, that it should be at some time wholly divided in act, and no longer divisible in potency.

"And there is a like consideration in the void. For it is possible for a place to be emptied from this body, but not as to be wholly void: for it remains filled with another body. And thus there remains always in the void potency conjoined with act. And it is the same in motion, and time, and other such, which do not have perfect being" (no. 1831).

3. When Is Something in Potency and When Not?

Something is in potency in the full sense of the word when it can be brought to act by a single act.

"Matter is then in potency a house when none of those things which are in the matter prevent the house from being produced immediately by one action, nor is there anything which must be added or taken away, before the matter is formed into the house. For example, it is necessary to transform the clay before bricks are made out of it; while from the trees something must be removed by chopping and added by joining, in order for the house to be put together. Whence clay and trees are not a house in potency, but the bricks and lumber already prepared....

"But those things which it is necessary to transform before they are immediately reducible to act, require another active principle, which, namely, prepares the matter, and which, meanwhile, is other than the perfecting principle which induces the ultimate form. Thus it is plain that earth is not yet a statue in potency, for it cannot by one act, nor one agent, be reduced to act; but first it is transformed by nature and is made into bronze, and then by art it is made a statue" (nos. 1836, 1838).

C. Relationship of Potency and Act
1. According to Priority and Posteriority

Speaking now of potency universally—whether it be a motive principle, a principle of immobility and rest, of activity existing without motion, such as is understanding—to all such potency, act is prior by notion and substance, and in a certain way by time (although in a certain way not, also).

a. As to Notion

"That by which another must be defined is prior to it by notion, as animal is prior to man, and subject to accident. But potency cannot be defined except through act. For the first notion of possible consists in this, that it befits it to act or to be in act—as he is called a builder who is able to build, and a speculator who is able to speculate, and that is called visible which is able to be seen, and so in others. Therefore it is necessary that the notion of act precede the notion of potency. And because of this, Aristotle manifested potency by defining it through act, but act was not able to be defined through anything else, but he manifested it solely inductively" (no. 1846).

b. As to Time

1) In passive potencies. "Act is prior in time to potency: in such a way, nevertheless, that in that which is the same as to species, there is first the agent or being in act before being in potency; but in the same as to number, it is first in time in potency before being in act.

"This is made manifest as follows. For if we should take this man who is already in act, he was, prior to this, according to time, matter which was man in potency. And likewise prior in time was the seed, which is the wheat in potency, before the wheat in act....But nevertheless certain things existing in act were prior according to time to those things existing in potency, namely, the agents by which they are reduced to act. For it is always necessary that that which is being in potency be being in act by the agent which is being in act. Whence, man in potency is made man in act by the man generating, who is in act. And likewise that which is musical in potency looks toward that which is musical in act, learning from the teacher who is musical in act....

"...It was said above of substance, namely, in Book VII, that everything that is made, is made from something, as from matter; and by something, as from an agent. And this agent is also the same in species with that which is made. This is plain in univocal generations. But in equivocal generations it is necessary that there be some likeness of the generator to the generated" (nos. 1847-49).

2) In certain active potencies. "It was said above that there are certain operative potencies which must be taken as performing or exercising themselves in their actions in advance. This is the case of those things which are acquired by habit or teaching. And concerning these he [Aristotle] states here that even in the same according to number, act precedes potency. For it is seen to be impossible that anyone become a builder who has not first built; or that one become a harpist, who has not first played the harp....For one cannot learn such an art except by exercising oneself in its act....

"...Since to learn is to become knowing, it is necessary that the one learning have something of science and art. Whence it is not unfitting if he should perform in some sense the activity of the art. For he does not do so perfectly, as one who already has the art. But in the reason itself there are naturally present in advance certain seeds and principles of the sciences and virtues, by virtue of which a man is able to some extent to produce the act of science and virtue before he has the habit of science and virtue—when he has it, he acts perfectly, but before imperfectly" (nos. 1850-51, 1854-55).

c. As to Substance

1) From things sometimes in potency, sometimes in act. To be first in substance is to be first in perfection, and this is attributed to form and end.

a) On the part of form. "Not only is act prior to potency by notion and time, but 'by substance,' i.e., by perfection. For by the name *substance* is customarily meant the form by which something is perfect. And this first point appears for the following reason: those things which are posterior in generation are 'prior according to substance and species,' i.e., in perfection, since generation always proceeds from the imperfect to the perfect, as, for example, man is posterior in generation to boy, for from the boy the man is made, and man is posterior in generation to the sperm. And this indeed because the full-grown man already has the perfect species, but the child and sperm not yet. Since, therefore, in the same according to number, act is in generation and time posterior to potency, as is evident from the above, it follows that act is prior to potency by substance and notion.

b) On the part of the end. "...The end for the sake of which something is done, is a certain principle. For it is first in the intention of the agent, since generation is produced for the sake of it. But act is the end of potency: therefore act is prior to potency, and a certain principle of it.

"...Aristotle manifests this first in *natural active* potencies, saying that animals do not see in order to have visual power; but rather they have visual power in order to see....

"He shows the same in *rational* potencies, saying that the reason why men have the power to build is to build; they have 'theoretical,' i.e., speculative, science in order to speculate. For they do not speculate in order to have theoretical science, except in the case of those who are learning, who meditate on the things of speculative science in order to acquire it. And these do not speculate perfectly, but in a certain way and imperfectly...since speculation is not because of any need, but is the use of science already had. But the speculation of those who are learning is because they need to acquire the science.

"...He shows the same in *passive* potencies, saying that matter is in potency until it arrives at form or species, but it is then first in act when it has species. And so it is in all other things which are moved because of an end. Whence, just as those who teach believe they have attained the end when they point out the disciple whom they have instructed performing the things which belong to the art, so nature attains the end when it reaches act. And thus it is plain that act is the end in natural motion.

"...If perfection and end did not consist in act, then there would seem to be no difference between some wise man, as was Mercury, and some fool, as was Paxonas....For through the act of science is someone shown to be knowing, and not by potency. For operation is the end of science. But operation is a certain act. Whence, the word *act* is derived from operation, as was said above" (nos. 1856-61).

This end need not be a product, a work; it may simply be the use of the potency.

"The ultimate end of certain active potencies is the sole use of the potency, and not something produced through the action of the potency. Thus the ultimate end of the visual potency is sight, and beyond it there is not made by the visual power any work that is produced. But in certain active potencies there is made some work beyond the act, as by the building art there is made a house beyond the actual building....

"...When through the action of the potency there follows something produced, that action perfects the thing produced, and not the producer. Whence it is in the product as its action and perfection, but not in the producer" (nos. 1862-64).

The most perfect act is that which perfects the agent. "But when there is not any work produced besides the action of the power, then the action exists in the agent and as its perfection, and it does not leave it to perfect something else without—just as sight is in the one seeing as his perfection, and speculation in the one speculating, and life in the soul, understanding by life the activities of life.

"Whence it is plain that felicity also consists in such an operation which is in the one acting, not one which goes out into an exterior thing, since happiness is the good of the one who is happy, and his perfection. For there is a certain life of the happy man, namely, his perfect life. Whence, just as life is in the living, so happiness is in the happy man. And thus it is evident that happiness does not consist either in building or in any such action which goes out into that which is external, but in understanding and willing.

"...From the aforesaid it is plain that substance and form and species are a certain act. And from this it is plain that act is prior to potency according to substance and form. And it is prior in time, as was said above, since there is always required previously the act according to which the generator or mover or maker is in act, before the other act by which what is generated or made is in act, after it was in potency—until one arrives at the first mover, which is in act only. For that which goes from potency into act, requires a preceding act in the agent, by which it is reduced to act" (nos. 1865-66).

2) Eternal things compared with mobile things in potency and act. "Eternal things are compared to corruptible things as act to potency. For sempiternal things, as such, are not in potency; but corruptible things, as such, are in potency. But sempiternal things are prior to corruptible things in substance and perfection. This, indeed, is plain. Therefore act is prior to potency in substance and perfection" (no. 1867).

2. According to Good and Evil

In this respect it is clear that in good things it is better to be in act than in potency; while in evil things, it is better to be in potency than in act. Thus it is better to be healthy in act rather than in potency, but sick in potency rather than in act. These two possibilities can represent two contraries of a same passive potency. On the other hand, things which are perpetually in act in a perfect sense, since they do not undergo any defect or corruption, likewise, as such, suffer no evil.

3. According to Understanding of True and False
a. From Viewpoint of Understanding Itself

In this respect it is clear that understanding, or arriving at the knowledge of something, is a clear case of going from potency to act in the same thing.

"Geometers find the true when they seek by dividing lines and surfaces. But division reduces to act that which was in potency. For the parts of the continuum are in potency in the whole before the division. Now if all things were divided accordingly as the finding of the truth requires, the conclusions sought for would be clear. But since in the first tracing of the figures such divisions are in potency, therefore there is not immediately made manifest that which is sought. [Examples of this would be the protracting of the base of a triangle and the drawing of a parallel line at the exterior angle of the triangle in order to prove the sum of its interior angles equal to two right angles; likewise the drawing of a line from an angle inscribed in a semicircle to the center in order to prove that every angle inscribed in a semicircle is a right angle.]...

"Thus, therefore [describing the two geometrical processes above], the Philosopher concludes that it is plain that when certain things are reduced from potency to act, then their truth is found. And the reason for this is because understanding is of act. And therefore, those things which are understood must be in act. Because of this, potency is known from act. Whence, those who reduce something to act, know, as is evident in the above descriptions. For it is necessary that in the same according to number, act should be posterior to potency according to the order of generation and time, as was expounded above" (nos. 1888, 1894).

b. From Viewpoint of Truth and Falsehood

What is intended to be stated here is that truth and falsehood are stated primarily according to act. This is shown first of all in continuous or composite substances, then in simple or immaterial substances.

1) Continuous substances. "For something to be true or false in things, is nothing other than to compose and divide. Whence he who thinks himself to divide what is divided in things, is true in his opinion—as, for example, he who thinks man not to be an ass. And likewise does he who thinks himself to compose that which is composed in things—as he who thinks man to be an animal. But he lies in his opinion who, on the contrary, has things other in his opinion than things are in their nature—as does he who thinks man to be an ass, and not to be animal—for when something is or is not, then there is stated the true or the false.

"This is to be considered as follows: For you are not therefore white because we truly think you to be white; but conversely, we therefore think you to be white because you are white. Whence it is plain that the disposition of the thing is the cause of truth in opining and expressing oneself.

"But he adds this in order to manifest what he had said above, namely, that true and false are in things to be composed and divided. For it is necessary that the truth or falsehood which is in expression or opinion be reduced to the disposition of the thing as to its cause. For when the intellect forms a composition, it takes two things, one of which is formal with respect to the other. Whence it takes it as existing in another, because of which predicates are held in the order of form. And therefore, if such an operation of the intellect should be reduced to the thing as to its cause, it is necessary that in composite substances the very composition of form to matter, or of that which is related as form and matter, or even the composition of accident to subject, correspond, as though a foundation and cause of the truth, to the composition which the intellect forms interiorly and expresses in words. For example, when I say, "Socrates is man," the truth of this enunciation is caused by the composition of the human form to individual matter, by which Socrates is this man. And when I say, "The man is white," the cause of the truth is the composition of whiteness to the subject. And the same is clear in division.

"...But in things there is found the following difference concerning composition and division. Certain things are always composed, and it is impossible for them to be divided—as to the rational soul there is always conjoined sensitive nature, and it is impossible that it be divided from it....But certain things are divided, and it is impossible for them to be composed—as in the case of black with white, and the form of ass with man. But certain other things are related to contraries, since they are able to be composed and divided—as in the case of man with white and also running.

"...It is plain that in those things which may be composed and divided one and the same expression may be sometimes true, sometimes false—as, for example, this statement *Socrates is sitting* is true when he is sitting, but the same is false when he rises. And the same is true of the opinion. But in those things which cannot be otherwise, namely, which are always composed or divided, it is not possible that the same opinion or expression be sometimes true, sometimes false, but that which is true, is always true, and that which is false, is always false. For example, this is true in this way: *Man is animal*; while this is false: *Man is ass*" (nos. 1896-1900).

2) Simple substances. "Concerning noncomposite and simple things, there is not true or false through composition or division which is made in things, but through knowing what something is, or not knowing. For when we attain to knowing *what something is* of some simple thing, then the intellect is seen to be true. But when we do not attain to knowing the *what something is*, but attribute something else to it, then it is false....Nor is this surprising, since being also is not the same in both. But the being of composite things arises from the components, but not the being of simple things. And truth follows being, since, as was had in Book II [see p. 62 above], there is the same disposition of things in being and in truth. Whence those things which are not alike in being, are not alike in truth....

"...Aristotle states in *De Anima* III that just as the sense concerning its proper objects is always true, so is the intellect concerning *that which something is*, as though with its proper object. And that the intellect does not err concerning the *what something is*, is so not only in simple substances, but also in composite.

"But how it is accidentally deceived concerning *what something is*, is to be considered. For it is not deceived concerning what something is except by composing or dividing. This occurs in composite substances in two ways. In one way, by the composition of the definition with the thing defined, or the division therefrom. For example, if one should say, "Ass is mortal rational animal," or "Man is not mortal rational animal," both are false. But in another way, accordingly as the definition is constituted out of parts which are not composible with each other—as if one were to assign this definition, *Man is a nonsensitive animal*. In the first way, therefore, the definition is called false, because it is not of this thing. In the second way, it is called false in itself, as the Philosopher taught above in Book V [see p. 165 above].

"But in simple substances there cannot be deception concerning the *what something is* accidentally except in the first way. For their *what something is* is not composed of several things, concerning the composition or division of which falsity might occur....

"All simple substances are being in act, and never being in potency, since if they were sometimes in act, and sometimes in potency, they would be generated and corrupted. But this cannot be, as was shown above, for such substances are forms only, whence also they are beings by nature: but being according to itself is neither generated nor corrupted. For everything which is generated, is generated out of something: but being, absolutely as being, cannot be generated out of anything. For there is not anything outside of being, but outside *such* a being, as, for example, outside of man there is some being. Whence this being may be generated in a certain way, but not being absolutely.

That, therefore, which is being according to itself, because it is form, upon which being follows, is not generable.   Whence it is not sometimes in potency, sometimes in act....

"How the ignorance [concerning simple substances] is, he [Aristotle] shows when he says that this ignorance is 'not a privation such as blindness,' which is the privation of the visual power.   Whence this ignorance would be similar to blindness if one did not have intellective power to attain to simple substances.   From this it is evident that, according to the judgment of Aristotle, the human intellect can arrive at knowing simple substances, which he appears to have left doubtful in *De Anima* III" (nos. 1901-16).

From the fact that simple, ungenerable things are always in act, and therefore cannot be sometimes in one way, sometimes in another in this respect, the truth concerning them is likewise stable and not subject to change.   Thus truth is more concerning that which is in act.

Chapter 12

One, and What Follows upon One
(*Metaphysics*, X)

A. One according to itself
    1. In how many ways one is said
        a. As denoting a continuum
        b. As denoting a whole
        c. As denoting a singular
        d. As denoting a species
    2. A property of one: to be a measure
        a. Measure in quantity and other accidents
        b. Measure as to one in substance
    3. Being and one are the same as to subject
B. One compared to many
    1. One and many, and what follows them
        a. How one is opposed to many
        b. What follows one and many
            1) Those things following one
                a) The same
                b) Alike
                c) Equal
            2) Those things following plurality
    2. Contrariety specially considered
        a. Contrariety is the greatest difference
            1) Contraries
                a) The nature of contrariety
                b) Contrariety compared to other oppositions
                    (1) Contrariety as opposition of privation and having

One, and What Follows upon One
(*Metaphysics*, X)

A. One according to itself
    1. In how many ways one is said
    2. A property of one: to be a measure
    3. Being and one are the same as to subject
B. One compared to many
    1. One and many, and what follows them
    2. Contrariety specially considered

Accidental being and the being which is the *is* of propositions having been treated in Book VI (chapter 9), and being per se as divided by the ten predicaments in Books VII-VIII (chapter 10), and being as divided into potency and act in Book IX (chapter 11), Aristotle now treats of one as converted with being in Book X.

In this treatment, he treats first of one according to itself; then in comparison to many.

A. One According to Itself
1. In How Many Ways One Is Said
a. As Denoting a Continuum

This may be so either by taking that which is continuous in any way, for example, two pieces of wood glued together, or that which is continuous by nature.

This latter way may be of two sorts: there may be either a uniform whole, as in the case of a straight line, or also of a circle; or a nonuniform whole, as in the case of a line with an angle. In a straight line, one part cannot move without the other, but in an angled line, one can imagine one part moving while the other is at rest, i.e., one arm of the angle staying fixed, the other sweeping nearer or away. The straight line is therefore more one than the angled line, as having the more unified motion.

b. As Denoting a Whole

This way is that in which that which is a certain whole, having form, adds a further unity to the unity of continuity—as a man or an animal is not only one as continuous, but one as to form. In this case, too, that which is so by nature rather than by art, is more one. What is the first such continuous whole? It is one moving according to unity both of place and time, i.e., all the parts move according to the same motion and at the same time.

"If some continuous and whole thing by nature is called one because its motion is one, then, if some thing which is continuous and a whole has within itself the principle of the first motion, this thing will be the first one in magnitude. Now, among motions, the first motion is local motion, and among local motions the first is circular motion, as is proved in *Physics* VIII. And among the bodies which are moved with circular motion, there is some one which has the principle of such motion, namely, the body which is both turned, and turns the others, according to the diurnal motion. Whence it is plain that this is the first magnitude which is one, since it has the first principle of the first motion" (no. 1928).

c. As Denoting a Singular

Whatever has one notion or reason, is one. Something may be grasped as one, either because it is a singular and one in number, or else because it is one in species.

d. As Denoting a Species

"That which is one species is indivisible, and is one according to science and knowledge. For there is not in diverse singulars some nature which is one in number, which might be called the species. But the intellect apprehends as one that in which all the inferiors agree. And thus, in the apprehension of the intellect, the species is made indivisible which in reality is diverse in diverse individuals" (no. 1930).

Obviously that which is first in those things which are one in notion or in reason is substance, since all other essences depend on it.

Therefore one is said in the following four ways:

1. that which is continuous according to nature;
2. that which is a whole;
3. that which is singular;
4. that which is universal as a species.

"And all these are called one for one reason, namely, by virtue of the fact of being indivisible. For, properly, one is indivisible being. But in the first two, something is called one because its motion is indivisible; but in the other two because there is an understanding or notion which is indivisible—and under this is also included the apprehension of a particular thing" (no. 1932).

Insofar, then, as a thing is indivisible in any one of the above ways, in that sense, too, it is one.

2. A Property of One: To Be a Measure
a. Measure in Quantity and Other Accidents

The notion of one is to be indivisible, and that which is indivisible in any genus, is the measure thereof. This occurs most properly in quantity; for measure is nothing else than that by which the quantity of a thing is known. This is either by one (as in one foot, one inch) or by number (as in three feet, three inches), which number is composed of unities.

This notion of measure is found first of all in discrete quantity, i.e., in the one which is the principle of number. One as measure, as referred to other forms of quantity, is rather something adventitious than the thing itself, as, for example, in the case of one hand smaller than the other.

By derivation, whatever is indivisible, and therefore one, in some genus, is taken as the measure in that genus. Thus, in dimensions, some indivisible length, such as the foot, is taken as a unit of measure.

The reason that it must be something indivisible is so that it may be constant, to which nothing may be added or subtracted. One as the principle of number is the perfect example of this. In the other genera of quantity, some basic minimum is chosen—since if one takes something too large, it is impossible to measure small variations.

One, then, is the measure of all things, since it is that at which division ends, and a thing is known by dividing it down to its component parts—whether they be quantitative parts, or specific parts such as matter and form and the elements.

Some things are absolutely indivisible, as is the unity which is the principle of number; others are indivisible according to convention, as in the case of inch or foot as units of measure. This is so because every continuous thing is divisible, at least mathematically, although not in nature—"for one finds a smallest (quantity of) flesh, as is touched upon in *Physics* I" (no. 1953). Furthermore, the measure must be of the same nature as that which is measured. Thus lengths would be measured by a length, surfaces by a surface, and so forth.

In relation to knowledge, whereas we may speak of our knowledge as measuring things, actually it is the things of nature which measure our knowledge, although, insofar as we are the makers of things by art, our knowledge measures them.

"For it is not because we sense or know something that it is therefore thus in the nature of things. But because it is thus in the nature of things, therefore we truly know, or sense, something, as is said in *Metaphysics* IX. And thus it happens to us, that in sensing and in knowing we are measured by the things which are outside us....

"But if there is any knowledge which is the cause of the thing known, it will be necessary for it to be its measure. Thus the knowledge of the artisan is the measure of the artifacts, since each artifact is perfect to the extent that it attains to the likeness of the art. And this is the relation of the science of God to all things" (nos. 1957, 1959).

In conclusion, then, it belongs to one to be a measure, since, as one, it is indivisible. This is true basically in quantity, and then in quality and other genera insofar as some indivisible in the genus is taken as the unit of measure and comparison. Finally, in quantity that which is absolutely indivisible is the unity which is the principle of number.

b. Measure As to One in Substance

Is one the very substance of a thing? That is, is one a subsisting substance as the Pythagoreans, and later the Platonists, came to hold, or is it rather said of something, in the sense that at the basis of things there is some element which, as indivisible, is one, as the naturalists held?

Plainly, one cannot be a subsisting substance, since being and one are universals predicable of many, and a singular substance cannot be predicated of many. Likewise it is clear that one is not itself a nature; rather, in every genus some nature is sought, of which one is said. Thus, while one is not a substance, in the genus of substance there will nevertheless be some substance which is most perfectly one and is, as such, the measure of the others.

3. Being and One Are the Same As to Subject

Being and one are the same as to subject, and differ solely as to notion. "For one adds indivision over and above being. It is, indeed, indivisible or undivided being which is called one" (no. 1974).

The three following reasons are given for the identity of being and one:

1. One follows all the predicaments, and is not in one and not in another. The same is true of being.
2. When one says one man, one does not intend to indicate by one something added to man, any more than being is considered to add anything not contained in the ten predicaments.
3. Each thing is one insofar as it is being; when it ceases to be one, it ceases to be.

What is to be said of being and one which, on the one hand, are not themselves the substances of things, nor, on the other hand, something added to things as is the case with accidents? The answer lies in the distinction between first and second substance. First substance is that which actually exists; second substance, namely, genera and species, are the universal natures derived from the singular substances. These universals in the mind are not, as the Platonists thought, actual subsisting things, nor, on the other hand, are they accidents. They are, rather, universal or common ideas, applicable to many, or, in the case of being and one, applicable analogously to everything that is.

This one which is applicable to all that is being, is plainly not the one which is in the genus of quantity, and is the principle of that accident which is number. The reason is that the number of something (e.g., five of fingers) does add something to the concept, finger, in the sense of relating a plurality of fingers according to a certain measure, different, for example, from four or six.

B. One Compared to Many
1. One and Many, and What Follows Them
a. How One Is Opposed to Many

"Although one and many are opposed in many ways,...nevertheless one way, and the more important, is accordingly as one and many are opposed as divisible and indivisible, since this mode of opposition is considered according to the proper notion of each. For the notion of many consists in the fact of things being divided from each other, or divisible" (nos. 1983, 1984).

To what genus of opposition does the opposition of one and many belong? There are four genera of opposition: contradiction, relation, privation, and contrariety. One and many will be seen to be opposed as contraries.

"That, indeed, they are not opposed according to contradiction, is plain, since neither is verified of nonbeing. For nonbeing is neither one nor many. But it would be necessary for one part of the contradiction to be true both of being and nonbeing, since one part of a contradiction, the negating part, extends to nonbeing [e.g., in the case of blue and nonblue, all nonbeing is also nonblue: two contradictories necessarily include not only all being, but also all nonbeing within their scope]. Likewise it is plain also that they are not opposed as things said toward something , i.e., as relation. For one and many are said absolutely.

"But although he [Aristotle] has said that one and many are opposed as indivisible and divisible, which are seen to be opposed according to privation and having, he concludes nevertheless that one and many are opposed as contraries. For the opposition which is according to privation and having, is the principle of the opposition which is according to contrariety, as will be evident below. This is so because one of two contraries is always privation, although not pure privation. For thus it would not share in the nature of the genus, since contraries are in the same genus. It is necessary, therefore, that both contraries be a certain nature, although one of them may share in the nature of the genus with a certain defect, just as black is related to white....Since, therefore, one does not signify pure privation—for it does not signify indivision itself, but being which is undivided—it is plain that one and many are not opposed according to pure privation and having, but as contraries" (nos. 1987-88).

There is an apparent difficulty which arises, in that privation seems to follow having; and indivisible, divisible; and therefore one, the many. But it has been previously stated (see p. 123 above) that one is the principle of many, and that through which it is known. For example, if one does not know one, one cannot know five.

"To see, therefore, the solution of the objection, it must be considered that those things which are prior according to nature and more known, are posterior and less known as to us, in that we receive the knowledge of them through sense. But composite and confused things fall on sense first, as is stated in *Physics* I. Whence it is that composite things fall first on our knowledge. But the more simple things which are prior and more known according to nature fall on our knowledge afterward. Whence it is that we do not define the first principles of things except through the negations of posterior things. Thus we say that a point is that which has no part; and we know God through negations, insofar as we say God to be incorporeal, immobile, infinite.

"Thus, therefore, although one is prior according to nature to many; nevertheless, according to our knowledge it is defined and named from the privation of division. And because of this the Philosopher says that 'one is said,' i.e., is named, 'and shown,' i.e., known, from its contrary, as indivisible from divisible. The reason is from the fact that many is more sensible than one, and the divisible more than the indivisible. Whence many is prior in notion to indivisible, not, indeed, according to the order of nature, but because of sense, which is the principle of our knowledge" (nos. 1990-91).

But even against the supposition of one and many being opposed as contraries there arise difficulties. For example, normally one contrary does not constitute the other, but rather destroys it. Yet one constitutes, and is the principle of, many. The answer to this lies in the distinction between one taken formally and one taken materially. Thus body as such, without soul, is opposed to animate; but body as the matter in that which is animated, is a part of animate. Thus, too, one taken formally as indivisible, is opposed to the divided many; but taken materially as the matter of many, it is not opposed to, but a part of, many. In the same way, two, as a formal species of number, differs from three, but as a material part of the latter, it does not.

Likewise a difficulty arises in saying that many is prior in notion to one. For since one is in the notion of many—many being nothing other than an aggregate of ones—then, if one is posterior in notion to many, it follows that in the notion of one and many there is a certain circular-ity. Thus it would be necessary through many to know one, and conversely. The same would be both better known and less known, which is impossible.

"It should be said, therefore, that nothing prevents something being prior and posterior to the same according to notion, according to different things considered in it. For in multitude one can consider both that it is multitude and the division itself. By reason, therefore, of division it is prior to one according to notion. For one is that which is not divided. But as it is many, it is posterior to one according to notion, since many is called an aggregation of unities.

"The division, however, which is presupposed to the notion of one, accordingly as it is convertible with being, is not the division of continuous quantity, which is preunderstood to the one which is the principle of number. But it is the division which contradiction causes, insofar as this being and that are said to be divided, in that this is not that [see p. 77 above].

"Thus, therefore, there falls first in our intellect, *being*, and then *division*; and after this, *one*, which takes away division, and finally *many*, which is made up out of unities. For although those things which are divided be many, nevertheless they do not have the notion of many except after there has been attributed to this and that one that it is one. Likewise, too, nothing prevents its being said that the notion of many depends on one, accordingly as it is measured by one, which already pertains to the notion of number" (nos. 1996-98).

b. What Follows One and Many

As was stated in Book V (see chapter 8), where the different ways in which contrariety is said were treated, upon one there follows the same, and like, and equal. For the same is one in substance; like is one in quality; equal is one in quantity. In respect to many, there is, to match these, diverse, that which is not one in substance; unlike, that which is not one in quality; unequal, that which is not one in quantity.

1) Those things following one.
a) **The same.** There are three ways in which things are said to be the same:

1. <u>In supposite alone.</u> In the same substance, when it is stated, "Socrates is white," or "musical," these predicates are the same as Socrates in the sense that they are in the same supposite.
2. <u>In species alone.</u> As Socrates and Plato are the same in that they have the same nature or species.
3. <u>In both supposite and nature.</u> As Socrates is the same as Socrates.

b) **Alike.** There are four ways in which things are said to be alike:

1. (This way corresponds to no.2 of the same.) When things not numerically the same are one in quality, i.e., similar or alike as to figure or proportion. Thus one rectangle would be similar to another rectangle which had equal angles and proportionate sides; many unequal straight lines would be alike. (For them to be the same in the mathematical sense, the lines in the rectangle would have to be equal.)

   "Now one may consider here that when there is unity according to the perfect notion of species, there is said to be identity; but when there is unity not according to the whole notion of the species, there is said to be similarity. Thus one might say that those things which are one in genus, are similar, but those which are one in species are the same. [Thus two rectangles with equal, and not merely proportionate, sides would be the same in species.]" (no. 2009).
2. When things agree in some form, which is susceptible to more or less, in an equal way. Thus, two whites of this sort would be called similar.
3. When things agree in one form, but according to more or less, they are still called similar, since they have the same species of quality, as in the case of things more white and less white.
4. When things agree in more ways than they disagree, at least in appearance, as pewter might be said to be like silver.

c) **Equal.** This mode following one is not treated because it is not said in many ways other than in quantity.
2) Those things following plurality. The modes following plurality or many are proportionate to the modes following one. Thus, just as the same is taken in three ways, so is diverse:

1. That which is other as opposite to the same. Everything, compared to something else, is either the same or diverse.
2. That which has not both one matter and one notion, as two men are thus diverse.
3. As unequal lines are diverse, i.e., having neither matter nor notion in common.

The same and diverse, or different, although originating in substance, nevertheless are extended to all genera of being, as is true of essence also. Nevertheless, they do not extend to nonbeing, since, just as one and many are contraries, both of which are true of natures, so too of same and diverse. (Nonsame, however, can be true of nonbeing.)

What is the difference between difference and diversity? Anything not the same as some other is diverse; but that which is different, is different in respect to something, and therefore presupposes a common ground in those aspects in which it does not thus differ, i.e., it is the same in some respects.

"That which is different from something, must be different by something. Whence it is necessary that that by which things which differ, differ, be some same thing in those things which do not thus differ. But that which is the same in several is either a genus or a species. Whence every different thing differs either by genus or by species.

"Those things differ indeed as to genus which do not have a common matter. For it was said above in Book VIII [see chapter 10] that although matter is not a genus, nevertheless it is from that which is material in a thing that the genus is taken. For example, sensible nature is material in man with respect to notion. And therefore that which does not communicate with man in sensible nature is of another genus.

"And since those things which do not communicate in matter, are not reciprocally generated, it follows that those things are diverse in genus whose generation is not reciprocal. It was necessary to add this because of those things which do not have matter, as is the case with accidents. Thus those things are of diverse genus which are in diverse predicaments, as line and whiteness, one of which is not made from the other.

"But those things are said to differ in species whose genus is the same, and which differ according to form. Now that is called a genus which is predicated of two things differing as to species, as in the case of man and horse. Now contraries differ, and contrariety is a certain difference" (nos. 2018-21).

2. Contrariety Specially Considered
a. *Contrariety Is the Greatest Difference*

1) Contraries.
a) <u>The nature of contrariety.</u> What is contrariety? First of all, there must be some greatest difference. This is so because whatever things differ according to more or less, must have some greatest difference, since one cannot go to infinity. But certain things do differ according to more or less. Contrariety is that greatest difference.

This is shown inductively. Things which are of a different genus are not said to have some greatest difference, since they do not have some common ground. But two things of the same genus which differ as to species, do—as, for example, two colors. In the realm of color one can go from black to white through various shades of diminishing darkness, but once one has arrived at white one can go no farther. It is thus the greatest difference from the other extreme, namely, black. These ultimates in the same species are called contraries.

Since it is impossible to go farther beyond these, and that which is perfect is that beyond which there remains nothing farther to be pursued, these greatest differences are also perfect differences. Because of this, there cannot be more than one contrary to a given thing, just as the distance of a line is between two points only.

b) <u>Contrariety compared to other oppositions.</u>
(1) Contrariety as opposition of privation and having. This is so because in all contrariety there is included privation and having. However, they are not the same: not every privation, i.e., not every lack of something which might be, is contrary, but only the perfect lack.

"Now since privation according to that which it is, is not susceptible of more or less, one cannot speak of a perfect privation except by reason of some nature which has a perfect distance in relation to the had. Thus not every privation of white is contrary to white, but the privation most distant from white, which must be based in some nature of the same genus, most distant from white. And according to this, we say that black is contrary to white" (no. 2038).

By extension, those things are called contrary which are related to the basic contraries. Thus there is first that which includes privation and having, e.g., white and black, hot and cold; then what actually brings this about, e.g., one heating or freezing; then the receiver of the same, as that which is heated or frozen; finally those things from which such contraries follow, as fire and water in relation to their having heat and coldness in them.

(2) Contrariety is not same as contradiction. "The reason for this is because contradiction is included in all other [species of opposition, including contrariety] as prior and more simple. For it is impossible for opposites according to any genus of opposition to coexist. This, indeed, occurs from the fact that one of the two opposites has in its notion the negation of the other. Thus, it is of the notion of that which is blind to be nonseeing; and of the notion of black that it be not white. And likewise it is of the notion of a son that he be not the father of him of whom he is the son. But it is plain that there is no middle in contradiction. For it is necessary either to affirm or deny, as was made clear in Book IV. But it is fitting for contraries to have a middle. And thus it is plain that contrariety and contradiction are not the same" (nos. 2041-42).

(3) Privation as a certain contradiction. "That is called privation in one way, when something does not have what it is in no way intended to have, as if we should say that a stone does not have sight. In another way, something is said to be deprived of something if it does not have what it is intended by nature to have—as, for example, in the case of an animal if it should not have sight. And this may be in two ways: in one way, in whatever way it does not have it; in another way, when it does not have it at a determinate time, or in some determinate way. The reason is that privation is said in many ways, as was had above in Books V and IX [see chapters 8 and 11].

"From these considerations, therefore, it is evident that privation is a certain contradiction. And that it is indeed contradiction is evident from the fact that something is said to be deprived of something from the fact that it does not have it.

"But that it is not absolute contradiction, but rather a certain contradiction, is plain from the fact that contradiction in its notion does not require either the aptitude, or even the existence, of some subject. For it is verified of being and of any nonbeing whatever. We say, indeed, that an animal does not see, and wood does not see, and nonbeing does not see. But privation necessarily requires some subject, and sometimes it also requires an aptitude in the subject. But what is wholly nonbeing is not said to be deprived of anything....

"And therefore contradiction cannot have a middle, but privation has a middle in some way. For it is necessary that everything be either equal or nonequal, whether it be being or nonbeing. But it is not necessary to say of everything that it is either equal or unequal [as deprived of an equality it should have], for this is necessary solely in that which is susceptible of equality.

"Thus, therefore, the opposition of contradiction is wholly immediate, while the opposition of privation is immediate in a determinate subject, but not immediate absolutely. From which it is evident that contrariety, whose nature it is to have a middle, is closer to privation than to contradiction. Yet it is still not had that privation is contrariety" (nos. 2043-49).

(4) Contrariety is privation. Generations are from contraries in matter, and every contrary is privation of a sort. Therefore, one of two contraries will always be privation. Yet every privation is not contrariety. The reason for this is that even things close together may be described as privation—as gray may be said to be lacking in white. But only the extremes or ultimates, or greatest distances, may be a privation which is a contrary.

"Privation does not signify some specific nature in a subject [at a specific distance, near or far, from the form], but presupposes only a subject with an aptitude. A contrary, however, requires a determinate disposition of the subject, according to which it is at the maximum distance from the form" (no. 2051).

There is a twofold privation:

1. One privation has an immediate order to the subject of the form, and therefore there is a reciprocal transmutation, as between darkness and light, light and darkness.
2. The other is compared to the subject *through* the form, of which it is a certain corruption, as blindness is the corruption of sight, death of life. In such there is no reciprocal conversion, as was had in Book IX.

Contrariety is of the former sort, namely, that which is susceptible of reciprocal or reversible transformation.

Since the privation which is found in one of two contraries may be either in any way at all, or in some certain way, at some certain time (e.g., at some certain age), in some certain part (e.g., a principal part), and so forth, it is possible for certain contraries to have a middle.

"Between good and evil, there is a middle. For there is some man neither good nor evil. This is because man is called good according to virtue. For virtue is that which makes its possessor good. But not everyone who lacks virtue is evil. But if at the age at which he should have virtue, a man should not have it, he is called evil. Or, likewise, if anyone should lack virtue as to certain minimal acts, and as though of indifferent importance to life, he is not called evil—but only should he lack virtue as to the principal and necessary acts for life. But even and odd in numbers do not have a middle, since a number is called odd from the fact that it in any way lacks being even.

"Another difference in privation is that a certain privation determines a subject for itself, while another does not. For it was said above that that which lacks something, even should it not be intended to have it, is sometimes called deprived. But from this diversity of privation there is able to occur in some contraries that they should have a middle or not have one. Thus, if we were to say that, when man is called good according to the political virtues, if the evil which includes the privation of good should require a determinate subject, the rustic who does not participate in civil conversation is neither good nor evil by civil goodness or malice. Thus, therefore, it is evident from the aforesaid that one of two contraries is stated according to privation" (nos. 2056-57).

Finally, that one of two contraries is privation may be shown if the two basic contraries from which the others are derived, namely, one and many, involve privation. For the same and diverse, similar and dissimilar, equal and unequal, follow upon one and many. But one and many are opposed as divisible and indivisible, i.e., that which lacks division. And therefore, all contraries include privation.

c) Certain difficulties from what determined. Since it has been stated that one thing is contrary to one, two difficulties seem to arise: first, one and many are opposed, but to many there is also opposed few; secondly, equal appears to be opposed by both large and small.

Starting with the second of these difficulties, what of the opposition of equal to large and small? That is, can it be opposed to both, thereby having more than one contrary to equal, while there is supposed to be only one contrary to one, occupying the greatest difference? This is resolved by recognizing that while equal is indeed opposed to large and small, it is nevertheless not opposed as a contrary, since it is in the middle here, and is therefore not a perfect, or extreme, difference.

What kind, then, of opposition is it? It is not the opposition of contradiction, but rather that of privation.

"This particle *not*, which is included in the notion of equal, when we say that to be equal which is not more, not less, is not a negation absolutely, but necessarily is a privation. For a negation is said absolutely of whatever thing in which there is not its opposite affirmation. This does not happen in the present case. For we do not call equal everything which is not more nor less, but we state this only in those things in which there is an aptitude for being more or less.

"This, therefore, is the notion of equal: to be that which is neither large nor small, yet has the aptitude to be either large or small, as other privations are defined. And thus it is plain that equal is opposed to both, namely, to large and small, as a privative negation" (nos. 2069-70).

Thus equal is a middle between large and small, as there is a middle between good and evil, although it is unnamed. The reason for this is that there may be many varying degrees of that which is neither good nor evil, just as there may be many varying degrees between black and white. But equal is one determined thing. It should be noted here that middles of this sort are not between just any two things whatever, but between things in the same genus, having a same common distance between them.

What of the opposition between one and many? How can many be opposed to few and also to one? Certainly this would not seem to make one the same as few. Many must therefore be taken in different senses. In one sense, many can be taken to mean a plurality which exceeds, either absolutely, insofar as something is called much or many if it exceeds the usual plurality, as for example, in the case of much rain, or many showers; or else in a certain respect, as ten men are many in comparison to three. By contrast, few will be a plurality which is in defect, less than the usual, or less than many.

In another sense, many may be taken absolutely, as anything more than one. This is the many which is opposed to one.

"In another way, many is said absolutely, as number is called a certain multitude. And thus many is opposed only to one, but not to few. For many according to this present meaning is as though the plural of that which is called one. This meaning is as if we should say one and many in the sense of saying one and ones plurally, as we say white and whites, and as the measured are referred to the measurable. For many is measured by one, as will be said below. And according to this meaning, from many one speaks of multiples. For it is plain that according to any number something is said in a multiple way—as from two, double; and from three, triple; and so forth. For each number is many in this way, since it is referred to one, and since any of them is measurable by one. And this is so accordingly as many is opposed to one, but not accordingly as it is opposed to few.

"Whence even two, which is a certain number, is many accordingly as many is opposed to one. But accordingly as many signifies a plurality which exceeds, two is not many, but few. For nothing is fewer than two, since one is not few....For few is a plurality having defect. But the first plurality having defect is two. Whence two is the first few" (nos. 2082-83).

How then are one and many opposed? They are opposed as relatives, not as relatives which are mutually related, as in the case of father-son, master-servant, but as relatives in which one thing is referred to the other only, as knowledge is referred to the knowable, but not conversely—in the sense that being known adds nothing to the knowable, while knowing does add something to the knower.

"One is opposed to many, as the measure to the measurable, which, indeed, are opposed as toward something [relation]. Nevertheless this is not so in such a way that it is of the number of those things which are toward something according to themselves. For it was stated above in Book V [see p. 148 above] that things are toward something in two ways. For certain things are referred to each other mutually, as master and servant, father and son, large and small; and he [Aristotle] states these to be toward something as contraries. And they are toward something according to themselves, since, in the case of both, what it is that they are is said toward the other.

"But other things are not toward something mutually, but one of them is said toward something, not because it is referred to something, but because something is referred to it, as in the case of knowledge and the knowable. For the knowable is said relatively, not because it is referred to knowledge, but because knowledge is referred to it. And thus it is evident that they are not relative according to themselves, since the knowable is not as what is referred to another, but rather the other is said in relation to it....

"...And since it is of the notion of measure that it be the smallest in some way, therefore it is first stated that one is less than many and even than two, although it is not few. For it does not follow that if anything be less that it be few—although it is of the notion of few that it be less—since every few is a certain plurality.

"Now it should be known that the absolute plurality or multitude which is opposed to the one which is convertible with being, is as though the genus of number, since number is nothing other than plurality and multitude measurable by one. Thus, therefore, one, accordingly as it is absolutely called indivisible being, is convertible with being. But accordingly as it takes on the notion of measure, it is thus determined to some genus of quantity, in which there is properly found the notion of measure.

"And likewise plurality or multitude, accordingly as they signify divided beings, are not determined to any genus. But accordingly as they signify something measured, they are determined to the genus of quantity, whose species is number. And therefore he [Aristotle] says that number is plurality measured by one, and that plurality is as the genus of number.

"And he does not say that it is the genus absolutely, because just as being is not a genus, properly speaking, so neither is one which is convertible with being, nor the plurality opposed to it. But it is a quasi genus, since it has something of the notion of genus, insofar as it is common.

"Taking thus, therefore, one which is the principle of number, and which has the notion of measure, and number which is a species of quantity, and is multitude measured by one, one and many are opposed, not as contraries, as was said above of the one which is convertible with being, and of the plurality opposed to it, but they are opposed as certain of those things which are toward something, one of which, namely, is stated relatively since the other is referred to it. Thus are opposed, therefore, one and number, insofar as one is a measure and number is measurable.

"And since such is the nature of these relatives that one is able to be without the other, but not conversely, therefore this is found in one and number, that if there is number, there must be one. But it is not necessary that wherever there is one there be number. For if there be some indivisible, such as point, one is there, but not number. But in other relative things of which both are said according to themselves toward something, neither is without the other. For there is not a master without a servant, nor a servant without a master" (nos. 2087-94).

In conclusion, then, plurality as measured is opposed to one as measure, but not to few. Rather, to few, which signifies a plurality

which is exceeded, there is opposed the many which signifies a plurality which exceeds. At the same time, plurality is opposed to one in two
ways.

"In one way it is opposed to it, as was said above, as the divisible to
the indivisible. And this is so if one should take in common the one
which is convertible with being, and the plurality which corresponds to
it. But plurality is opposed in another way to one, as toward something, just as is knowledge to the knowable. And this is the case if one
should take the plurality which is number and the one which has the
notion of measure and is the principle of number" (no. 2096).

2) The middle of contraries.

a) <u>Middles in same genus with contraries.</u> Middles are in the
same genus with their contraries, since the definition of middles is that
they are those among which that first comes which is changing from
one extreme before arriving at the other extreme. This may be seen in
musical notes and colors, for example.

b) <u>Middles are between contraries.</u> Middles are between contraries, since change is made from one extreme to another and middles by
definition are on the route between extremes. These extremes cannot
be contradictories, since such have no middle—every subject, whether
being or nonbeing, being one or the other. Nor can they be relatives,
such as knower and knowable, which, not being in the same genus, are
not related as contraries; but only such as are so related: for example,
large and small, which have a certain middle in equal.

c) <u>Middles are composed from contraries.</u> Since contraries are in
the same genus, they must be constituted contrary species by prior
contrary differences.

"For it is necessary that of contraries there either be some genus or
none. But if there were no [same] genus of contraries, they would not
have a middle, since a middle is not except of those things which are of
one genus, as is evident from what has been said. But if there is, of
those contraries of which there is a middle, some genus prior to these
contraries, it is also necessary that there be contrary differences prior to
the contrary species, which produce and constitute the contrary species
out of the one genus. For species are constituted out of the genus and
the differences.

"And he [Aristotle] manifests this by an example. Thus, if white
and black should be contrary species and have one genus which is
color, it is necessary that they should have certain constitutive differences—in such a way that white be color-dispersing-sight, and black be

color-gathering-sight. And thus these differences, gathering and dispersing, are prior to white and black. Whence, since there is contrariety in both places, it is plain that contraries are prior to themselves. For contrary differences are prior to contrary species. And the former are also more contrary, since they are causes of contrariety to the species themselves.

"Nevertheless it should be considered that dispersing and gathering of sight are not true constitutive differences of white and black, but more their effects. Nevertheless there are set down, in place of differences, the signs of the latter. Thus it happens that through accidents there are designated differences and substantial forms" (nos. 2105-7).

In keeping with this, middle species between the contrary species will have middle constitutive differences, mediate between the contrary differences which are called the prime contraries. Thus, while the contraries will be constituted out of one or the other of extremes, the middles will be composed of both.

"That into which change first takes place is more and less with regard to both extremes [i.e., as a change begins from black to white, it is less black than absolute black, more black than absolute white]. And because of this it is necessary that it be the middle of contraries. And thus it follows that all middles are composed out of contraries. For the same middle which is more and less with respect to both extremes must be composed from the simple extremes, with respect to which it is called more and less" (no. 2110).

In this way, then, all the species of the genus, whether contrary or mediate, are from the prime contraries, namely, the differences.

b. How Contraries Differ in Species and Genus

1) Difference according to species. The difference diversifies the genus, somewhat as form diversifies matter. The likeness, however, is not absolute, since the genus may be predicated of the species, but the matter may not be predicated of the composite—since it is only a part of the composite.

"Matter is diversified by forms otherwise than the genus by differences. For the form is not that which is matter, but makes a composition with it. Whence matter is not the composite, but something of it. But difference is added to genus not as though part to part, but as though whole to whole. Whence the genus is that which is the species, and not solely something of it. For if it were a part, it would not be predicated of it.

"But nevertheless, since the whole may be denominated by one alone of its parts, as, for example, if a man should be denominated as having a head, or having hands, it occurs to the composite to be denominated from matter and form. And indeed the name by which some whole is denominated by what is material in it, is the name of the genus. But the name by which it is denominated by the formal principle, is the name of the difference. Thus man is named an animal from sensible nature, a rational being from intellective nature. Just as, therefore, having hands belongs to the whole, although the hand is a part, so the genus and difference belong to the whole, although they be taken from the parts.

"If, therefore, one considers in genus and difference that from which both are taken, the genus is related to the differences in the same way as matter to the forms. But if one considers them accordingly as they name the whole, then they are related differently. Nevertheless, this is common to both [i.e., to genus and matter], that just as the essence of the matter is divided by the forms, so the nature of the genus is diversified by the differences. But this separates them both: that matter is in both the divided things, nevertheless it is not both of them; while the genus is both of them—since matter names a part, but genus the whole....This animal is horse, and this animal is man.

"And he [Aristotle] states this against the Platonists, who laid down the common things to be separated, as though the common nature were not diversified, supposing the nature of the species to be something other besides the nature of the genus....Whence it is necessary that that common thing, such as animal, be according to itself *this* such thing according to one difference, and *that* such according to another, as that this be horse, and that man....

"Through this, then, which the Philosopher here says, there is not only excluded the opinion of Plato, positing the one and the same common thing to exist per se, but there is also excluded the opinion of those who say that that which pertains to the nature of the genus does not differ in species in the different species, as that the sensible soul is not specifically different in man and horse" (nos. 2114-19).

This difference which diversifies the genus, is the difference of contrariety. In effect, it cannot be the difference of contradiction, since its opposites are not in the same genus—negation positing nothing. The same is true of privative opposites, since they suppose only a negation in some subject—as a stone is nonseeing. Among relations, those which are not mutual, such as knowledge and the knowable, are not in the same genus, but only those which are mutual are, and this because they are like contraries. Thus, only contrary opposites divide the genus. There may be several successive divisions of a general genus until one arrives at the most special species, i.e., the species which cannot be divided into further species by any further formal differences, but now can be divided only materially into particular individuals of the same species.

2) Contrariety as not difference as to species.

a) <u>Contraries in the same species.</u> Why do certain differences, such as to be able to fly, and to be able to walk, constitute different species, while others, such as black and white, masculine and feminine, do not? This is explained by noting that there are differences according to form, and differences according to matter, and masculine and feminine, white and black, are examples of the latter—which do not constitute specific differences.

"Just as diversity of form makes a difference of species, so diversity of individual matter makes a difference of individuals. But white is not predicated of man except by reason of the individual. For man is not called white unless because *some* man is called white, such as Callias. And thus it is evident that man is called white per accidens, since it is not insofar as he is man, but insofar as he is this man, that he is called white. But this man is called such because of the matter. Whence it is evident that white and black do not pertain to the formal differences of man, but only to the material. And because of this, a white man and a black man do not differ in species, just as neither do a bronze circle and a wooden circle differ in species....

"...Masculine and feminine are properly passions of animal, since animal is placed in the definition of both. But they do not befit animal according to substance and form, but on the part of matter and the body....For from one seed diverse things according to the species are not produced. Whence it remains that masculine and feminine do not differ according to form, nor are they diverse according to species" (nos. 2132, 2134).

b) <u>Contraries leading to difference of genus.</u> "Contraries are diverse in species, as was shown above....Corruptible and incorruptible are contraries. This he [Aristotle] proves from the fact that the impotence opposed to a determined potency is a certain privation, as was had in Book IX. But privation is the principle of contrariety. Whence it follows that impotence is contrary to potency. But corruptible and incorruptible are opposed according to potency and impotence. But they are opposed in different ways. For if potency is taken in a common way, accordingly as it refers to being able to do or to undergo something, thus corruptible is said according to potency, and incorruptible according to impotency. If, however, potency is said accordingly as is meant not to be able to deteriorate, thus, conversely, incorruptible is said according to potency, and corruptible according to impotency.

"Now although it would seem that one should conclude from this that corruptible and incorruptible differ according to species, he [Aristotle] concludes that they are diverse in genus. And this because, just as form and act belong to species, so matter and potency belong to genus. Whence, just as the contrariety which is according to forms and acts produces a difference according to species, so the contrariety which is according to potency produces a diversity of genus" (nos. 2136-37[2]).

What of the theoretical objection that in the same species one thing might be corruptible, another incorruptible, or the same thing corruptible at one time, incorruptible at another?

"Corruptible does not inhere, in any of those things of which it is predicated, according to accident—because what is according to accident may also not inhere. But corruptible is necessarily in those things in which it is. Now if this were not true, it would follow that one and the same should be at one time corruptible and at another incorruptible, which is impossible according to nature. This does not, however, exclude that the divine power should incorruptibly preserve certain things corruptible according to nature....

"And from this it follows necessarily that corruptible and incorruptible are diverse in genus. For it is plain that the contraries which are in a same genus are not of the substance of that genus. For rational and irrational are not of the substance of animal. But animal is both in potency. Now whatever genus is taken, it is necessary that corruptible and incorruptible be in its notion. Whence it is impossible that they should communicate in any genus. And this comes about reasonably. For of corruptible and incorruptible things there cannot be one matter. But genus, physically speaking, is taken from matter. Whence it was said above that those things which do not communicate in matter are diverse in genus. Logically speaking, however, nothing prevents that they should agree in genus, insofar as they agree in one common notion, either of substance, or quality, or some such" (nos. 2140-42).

Nevertheless, all contraries cause a specific difference in some sense. Thus, although black and white do not cause different species of man, they do cause different species of color, just as masculine and feminine do of sex. In the same way, although animate and inanimate differ generically in relation to the species derived from them, yet, as to the genus which is divided by them, they differ specifically. "For all differences of a genus are constitutive of certain species, even though those species may be generically diverse" (no. 2144).

"But corruptible and incorruptible divide being per se: since corruptible is that which is able not to be, and incorruptible that which is not able not to be. Whence, since being is not a genus, it is not surprising if corruptible and incorruptible do not fit in any genus [except a quasi genus?]" (no. 2145).

Chapter 13

The First Principles of Being
(*Metaphysics*, XI-XII)

A. Survey
  1. Considerations before that of substance
    a. Questions as to subject matter of science
      1) As to consideration itself
      2) As to things considered
    b. What pertains to this science
      1) To consider all beings
      2) To consider first principles of demonstration
        a) In general
        b) In particular, the principle of contradiction
          (1) Its defense
          (2) Various positions
            (a) All propositions are false
            (b) All propositions are true
          (3) Source and remedy of these positions
            (a) The axiom: Nothing comes from nothing
            (b) Different people judge same differently
      3) Metaphysics compared to particular sciences
        a) What is proper to each particular science
        b) How particular sciences differ from each other
        c) Metaphysics compared with particular sciences
          (1) As to mode of separation
          (2) As to nobility
          (3) As to universality

The First Principles of Being
(*Metaphysics*, XI-XII)

Just as it is fitting that there be a certain universal and first science to treat those things which exceed the scope of the particular sciences, and which are, namely, the common things which follow being in common, so also it is fitting that this science treat of separated substances, which likewise exceed the scope of the particular sciences.

Metaphysics, therefore, after having examined being in common, approaches the question of separated substances, "to the knowledge of which are ordained not only those things which have been treated in this science, but also those things which are treated in the other sciences" (no. 2146).

This treatment comprises the following two parts:

1. a survey of things useful for this, as stated both in the *Physics* and the *Metaphysics*;
2. the actual inquiry concerning separated substances.

A. Survey
1. Considerations before That of Substance
a. Questions As to Subject Matter of Science

1) As to consideration itself. Although this science considers more than one principle, it does so, nevertheless, from one single viewpoint, and therefore remains one science. It likewise considers the common principles of demonstration, such as *The same thing cannot be both affirmed and denied* and other such, since the terms of these principles, e.g., being and nonbeing, whole and part, same and different, and so forth, belong primarily to the consideration of this science.

This science is likewise of all substances, "although of certain ones more principally, namely, of separated substances" (no. 2153), insofar as all agree in one genus, which is that of being per se. "The truth is that wisdom considers substances and accidents, insofar as they agree in being; but substances principally, as the per se first being, and concerning these it demonstrates accidents" (no. 2155).

What are the causes touched upon in this science? Since it is of immobile things, namely, separated substances, it would seem to exclude the final cause, which is a cause of motion. Yet just the opposite is true.

"This science does not seem to be about 'that for the sake of which,' i.e., the final cause, because the end has the notion of good. But the good consists in operations, and in those things which are in motion. Whence, in immobile things, as, for example, in mathematics, nothing is demonstrated through the final cause. And it is plain that the end is that which first moves. For it moves the efficient cause. But a first mover does not seem to exist in immobile things.

"But the truth is that this science does consider the aforesaid [four] genera of causes, and especially the formal and final causes. And furthermore, the end, which is the first mover, is wholly immobile, as will be shown below" (nos. 2156-57).

How does this science treat of sensible substances? "Now the truth of this question is that this science determines concerning sensible substances insofar as they are substances, not insofar as they are sensible and mobile. For this properly belongs to natural science. But the proper consideration of this science is of the substances which are not ideas, nor separated mathematical things, but first movers, as will be evident below" (no. 2159).

2) As to things considered. Although this science treats of being, and the universal principles of being, it should be remembered that it does not treat of abstractions, but of existing singulars, the singulars which are causes, and the singulars which are caused.

"The truth is that there is nothing existing in the nature of things except singulars, but [genera and species exist] only in the consideration of the intellect abstracting common things from proper" (no. 2174).

Science is of universals, not in the sense of universal beings being its object, but in the sense of a consideration of the universal aspects of singular things. Although material singulars are not intellectually knowable as such, immaterial singulars are, and certain of them are principles of other things.

"And the truth is that, although universals do not exist of themselves, nevertheless, the nature of those things which do subsist of themselves is to be considered universally. And according to this, genera and species are had in the predicament of substance, and they are called second substances. Science is concerning these. Certain substances existing of themselves are also principles, which substances, since they are immaterial, pertain to intelligible knowledge, although they exceed the comprehension of our intellect" (no. 2189).

Although the intrinsic principles of things, i.e., matter and form, are many, the absolutely first principle, upon which all others depend, is one.

"And the truth is, speaking of extrinsic principles, that they are one in number, since that which is the first principle of all is the agent and the end. But intrinsic principles, namely, matter and form, are not one in number for all, but according to analogy, as will be shown below" (no. 2193).

b. What Pertains to This Science

1) To consider all beings. The first question is whether the consideration of all beings can be reduced to one single aspect.

"It is necessary for the present consideration to inquire whether all things may be reduced in some way to one....Since the science of philosophy [i.e., first philosophy or metaphysics] is of being insofar as it is being, in such a way that it considers being according to the universal notion of being, and not according to the notion of some particular being, and since being is said in many ways and not in one way, if such a multiplicity should be pure equivocation, which would not be stated according to something common, all beings would not fall under one science. For it is necessary that one science be of one genus.

"But if this multiplicity should have something common, all being may be under one science. Whence, in line with the question by which it was sought whether this science is one, since it is of several and diverse things, it is necessary to consider whether all beings may be reduced to something one, or not" (no. 2194).

The mode by which all beings may be reduced to one is, of course, that of analogy, or proportion. This is based on there being one first thing to which a certain meaning belongs, and then other things which are called the same, not by virtue of being the same, but by virtue of having a meaning related to that first thing. Thus, while healthy is said properly of the living body, it is said of urine as signifying health, of a potion as productive of health.

"It is plain that things which are said thus, are halfway between univocal and equivocal statements. For in univocal statements, one name is predicated of different things according to a notion which is wholly the same. Thus *animal*, said of horse and ox, signifies an animated sensitive substance. But in equivocal things, the same name is predicated of different things according to a notion which is wholly diverse, as is evident of the name, *dog*, as it is said of the star and of a certain species of animal.

"But in those things which are stated according to the aforesaid mode [i.e., analogy], the same name is predicated of different things according to a notion which is partly the same, partly different. It is different, indeed, as to the different modes of relation. It is the same, as to that to which the relation is made, for to be significative [of health], and to be productive [of health], are different. But the health [to which these are referred] is one. And because of this, such things are called analogous, since they are in proportion to one.

"And it is likewise of the multiplicity of being. For that is called being absolutely which has being in itself, namely, substance. But other things are called beings, because they are *of* that which is per se, being either a passion, or a habit, or some such thing. For quality is not called being because it has being, but because through it substance is said to be disposed. And it is likewise of the other accidents. And because of this, he [Aristotle] says that they are *of* being. And thus it is evident that the multiplicity of being has something common, to which a reduction is made....

"...And it makes no difference whether the reduction is made to being or one. For if one should say that being and one are not the same, but differ in notion, accordingly as one adds indivisibility over being, nevertheless it is plain that they are convertible with each other, since every one is in some way being, and every being is in some way one. And just as substance is properly and per se being, so it is properly and per se one" (nos. 2197-99).

2) To consider first principles of demonstration.

a) In general. Not only does this science consider all beings, under the aspect of being, with relation to one first being, substance, but it also considers the first principles of demonstration, and particularly the first of all, the principle of contradiction.

The reason for the consideration of these principles by this science is that the particular sciences use them only as applicable to their matter, but not in common.

"For this principle, *If you take equals from equals, the remainders are equal* [Common Notion 3 of Euclid], is common to all quantitative matters, in which there is found equal and unequal. But mathematical sciences take such principles for their own consideration concerning some part of quantity which is their fitting matter. For there is not any mathematical science which considers the common aspects of quantity as it is quantity. For this belongs to first philosophy [see p. 144 above].

"But the mathematical sciences consider what belongs to this or that quantity, as arithmetic those things which are of number, and geometry those things which are of magnitude. Whence the arithmetician takes the aforesaid principle accordingly as it pertains to numbers only, while the geometer takes it as it pertains to lines or angles. But the geometer does not consider this principle concerning beings as they are beings, but concerning being as it is continuous, either according to one dimension, as line; or according to two, as surface; or according to three, as body. But the first philosopher does not focus on the parts of being insofar as anything happens to each of them [e.g., as quantity happens to be discrete or continuous], but when he speculates on each of such common things, he does so concerning being as it is being....

"...Natural science is in the same position as to this as mathematics, since natural science speculates on the accidents of beings, and principles, not insofar as they are beings, but insofar as they are moved. But the first science is of them as they are beings, and not according to anything other. And therefore natural science and mathematics must be parts of first philosophy, as a particular science is said to be a part of the universal" (nos. 2208-9).

The first principles belong, therefore, to the consideration of the first philosopher, because they are self-evident, and composed of common terms known to all.

"Now, that such common principles should pertain to the consideration of the first philosopher is for this reason: since all the first propositions are per se, whose predicates are of the notion of the subject, it is necessary, in order that they be self-evident to all, that the subjects and predicates be known to all. But such are the common things which fall in the conception of all, as are being and nonbeing, and whole and part, equal and unequal, like and diverse, and similar things, which belong to the consideration of the first philosopher. Whence it is necessary that all the propositions which are constituted out of such terms belong principally to the consideration of the first philosopher" (no. 2210).

b) In particular, the principle of contradiction.

(1) Its defense. Just as being and nonbeing are the first concepts which fall upon the consideration of the intellect, so also the first principle to do so is that composed of them: *The same thing cannot both be and not be, at one and the same time, in the same way, and so forth.* It is impossible for anyone to think this principle false: to do so he would have to be able to think contradictories to be simultaneously true, to hold contrary opinions simultaneously.

How is this principle shown to be true when attacked? Obviously it cannot be proved by any better known principle, since nothing can be better known. Someone who would admit it because of some other principle would be, actually, although not conscious of it, admitting the better known on the basis of the less known. In reality, since nothing can be better known, the only way that someone denying the principle could be shown the principle would be from the same principle expressed in other terms. It would seem to be another principle, but would not actually be so, since all principles depend on this first.

In order to vindicate first principles it is indispensable that human beings agree on *words'* having some definite meaning. This being the case, having predicated something of something, e.g., by saying, "Socrates is man," one cannot, without contradicting oneself, add, "Socrates is not man." Otherwise, since it is true to say, "Socrates is not a horse," it will be equally true to state, "Socrates is a horse," i.e., its contradictory, if contradictories may be simultaneously verified. All these are *ad hominem* arguments, i.e., they may prove to someone something which is actually better known than the proof.

(2) Various positions.

(a) All propositions are false. This position arises from the outlook of Heraclitus to the effect that an affirmation and negation about something were both true, and also that there was a middle between them. Since one can then hold a position which is neither an affirmation nor a negation about some thing, it follows that all propositions

must be false. Obviously, if nothing is true, nothing can be conceded as a starting point from which to argue, and discussion cannot begin. Even more basically, if an affirmation and a negation about the same thing may both be true, then words mean nothing and it is useless to talk. Quite simply, however, if all propositions are false, then the proposition which says so is false, and the position is self-destructive.

(b) All propositions are true. This position arises from the outlook of Protagoras that everything is as it appears to be to each, and that "man is the measure of all things." Although this position destroys the principle of contradiction in theory, nevertheless it is not followed out in practice. For example, its proponents would not accept the contradictory opinions of a doctor and a layman as having equal weight concerning a sickness. It is likewise self-destructive in that the proposition which affirms this position to be false must, according to the position, be accepted as true.

(3) Source and remedy of these positions. What is the source of such opinions? Aristotle supposes that they arise from two things:

(a) The axiom: Nothing comes from nothing. This opinion of the natural philosophers, combined with the inability to explain becoming, could lead one to hold, either that nothing becomes and all change is an illusion, as Parmenides held, or that everything preexists in everything, as Anaxagoras held, and which could lead to the opinion that all judgments were true, since everything was in everything.

Aristotle solves the difficulty of becoming and the axiom, *Nothing comes from nothing*, by the recognition of potency.

"For it is expounded in *Physics* I how something is made from being, and how from nonbeing. For it is stated that something is made from nonbeing in act and from being in act, accidentally. But from matter, which is in potency, something is made per se. For it is accidental to the making that the matter from which something is made should have been subject to form and privation. And thus it is not necessary that that from which something is made be simultaneously being and nonbeing in act; but that of itself it be potency to being and nonbeing, i.e., to form and privation" (no. 2228).

(b) Different people judge same differently. These judgments lead to the opinion that things are as they seem to each. In reality it is clear that human beings do not actually rate a defective faculty on a par with a healthy one in such judgments, any more than a person, because he saw two images by displacing one of his eyes, would think he saw two things.

The opinion that all propositions are true, since everything is as it appears to each, is the counterpart of the opinion that all propositions are false, since all things are in a state of flux and there is nothing fixed and determined in nature. What of this latter opinion? First of all, it should be noted that the principal bodies of the universe, the heavenly bodies, show a formidable regularity. Likewise, things that move have plainly not arrived at a given terminus, and consequently, until they do, it is possible to make a true statement to the effect that they have not—unless one should try to consider the thing in motion to the terminus the same as having already arrived. Furthermore, things do not actually grow and change continuously, as time-lapse photography shows.

Then, even when things vary quantitatively, as a man grows fat or thin, nevertheless they may remain the same qualitatively, as the man remains the same man—and it is the what, rather than the how much, by which a thing is identified. Why, also, would a doctor prescribe this remedy rather than that, if all things are constantly changing their identity? Finally, if human beings' judgments vary, supposing this to be because of the varying of their faculties, this would not prove that things vary.

In all this it must be remembered that, if nothing is conceded, no discussion can take place. Meanwhile, as mentioned, he who states with Heraclitus that all opinions are false, makes his own opinion false; he who states with Protagoras or Anaxagoras that all opinions are true, makes the denial of his own opinion true.

3) Metaphysics compared to particular sciences.

a) <u>What is proper to each particular science.</u> Each of the particular sciences circumscribes a certain area of being, whose particular principles and causes it seeks. Concerning its subject, it supposes its existence and nature, which latter it uses, when framed in a definition, as a middle term to demonstrate things of the subject. The subject that is supposed is had either from the senses, or from another more universal science (as mathematics takes quantity from metaphysics).

"Certain sciences take the *that which something is* from sense, insofar as from sensible accidents they arrive at the knowledge of the essence of the thing. Others, indeed, take the *what something is*, by supposing it from other sciences, as the particular sciences do from the universal.

"And thus it is plain that in the particular sciences there is not a demonstration of the substance of the thing, nor of the *what something is*. Both of these, therefore, concerning which the particular sciences do not intrude, pertain to the universal science, i.e., to consider concerning the substance and being and quiddity of a thing" (nos. 2250-51).

b) **How particular sciences differ from each other.** Natural science differs from practical science, whether active or factive.

"In order to know this difference, one must take what was had above in Book IX, namely, that to act and to make differ. For to act is properly said according to the operation which remains in the agent, and does not go out into exterior matter, as in the case of understanding and feeling and the like. But to make is according to an operation going out into exterior matter, which is changed, as in the case of heating, sawing and other things. There is, therefore, an active science, from which we are instructed in rightly exercising operations which are called actions, as in moral science. But factive science is that by which we rightly make something, as in the art of the smith and other such.

"Now natural science differs from both these operative sciences, since the factive sciences do not have the principle of motion in that which is made, but in the maker. And this principle is like art, which is as a directive principle, or some power which is as an executive principle. And likewise the 'practical sciences,' i.e., the active, do not have the principle of motion in that which is done, but more in the ones doing.

"But those things which pertain to the consideration of natural science are things having the principle of motion within themselves, since nature is the principle of motion in that in which it is. It is plain, therefore, that natural science is not active, nor factive, but speculative....Whence, if it is not active, nor factive, it follows that it is speculative." (nos. 2253-55).

Mathematics differs from natural science. "Since it is necessary for each science to know in some way the *what something is*, and to use it as a principle in demonstrating, it is necessary that according to the different mode of definition the sciences be diversified....

"...Natural science is of those things in whose definitions sensible matter is placed [e.g., snub-nosed]. But mathematics is of other things, in whose definition sensible matter is not placed [e.g., concave], although they have being in matter" (nos. 2256, 2258).

c) **Metaphysics compared with particular sciences.**

(1) As to mode of separation. "There is a certain science of being as it is separable; for it does not pertain to this science only to deter-

mine concerning being in common, which is to determine concerning being as being, but it also pertains to it to determine concerning the being separated from matter according to being. Whence one must consider whether that science to which these two pertain is the same as natural science, or differs from it.

"And that it is different, he [Aristotle] shows: for natural science is about those things which have within themselves the principle of motion. Thus it is necessary that natural things have determinate matter, since nothing is moved except that which has matter. But mathematics speculates concerning immobile things, since in those things whose notion is taken without sensible matter, their notion must likewise be without motion, since motion is not except in sensible things.

"But those things concerning which mathematics considers, are not separable from matter and motion according to being, but according to notion only. It is therefore necessary that, concerning that being which is separated from matter and motion according to being and is wholly immobile, there be a certain science other than mathematics and natural science.

"And I say this [i.e., Aristotle says this] if there be nevertheless some such substance besides sensible things which is wholly immobile. And he [Aristotle] says this because it is not yet proved that some such substance exists. But he intends to show this.

"If, however, there is some such nature in beings, namely, which is separate and immobile, it is necessary that 'such a nature be somewhere,' i.e., that it be attributed to some substance. And that which has this nature will be something divine, and something which is above all things; for the more something is more simple and formal in things, so much the more it is more noble and prior and more the cause of others. And thus it is evident that this science which considers such beings should be called divine science and science of the first principles.

"And from this he [Aristotle] further concludes that there are three genera of speculative sciences, namely, natural, which considers those mobile things which receive sensible matter in their definition; and mathematics, which considers immobile things, which do not take sensible matter in their definition, although they have existence in sensible matter; and theology [i.e., metaphysics], which is about beings wholly separated" (nos. 2259-64).

(2) As to nobility. "He [Aristotle] states that the speculative sciences are most noble among all the other sciences, since in them knowledge is sought for itself, but in the operative sciences knowledge

is sought because of a work. And in the speculative sciences, the last, namely, theology, since it is about more noble beings, is more noble. For by so much the more is each science more noble as its knowable object is more noble" (no. 2265).

(3) As to universality. "Now if there is another nature and substance besides the natural substances, which is separable and immobile, there must be another science of it, which is prior to natural science. And since it is first, it must be universal. For it is the same science which is about the first beings, and which is universal. For the first beings are the principles of the others" (no. 2267).

c. On Imperfect Being

1) **Accidental being.** This accidental being, such as musical grammarian, which has no determinate cause in nature, is considered by no science. Architecture does not concern itself with the fortunes of those who live in the house once built, nor do shoemakers concern themselves with the fate of those who buy their shoes.

The only science which concerns itself with such accidental connections is sophistics, which uses accidental connections as though they were per se. "Whence there is made the fallacy of accident, which is most efficacious in deceiving even the wise man, as is said in *De Sophisticis Elenchis* I" (no. 2275).

Such accidental connections happen in the lesser part, conjoined without necessity or without being for the most part. "But every science is of that which is always or for the most part, as is proved in *Posterior Analytics* I. Whence it is plain that science cannot be of that which is accidental" (no. 2279). On the other hand, if such accidental things could not happen, then everything would be from necessity, and there would be no distinction between undetermined and necessary events. The outcome of future events, such as a World Series, would already have been irrevocably decided in their causes stretching back into the past.

Concerning the being which is in the mind, the *is* which links together the terms of a proposition, this being is omitted since the present study is of being which exists independently, outside the mind. Concerning accidental causes, e.g., the cause of finding a buried treasure, they are infinite—and, as such, unknowable.

2) Motion.
a) In itself.

(1) What is motion? In order to state the nature of motion, certain preliminary concepts are supposed:

1. Being as divided into act and potency. "Of beings, a certain one is in act, as is the first mover, which is God; a certain one is in potency only, as is prime matter; and a certain one is in potency and act, as are all intermediate things" (no. 2289).
2. Being is divided into the ten predicaments.
3. Motion does not have any nature separated from other things. Each form, insofar as it is in a state of becoming, is an imperfect act which is called motion. Thus something moves toward whiteness when it begins to become white in act. Thus, too, since motion can be in several predicaments, it is not a separate predicament itself, but is an imperfect state of whatever predicament in which it is found. As there is no common genus of the predicaments, there is no common genus of motion.
4. In every genus, something is found in two ways: according to perfection and imperfection. This is because of the fact that "all genera are divided by contrary differences, and of contraries, one of them is always as that which is perfect, the other as imperfect" (no. 2292).
5. The species of motion and change follow the species of being. This does not mean that motion is found in every species of being, but that it will follow being as a certain imperfect type of being.

Since being according to each genus is divided by potency and act, the definition of motion is as follows: motion is the act of that which is in potency, as such.

"A thing is only reduced by motion from potency to act, from that potency which is signified when it is said that something is mobile, i.e., able to be moved" (no. 2295).

A thing is in potency, as such, only so long as it is in motion toward its term: once it arrives, it is no longer in potency thereto. But before it moves, it is not in act. Thus, the state of a thing in motion, the act of a thing in potency as such, does not exist before it moves, nor after. Thus a house is able to be built (prior potency), being built (motion), and built (act).

Motion is not potency alone, because otherwise everything in potency would be in motion: it would thus be in motion before it was in motion. On the other hand, it is not perfect act, but the act of something imperfect, namely, possible being, being in potency.

"Whence, perfect acts are not the acts of something existing in potency, but of something existing in act. But motion is of something existing in potency in such a way that it does not remove potency from it. For as long as there is motion, there remains the potency in the mobile thing towards that towards which it tends through motion. But only the potency to be moved is removed by motion—and nevertheless not wholly, because what is moved remains still in potency to be moved, since everything which is moved, will be moved, because of the division of continuous motion, as is proved in *Physics* VI. Whence it remains that motion is the act of something existing in potency, and thus is an imperfect act, of an imperfect thing.

"And because of this it is difficult to grasp what motion is. For it seems that it is either necessary to place motion in the genus of privation [as undetermined]...or in the genus of potency, or in the genus of simple and perfect act—none of which happens to be motion. Whence it remains that motion is that which was said: namely, act, and that it not be called perfect act. This, indeed, is difficult to see, but nevertheless is what occurs, since, this being laid down, there follows nothing unfitting" (nos. 2305-6).

(2) Where is motion? Motion is *in* the mobile thing, since it is the act of the mobile thing as mobile, and everything is in that of which it is the act. It is also the act of the *mover*. Thus the same motion is both the act of the mover and of the mobile thing. For the mover is so called as being able to move, and motion is the reduction to act. But the motion is in the mobile thing, as its act also.

"For the one motion, according to its substance, is the act of both, but differs by reason. For it is the act of the mover, as that by which; but of the mobile thing, as that in which—and not the act of the mobile thing as that by which, nor of the mover as that in which. And therefore the act of the mover is called action; but that of the mobile thing, passion.

"But if action and passion are the same according to substance, it seems that they are not different predicaments. But it should be known that the predicaments are diversified according to the different modes of predicating. Whence the same thing, accordingly as it is differently predicated of different things, belongs to different predicaments. For place, accordingly as it is predicated of that which makes something in place, pertains to the genus of quantity. But accordingly as it is predicated denominatively of that which is in place, it constitutes the predicament, *where*. Likewise motion, accordingly as it is predicated of the subject in which it is, constitutes the predicament of passion. But accordingly as it is predicated of that by which it is, it constitutes the predicament of action" (nos. 2312-13).

b) Infinite, passion of motion and of universal quantum.

(1) How infinite is said to be in act. Every finite thing is able to be gone through by division; for example, by continuing to take away a given quantity from a given length. Whence the infinite is properly that which cannot be gone through by measuring. To be unable to be gone through can be in one of four ways:

1. because it is impossible by nature, as in the case of point or unity. Or else it may not be in the genus of quantity, as a word is invisible since it is not in the genus of visible things.
2. because it has not yet been gone through, in the sense of infinite as meaning unfinished.
3. because it can scarcely be gone through, as some trial might be called infinitely long.
4. because, while it is in the genus of things which have a going-through or term, it does not have such yet, as would be the case with an unterminated line. This is the quantitative infinite truly and properly.

(2) How infinite is in potency. The infinite is in potency in one way by addition, as in the case of numbers. "For to any given number it is always possible to add unity, and thus number is increasable to infinity" (no. 2319).

Another way is by subtraction and division, as magnitude is said to be divisible to infinity.

A third way involves both, as time is said to be infinite both by division, since it is continuous, and by addition, since it is a number. And motion is infinite in the same way.

There is no quantitative infinite in act, since every body has a certain determinate range of magnitude; every number can be counted through. The infinite in sensible things is a potential infinite.

"[The infinite in potency] is found in magnitude and motion and time, and it is not univocally predicated of them, but according to prior and posterior. And always that which is in them in a posterior [or subsequent] way, is said to be infinite according to that in which the prior is infinite. Thus motion is so according to magnitude, in which something is moved locally, or is increased, or altered. And time is called infinite according to motion.

"This is to be understood as follows. For the infinite by division is attributed to the continuum, which is first attributed to magnitude, from which motion has continuity. This is plain in local motion, since the parts in local motion are taken according to the parts of the magnitude. And likewise it is plain in the motion of increase [growth], since it is according to the addition of magnitude that growth is reckoned. But in alteration [change in quality], it is not thus manifest. But nevertheless it is truly there in some way; since quality, according to which alteration takes place, is divided per accidens with the division of magnitude. And furthermore the intensification and diminishing of quality is reckoned accordingly as the subject which has magnitude in some way, either more or less, perfectly shares the quality. But following upon the continuity of motion there is the continuity of time. For time, according to itself, since it is a number, does not have continuity, but only in its subject—just as ten measures of cloth are continuous in that the cloth is a certain continuous thing. In the same way, therefore, infinite is said of these as continuous" (no. 2354).

c) **Parts of motion.**

(1) Division of change. "That [change] which is from nonsubject to subject, existing between contradictory terms, is called generation. But this happens in two ways. For the change is either from nonbeing absolutely to being absolutely—and then there is generation absolutely. And this is when a mutable subject is changed according to substance. Or it is from nonbeing to being, not absolutely, but in a certain respect, as, for example, from that which is not white to that which is white—and this is a certain generation and *secundum quid.*

"But that mutation which is from a subject to a nonsubject is called corruption. And likewise in it there is distinguished absolutely and *secundum quid*, as in generation....

"...Now changes are three: two of which, which are according to contradiction, namely, generation and corruption, are not motion. It remains therefore that the sole change which is, namely, from subject to subject, is motion. And since those subjects between which motion is must be opposite, it is necessary that they be contrary or intermediate—since privation, although it may be shown affirmatively, as in the case of nude, toothless, and black, nevertheless is reduced to a contrary—privation being the first contrary, as was shown in Book X. He also says black not to be privation absolutely, but insofar as it defectively participates in the nature of the genus" (nos. 2366-67, 2375).

(2) Division of motion. There are three genera of being in which there can be motion; namely, quantity, quality, and where.

There cannot be motion according to substance, since motion is a change from subject to subject, which subjects are contrary or intermediate. But since nothing is contrary to substance, there cannot be motion in substance, but generation and corruption only, whose terms are opposed according to contradiction. The reason nothing can be contrary to substance is that contraries must have a same subject. There can be, however, contrariety between substantial forms, in the sense that one form may have that of which another form is deprived, as between animate and inanimate, rational and irrational. Absolutely speaking, one form or species does not oppose another, because there is not continuity between them, just as there is not between numbers.

There cannot be motion in relation, except accidentally, insofar as a motion in another causes relation. For example, equal or unequal come about by a change in quantity in another, similar or dissimilar by a change of quality, left or right by a movement in place.

There cannot be motion in action and passion. In other words, since action and passion *are* motion, the same motion, to have motion in them would be to have motion in motion, and change would have to change. This would be similar to leaving New York for Chicago, and having New York become Chicago in the course of the trip. Thus, by the change of change and the motion of motion, motion itself would become impossible. There can be, of course, different changes going on at the same time, but not change of change.

Motion exists, therefore, in those genera where there are contrary terms, namely, in quantity, quality, and where. This quality is accidental quality, not substantial form. It is, even more specifically, possible quality, that species of quality capable of producing an affection in the way of perception, such as do sweetness or heat (see *Predicaments*, 9b 5).

What is said to be immobile? Things are said to be immobile in three ways:

1. that which is entirely immovable, as is God;
2. that which is hardly movable, such as a large stone;

3. that which is movable by nature, but cannot be moved at the moment; and such a thing is said properly to be at rest, because rest is "the contrary of motion in that which is susceptible of motion" (no. 2403).

(3) Designations accompanying motion. Certain designations accompany motion, especially local motion. Because of this, things are as follows:

1. *together* in place, which are in one first place, i.e., a circumscribed place.
2. *apart*, which are in different places.
3. *touching*, or in *contact*, whose extremities are together, e.g., two bodies whose surfaces are in contact.
4. *mediate* between two, if that to which something continuously changing will arrive at before its term, e.g., if something going from A to C reaches B before C, B is mediate.
5. *contrary* as to place, if most distant according to a straight line. Since between two points there can be an infinity of arcs of a circle of different lengths, it is only according to a straight line that the greatest and contrary distance is measured. The extremes of above and below in nature are according to the center and extremity of the universe.
6. *consequent*, or *following*, if coming after some first principle, either according to position, or according to species, or any other way—with no middle of the same genus in between. Such would be one house consequent upon another on a street.
7. *had*, if consequent and touching, as a man has his socks on.
8. *continuous*, if of two things which are touching and together there is one and the same terminus, as the parts of a line are continued at a point. One can indicate a point on a line, but this does not actually divide the line, the point itself having no extension.

The continuum is between those things which by nature can be one according to contact, since the continuum requires identity of terminus.

"Among the three—consequent, in contact, continuous—one is more prior and common than the other. Thus, whatever is consequent need not be in contact, but whatever is in contact is consequent. Likewise, what is in contact need not be continuous, but what is continuous is in contact....

"...Point and unity are not the same, as Plato would have it, defining point as unity having position. This is plain, since according to points one may have contact, but not according to unities, which are consequent to each other. Further, between two points there is always a middle, as is proved in *Physics* VI, but there is no need that there be a middle between two unities" (nos. 2414-15).

2. Consideration of Substance
a. This Science Treats Principally Substance

Since this science seeks the first principles of beings, and being is principally substance, this science must be principally of substance. While substances may be without accidents, accidents may not be without substance. Thus the first philosophers looked for the substance of things, inquiring whether it was fire, or water, or air, or some other concrete thing. The Platonists, however, turned to universals, thinking these abstractions actually to exist as such in the nature of things.

b. Treatment of Substance

1) Division of substance. There are the following three types of substance:

1. sensible substance;
   a. incorruptible (heavenly bodies);
   b. corruptible (plants, animals, and so forth);
2. immobile, nonsensible substance (not manifest to all).

How does the consideration of the three types of substance differ? "Sensible substances, whether corruptible or perpetual, pertain to the consideration of natural philosophy, which determines concerning mobile being. For such sensible substances are in motion. But separable and immobile substance pertains to the consideration of another science, and not to the same, if nevertheless there is no principle common to both substances. For if they should agree in something, the consideration of both types of substance will then belong to that science which considers that common thing. And therefore natural science considers sensible substances only as they are in act and motion. Hence this science [i.e., metaphysics] considers both concerning them and concerning immobile substances as well, insofar as they communicate in the fact of being beings and substances" (no. 2427).

2) Types of substance in particular.

a) Sensible substance.

(1) Matter. Of the principles of sensible substance, one of them is matter. Matter is found in sensible substances, and matter is necessary to sensible substance, since sensible substance is mutable.

"Since, therefore, every change is from contrary to contrary, it is necessary for some subject to underlie it, which is able to be changed from contrary to contrary. And the Philosopher proves this in two ways. The first is for the reason that one of the contraries is not changed into the other, for the blackness itself does not become whiteness. Whence if a change is to be made from black to white, it is necessary for there to be something besides the blackness, which is made white.

"He proves the same thing in another way, from the fact that in any change there is found something which remains. Thus, in the change which is from black to white, the body remains, while the other, namely, the contrary, for example, the black, does not remain. Whence it is plain that matter is some third thing besides the contraries" (nos. 2429-30).

It is the presence of matter which explains how things are able to come to be without violation of the principle, *Nothing comes from nothing*, and without one's having to hold that everything actually pre-exists in act.

"This difficulty the Philosopher solves by showing how something is made from being and nonbeing, saying that being is twofold, namely, being in act, and being in potency. Everything, therefore, which is changed, is changed from being in potency to being in act—as when something is altered from white in potency to white in act. And it is similar in the motion of increase and decrease, since something is changed from being in potency great or small, to great and small in act. Whence in the genus of substance all things are made from nonbeing and being. It is, however, from nonbeing per accidens, insofar as something is made from matter subject to privation, according to which it is called nonbeing. But per se something is made from being, not, however, in act, but in potency; namely, from matter, which is being in potency, as was shown above" (no. 2433).

This matter does not exist in the same way in all sensible substances.

"Those things which are 'changed according to substance,' i.e., which are generated and corrupted, have matter which is a subject of generation and corruption—which, namely, is in potency to forms and privations. But the heavenly bodies, which are eternal and ingenerable, while mobile according to place, have matter indeed, but not that which is a subject of generation, or which is in potency to form and privation; rather, it is in potency to the terms of local motion, which are that whence motion begins, and that whither motion tends" (no. 2436).

Although sensible things are made from matter, this does not mean that anything is made from anything. Rather, there is a certain order.

"For although prime matter is in potency to all forms, nevertheless it takes them on in a certain order. For it is first in potency to the elemental forms, and through them, according to the diverse proportions of combinations, it is in potency to different forms. Whence it is not possible immediately to make anything out of anything, except, perchance, through resolution to prime matter [i.e., by reducing the thing to prime matter and starting again from the beginning]" (no. 2438).

(2) Form. "In every change there must be some subject of change, which is matter, and something by which the change is made, which is the moving principle, and something into which the change is made, which is the species and form" (no. 2443).

That form was in the order of substance was not immediately recognized by the first natural philosophers.

"Matter, as to that which appears, seems to be substance and the existing thing [*hoc aliquid*]. Whence the first natural philosophers set it down as substance. And this they did because they saw that in artificial things which are made by contact and not by natural union, solely the matter and subject are seen to be substance; for the forms of artificial things are accidents. Likewise the nature of a thing is seen to be substance and the existing thing—for the nature of the thing is that in which natural generation terminates, i.e., the form, which is as a certain habit. Likewise a third substance is that which is composed from matter and form, as are singulars, such as Callias and Socrates" (no. 2446).

The forms of material sensible things cannot exist apart from those things, but begin and end with them.

"The moving causes exist before the things that are made. And this is necessary, because the moving causes are the principles of the motion which terminates at the thing made. But the formal cause, which is a cause as being the nature of the thing, begins to be at the same time with the thing of which it is the form. For health begins to be when the man is healed; and the figure of a bronze sphere then begins to be when the bronze sphere is made. Whence it is plain that the forms are not separated from composite substances. For if they were separated, they would have to be eternal, since there is of such neither generation nor corruption, as was shown; and thus they would preexist to those substances of which they are the forms.

"But although the forms do not preexist to the composite substances, one nevertheless should examine whether any form might remain afterwards, once the composite substance is corrupted. For in certain forms nothing prevents them from remaining after the composite substance; for example, if we should say the soul to be such....

"It should be considered that this is the judgment of Aristotle concerning the intellective soul; namely, that it did not exist before the body, as Plato laid down, nor was it destroyed by the destruction of the body, as the ancient natural philosophers laid down, not distinguishing between intellect and sense" (nos. 2450-52).

Although the forms of composite material things do not preexist, it is nevertheless not necessary to posit separated species, as Plato did, in order to account for the production of sensible substances.

"This is not necessary, because in the lower things themselves there is found a sufficient cause of the formation of all things which are produced. For the natural agent produces that which is similar to itself. Man generates man—not, indeed, the universal the singular, but the singular produces the singular. Whence it is not necessary to posit a universal man to be separated, from which this singular man receives or participates in the form of the species" (no. 2454).

In addition to the intrinsic principles of things—matter, form, and privation—there are also the extrinsic principles—the agent and the end. These are the same for all composite things, not as singulars, but analogously, in that all things will have form, but different forms; all will have an efficient cause, but different efficient causes.

"Thus, therefore, it is plain that, according to analogy, i.e., proportion, the elements of all things are three, i.e., matter, form and privation. For privations are called an element, not per se, but accidentally, since the matter, namely, to which it occurs, is an element. For matter existing under one form has in itself the privation of another form. But the causes and principles are four, if we add to the three elements the moving cause. He [Aristotle] does not mention the final cause, since the end is not a principle except as it is in the intention of the moving cause....

"He reduces the aforesaid four to three, in that the moving cause and the form are reduced to the same in species both in artificial things and in natural things" (nos. 2470-73).

The absolutely first principles, however, are absolutely the same for all.

"Among the four causes assigned, the moving cause is the first cause, because the mover is that which makes form or privation to be in matter. But in the genus of moving causes, one arrives at some one mover, as was shown in *Physics* VIII. That one and the same first mover, therefore, is the first principle of all things" (no. 2474).

Potency and act, likewise, are in a certain way the same for all, since they can be reduced to the four principles which are matter, form, privation, and the moving cause, in that form and the moving cause, and even privation, as something to which matter is in potency, represent act; while matter represents potency. Act and potency divide being universally, not as an individual act and potency, but as many acts and potencies taken in a universal sense.

"Of singulars there cannot be any principle other than a singular; for the universal is a principle of the effect taken universally, as man of man. But since there is not any man existing universally, there will not be any universal principle of universal man, but solely this particular principle of this particular thing, as if Peleus is the father of Achilles, and your father of you" (no. 2482).

Aristotle now summarizes what is true about the principles of sensible substances.

"Of all things there are in a way the same principles, or according to proportion. Thus we might say that in every genus there are found certain things which stand as matter and form and privation and mover; or that the causes of substances are the causes of all things, since if they [substances] are destroyed, other things are destroyed; or that the principles are an 'entelechy' [actuality], i.e., act and potency. For in these three ways there are the same principles of all things" (no. 2485).

b) Immobile substance. "The substances are three. Two of these are natural substances, since they are with motion—one eternal, as are the heavens, the other corruptible, as are the plants and animals. In addition to these there is a third which is immobile, which is not natural, concerning which one must now speak. For this consideration, there must first be shown that it is necessary that there be some eternal, immobile substance" (no. 2488).

How does Aristotle prove that such a substance must be? He does so in the *Metaphysics* on the supposition of the eternity of motion. The reasoning is as follows: If all substances were corruptible, none would be eternal. But some substance must be eternal. Why is this so? It is so because time is eternal, and time is the numbering of motion. Why is time eternal? It is eternal since, supposing time to have begun at a certain time, and to end at a certain time, then there was a time before time, and there can be a time after time. But since time is nothing other than the numbering of motion according to before and after, then time would have existed before itself, which is impossible. Therefore time always existed, and with it motion—not any motion, but that motion which is able to be eternal and continuous, namely, local motion; and in the realm of local motion, circular motion (as proved in *Physics* VIII).

In order to maintain the eternity of motion, there must be an eternal substance always moving and acting—a function which the separated universal species of Plato could not fulfill, since every active or motive principle must be singular. Furthermore, the substance of the first mover cannot be in potency, but must be solely in act. Hence it cannot be material, for matter is in potency.

What is Aquinas's attitude towards this positing by Aristotle of an eternal, actual, immaterial first mover because of the eternity of motion, which eternity the Catholic faith denies, holding the world to have begun in time?

"From this procedure...it is plain that Aristotle here is firmly of the opinion, and believed it to be necessary, that motion was eternal and likewise time.

"Nevertheless it should be known that the arguments put forward in *Physics* VIII, from the supposition of which he proceeds, are not demonstrations absolutely speaking, but probable reasons; unless, perchance they may be demonstrations against the positions of the ancient natural philosophers on the beginning of motion, which he intends to destroy.

"And, omitting any other reasons, which here he does not touch upon, it is plain that the argument which he here laid down to prove the eternity of time, is not demonstrative. For it is not, supposing that we hold time to have begun sometime, necessary to lay down a before except as something imaginary. For example, when we say that outside of the heavens there is not body, this outside which we state is nothing except something imaginary. Just as, therefore, it is not necessary to posit place outside of the heavens, although outside would seem to signify place, so also it is not necessary that time be before it began, or after it should cease, although before and after may seem to signify time.

"But although the arguments proving the eternity of motion are not demonstrative and concluding with necessity, nevertheless those things which are here proved concerning the eternity and immateriality of the first substance follow with necessity. For if the world is not eternal, it is necessary that it should have been produced in being by something preexisting. And if this be not eternal, it is necessary that it be produced by something. And since this cannot proceed to infinity, as was shown above in Book II, it is necessary to lay down some eternal substance, in whose substance there is not potency, and which is, consequently, immaterial" (nos. 2496-99).

What of the outlook of those who had the world emerge from potency, or even nothingness?

"This [beginning not from being in act] happens in two ways. In one way according to the opinion of certain ancients who were called the theologizing poets, as was Orpheus, and certain others who laid down the world to be 'generated out of night,' i.e., from a simple preexistent privation. In another way according to the later natural philosophers, such as the natural physicists and those following them, who, since they saw that according to nature nothing is made from nothing, laid down all things to be [initially] together in a certain confusion, which they called chaos, as Anaxagoras laid down. Thus they posited all things to be in potency, but not in act.

"But whether one proposes it in the latter way or the former, the same impossible situation arises if potency is absolutely prior to act. For those things that are in potency only, whether wholly under privation, or in a certain confusion, cannot be moved, in order to be reduced to act, unless there be some moving cause existing in act" (nos. 2502-3).

There was eventually a certain recognition of the necessity of a first mover. Thus Anaxagoras laid down intellect as a first moving principle; while Empedocles laid down strife and friendship; and Leucippus, the associate of Democritus, laid down atoms with self-motion, and Plato also posited motion to have always existed. From the perpetual circular motion of the heavens envisioned by Aristotle, combined with the alternating propinquity and remoteness of the heavenly bodies, such as the sun, moving in the zodiacal circle at a 23° angle to the equator, there would be perpetual generation and corruption (see no. 2511).

In conclusion, then, motion requires the perpetual existence of a first mover whose substance is act.

"For since everything which is moved, is moved by another, as is proved in physical science, if the heavens are perpetual, and motion is perpetual, it is necessary that there be some perpetual mover. But since in the order of movables and movers three types are found, of which the last is that which is moved only, and the middle is that which is moved and moves, it is necessary to lay down some eternal mover which is not moved. For it was proved in *Physics* VIII that, since it is impossible to go to infinity in movers and moved, it is necessary to arrive at some immovable mover; since, should one arrive at something moving itself, it is further necessary to arrive from this to some immovable mover, as is there proved.

"But if the first mover is eternal and not moved, it is necessary that it not be being in potency, since that which is being in potency is by nature apt to be moved, but that it be a substance existing of itself, and that it be substance in act. And this is what he had concluded above. But it was necessary to raise the question which existed among the ancients [as to a beginning from potency], in order that by its solution it might be more expressly shown by what order it is necessary to arrive at the first being, whose substance is act" (nos. 2517-18).

B. Nature of Eternal, Immaterial, Immobile Substance Which Is in Act

1. Its Perfection and How It Moves
a. Its Perfection

1) **How it moves.** "The first unmoved mover...must move as that which is desirable and intelligible [moves]. For these alone, namely, the desirable and the intelligible, are found to move without being moved.

"This is evident as follows. For there is a twofold motion: natural, and voluntary, or according to appetite. But that which moves with natural motion is necessarily moved, since that which moves naturally is that which generates and alters. For even heavy and light things according to place are moved per se by the generator. But that which generates and alters immediately must be in differing states. Whence it was said above that that which causes generation and corruption acts in other and in other ways. But in the motion which is according to will and appetite, the will and the appetite are as movers moved, as is evident in *De Anima* III. Whence it remains that solely that which moves as appetible is an unmoved mover.

"Now the first mover is said to move as that which is appetible, since the motion of the heavens is because of it, as for the sake of the end, caused by some proximate mover which moves because of the first immovable mover, in order to assimilate itself to it in causing, and to unfold in act that which is in the power of the first mover. For the motion of the heavens is not because of generation and corruption of the lower things as for an end, since the end is more noble than that which is for the end. Thus, therefore, the first mover moves as that which is appetible" (nos. 2519-21).

2) How it is perfect.

a) From notion of intelligible and appetible. How does the first mover come to be both the first intelligible and the first desirable thing?

First, the first mover is perfect in that it is intelligible. "Just as, therefore, from the ordination of mover and moved, it was shown that the first mover is a simple substance, and act, likewise, the same is found from the ordering of intelligible things. For it is plain that among intelligible things, substance is first, since we do not understand accidents except through substance, through which they are defined. And among substances, that is prior as intelligible which is simple rather than composite: for simple things are included in the understanding of composite things. And among the simple things, which are in the genus of substance, act is prior in intelligibility to potency, for potency is defined through act. It remains, therefore, that the first intelligible thing is a simple substance, which is act.

"And lest he should seem to fall into the opinion of Plato, who laid down as the first principle of things intelligible unity, he subsequently shows the difference between one and simple. And he says that one and simple do not mean the same, but one means measure, as was shown in Book X, while simple signifies disposition, according to which something is in a certain way, namely, because it is not constituted out of several" (nos. 2524-25).

Secondly, the first mover is perfect in that it is appetible. "That which is the good worthy of choice for itself, is related according to the same ordination. For that which is first in the genus of intelligible things, is also best in the genus of appetible things, or something corresponding to it proportionately is; which he [Aristotle] says, indeed, since things are intelligible in act accordingly as they are in the intellect, but appetible accordingly as they are in things. For good and evil are in things, as was said in Book VI.

"Thus, therefore, just as the notion of intelligible substance is prior to the notion of intelligible accident, so are the goods which correspond proportionately to these notions. Thus, therefore, that which is best will be the simple substance, which is in act, which is first among intelligible things. And thus it is plain that the first mover is the same as the first intelligible thing, and the first appetible thing, which is that which is best" (nos. 2526-27).

What of the objection that the good and the appetible have the nature of end, and there does not seem to be end, or final cause, in immobile things, e.g., in mathematics?

"He [Aristotle] says that this division, by which one distinguishes in how many ways end is said, shows that that for the sake of which, i.e., the end, can be in some way in immobile things. For something may be the end of another in two ways. One way is as preexisting, as the middle is stated to be the preexisting end of the motion of heavy bodies, and nothing prevents such an end from being in immobile things. For something can tend in its own way to share in some way in some immobile thing, and thus the first immobile thing can be an end. In another way something is said to be the end of another, as that which does not exist in act, but solely in the intention of the agent, through whose action it is generated, as health is the end of the operation of medicine. And such an end is not in immobile things" (no. 2528).

b) By first mover compared with first moved. The first mover, then, moves the first moved thing, the heavens, with a perpetual motion, which varies in its circular circuit as to place, but not as to substance. It is moved with a necessity dependent upon the will of the first mover, not an absolute necessity.

"From this principle, therefore, which is the first mover moving as the end, there depend the heavens, both as to the perpetuity of their substance, and as to the perpetuity of their motion; and consequently there depends from this principle the whole of nature, since all natural things depend upon the heavens and from such a movement of them.

"It should be noted also that Aristotle here states that the necessity of the first motion is not absolute necessity, but the necessity which is from the end, and the end is a principle, which he afterwards calls God.

284 of Metaphysics of Aquinas

Consequently, insofar as there is intended by motion an assimilation to it, and the assimilation to that which is willing and understanding, as he shows God to be, is to be expected according to the will and intelligence—as artificial things are assimilated to the artisan insofar as in them the will of the artisan is fulfilled—it follows that the whole necessity of the first motion is subject to the will of God" (nos. 2534-35).

c) **By that which moves as intelligible and appetible compared with what knows and desires it.** Just as the first mover is that which is most knowable and most desirable, so the knowledge of the first mover by others is that which is most pleasing to them.

"The act of the intellect as such is of that which is the best according to itself. For the intelligible good exceeds sensible good, as immutable and universal good does mutable and particular good. It also follows that the delight which is in the act of the intellect, is greater than that which is in the act of the sense. And consequently it is necessary that the greatest and most perfect intellectual activity be especially of that which is best, and thus there follows the greatest delight. Thus, therefore, it is plain that in that act of the intellect by which the first mover is known, which is also the first intelligible thing, there is the greatest delight" (no. 2538).

This knowledge of the first mover, which is that which is most delightful, is possessed, of course, most perfectly by the first mover itself, namely, God. This act of a living thing is life, and in this case the act is also the substance. And therefore God is his life, which is the knowledge of that which is best, the first being, containing all that is good.

b. Its Incorporeity

Since this first being is of infinite power, it can have no spatial finite magnitude; and infinite spatial magnitude is impossible. This is not the infinite of quantity, which is essentially the unfinished, the undetermined, but the negative infinite, that which is not limited to any determinate effect, nor subject to any intrinsic cause, as are all other things.

2. Number of Immaterial Substances Related to World

It is fitting that there be certain immaterial substances subordinated to the first mover, which would cause the fundamental motions of the heavenly bodies, which in turn cause motions in the lower things. "It appears quite fitting that the first motion of corporeal things, from which all others depend, should have as its cause the principle of immaterial substances, in order that there be a certain connection and order of sensible and intelligible things" (no. 2560). Then just as the first motion would come from the first immaterial substance, subordinated motions would come from subordinated immaterial substances. In effect, there are differing motions in the heavenly bodies, e.g., the obvious difference between those of the planets and the fixed stars, which require therefore different principles of motion.

The study of such matters belongs to astronomy. "It is most proper for this among the mathematical sciences. For it alone among them speculates concerning sensible and eternal substance, namely, the heavenly body. But the other mathematical sciences do not consider concerning any substance, as is evident of arithmetic, which is concerned with numbers, and geometry, which is concerned with magnitude. But number and magnitude are accidents" (no. 2563).

Supposing, however, certain immaterial substances as causes of various heavenly motions, the number of the former would not necessarily have to be restricted to the number of the latter. "For there can be stated to be certain separated substances higher than any proportion of them as ends to celestial motions. And it is not unfitting to lay this down, for immaterial substances are not because of corporeal things, but rather the converse is true" (no. 2589).

3. Activity of First Immaterial Substance
a. As Intelligible Good and Intellect

What does the first substance know? Plainly it must know that which is best, namely, itself; and this not in potency, but in act. "Since, therefore, it is that which is most noble and most powerful, it is necessary that it know itself, and that in it understanding and that which is understood be the same" (no. 2613).

In knowing itself, the first substance knows all other things. "This is evident as follows. For since he [God] is his own understanding, and this is most worthy and most powerful, it is necessary that his understanding be most perfect: therefore he understands himself most perfectly. But the more perfectly some principle is understood, so much the more its effect is understood in it: for the things which proceed from a principle are contained in the power of the principle. Since, therefore, from the first principle, which is God, there depend the heavens and the whole of nature, as was said, it is evident that God, in knowing himself, knows all things" (no. 2615).

b. As the Good and the Appetible

The first mover moves as that which is good and desirable. The good as end can be in two ways: the extrinsic end to which a thing moves; the intrinsic end which is the form of the thing. In which way is God the good and end of the universe?

"The good, accordingly as it is the end of something, is twofold. For there is the end which is extrinsic from that which is for the end, as we say place to be the end of that which moves to the place. There is also the end within, as the form is the end of generation and alteration, and the form once attained is a certain intrinsic good of that of which it is the form. But the form of some whole, which is one through a certain order of parts, is its order, whence it remains that it is its good.

"The Philosopher therefore asks whether the nature of the whole universe has that which is its good and its best, i.e., its proper end, as though something separated from it, or has its good and that which is best in the order of its parts, by which the good of some thing is its form.

"...He [Aristotle] shows that the universe has both a separated good and the good of order....He says therefore that the universe has a good and an end in both ways. For there is a certain separated good which is the first mover, from which depend the heavens and the whole of nature, as from the end and the appetible good, as was shown. And since all things whose end is one, must necessarily agree in the order to the end, it is necessary that in the parts of the universe some order be found. And thus the universe has both a separated good and the good of order....The whole order of the universe is because of the first mover, in order that, namely, there be unfolded in the ordered universe that which is in the intellect and will of the first mover. And thus it is necessary that the whole ordering of the universe be from the first mover....[Also,] that all things are ordered to each other is evident from the fact that all things are ordered together to one end" (nos. 2627-32).

Things are, however, ordered to the end in different ways, just as, in a household, the children, the servants, the domestic animals, are ordered to the one end in different ways.

"Just as there is imposed an order in a family by the law and precept of the father of the family, who is a principle to each of the things ordered in the house of carrying out those things which pertain to the order of the house, so nature in natural things is the principle to each thing of carrying out that which pertains to it of the order of the universe. For just as he who is in the house is inclined to something through the precept of the father of the family, so is any natural thing through its own nature. And the nature of each thing is a certain innate inclination in it from the first mover, ordering it to the due end. And from this it is evident that natural things act for the end, although they may not know the end, since from the first understanding they acquire an inclination to the end" (no. 2634).

Even though the divine intellect must move for an end, this end is not different from itself.

"The same thing can be understanding and that which is understood, and the intellect may move because of itself—which is found in a certain way in those things which act through intellect as do ourselves. For the art of medicine acts for the sake of health, and health [in the mind of the one healing] is in a certain way the art of medicine itself, as was said above" (no. 2648).

Finally, the first mover, which is the cause of contrariety in things as representing the perfection of the first substance by their diversity, has nothing contrary to itself, since this is the characteristic of things in potency. Rather all things are united in a single connected unity, and not many disconnected principles.

"And this [latter] cannot be, since beings do not wish to be disposed ill. For the disposition of natural things is such as to be the best that might be. And we see this in single things, that each is in the best disposition of its nature. Whence this must be thought to be all the more so in the whole universe.

"But a plurality of rulers is not good, just as, for example, it would not be good if there were different families in one house which did not communicate with one another. Whence it remains that the whole universe is as one rule and one kingdom. And thus it is necessary that it be ordered by one governor. And this is what he [Aristotle] concludes: that there is one ruler of the whole universe, namely, the first mover, and the first intelligible thing, and the first good, which he has called above God, who is blessed forever and ever. Amen" (nos. 2662-63: end of Aquinas's exposition).

Appendix

First Philosophy

What is the scope of this first philosophy elaborated by Aristotle, and expounded by Aquinas? By virtue of endeavoring to reach the first causes of all being, nothing is excluded from the scope of this enterprise.

As a preamble thereto, Aristotle himself investigates all the areas of human knowledge, starting with the study of reasoning in the *Organon* which comprises his works on logic, of which he is the acknowledged founder. Subsequently there are the series of his works on the natural sciences, developing from the systematic study of nature—the physical world with which the human being first comes in contact. He utilizes the perception of its order first for the practical purposes of living, elaborating such arts as fishing, farming, weaving, building, and so forth.

Following the subsequent acquisition of leisure through such arts, there begins, from the same perception of the order in the physical world, the effort by the mind to grasp the first causes of that order—such effort meriting the name of first philosophy by the fact that the first causes are sought.

In this pursuit, Aristotle begins with the physical world immediately evident to us, looking, through the analysis of motion, for a First Mover, himself unmoved. In the process of doing this, Aristotle, in his *Physics*, investigates the efforts of his contemporaries and predecessors in the search for the explanation of the universe in which we live. (Today's theoretical physics acknowledges that it is engaged in the same search begun in Aristotle's time, underlining the efforts of philosophers such as Democritus who first posited atoms as the basic explanation of the universe.)

In the course of his *Physics*, Aristotle deals with the quantitative analysis of physical reality, investigating the same notions which are incorporated into modern mathematical physics, as physics has become since the inauguration of the mathematical element as intrinsic to physics by Galileo and Newton. Likewise the cosmology of the physical world is investigated by Aristotle in his work, *On the Heavens*.

He is at one with contemporary cosmologists in the acknowledgment of the overall order of the universe and in their pursuit of a single all-embracing explanation of that order, referred to as the theory of everything. Contemporary physics, however, has circumscribed in advance what an acceptable theory of everything will be: it must be in physico-mathematical terms, i.e., an expression of the physical, tangible world, mathematically stated. Such an expression is, for example, Einstein's $e = mc^2$, equating mass and energy, both physical realities, by virtue of the former's equaling the latter when the former is multiplied by the square of the speed of light, a mathematical computation.

Such notions are encompassed in Aristotle's pursuit of the first causes of reality. His vision, however, is vaster. He states that if physical reality is everything, then physical science's statement of first causes will constitute metaphysics, the statement of the causes of all being. However, should physical reality not be ultimate, then a further science beyond the physical, embracing both the physical and the higher-echelon nonphysical, or immaterial, will be required, a metaphysics beyond, and embracing, physics.

The metaphysics of Aristotle, as expounded by Aquinas, is thus seen to encompass the domain of physics, the domain of the theory of everything, and more, envisaging a first cause of all being, both material and immaterial.

What is the nature of this first cause? Since its postulation is required to furnish an explanation of the order in the universe, the latter indispensably admitted and utilized by science, it must be an ordering force, an intelligence. The existence of such an intelligence obviously cannot be denied a priori, since such a denial would leave the denier open to be called upon to prove, in the face of recognized cosmic order, the nonexistence of an orderer or designer.

This science does not attempt to do. Nor does it go to the opposite extreme of affirming the order of the universe as the product of non-design, or chance. This latter affirmation is excluded by the fact that science, in the anthropic principle, rates the odds of such as trillions to one.

What then does science do? Nobel prizewinners in physics, such as Richard Feynman and Steven Weinberg, opt for the whole spectrum, namely, the positing of a range in explaining the order of the universe extending from the major probability of a designer to the minute possibility of chance, leaving the question of the cause of the order of the universe as unexplained because unexplainable—a window having always to be left open to chance and pointlessness.

Whether in the face of the universally acknowledged objective order in the universe such a restraint in acknowledging a supreme intelligence, or God, as the first cause of that order is rationally tenable or not, it does not constitute a conflict with those who, whether for intellectual reasons or reasons of faith, or both, are convinced of the existence of God as the explanation of the order of the universe. Such are more coherent in their subsequent deduction of the order of the universe (the order upon which science depends to operate) than those who feel compelled to withhold acknowledgment of any definitive explanation, or the rare few who come down, with no proof possible and no shred of probability, on the side of chance.

Therefore one finds oneself, insofar as one subscribes to Aristotle's metaphysics, operating in a descending way which encompasses modern science. In effect, the latter starts deductively from hypotheses which fulfill the criterion of predictability, which in turn indicates that they are somehow tapped into the order of the universe. Aristotelian metaphysics possesses in addition a coherent and unshakable explanation of that order, namely, God as first cause. Between God as first cause there is also coherently posited immaterial substances, separated from matter, as nonindispensable intermediaries. The cosmic link between the immaterial and the material is the human being who, in a material body, possesses an immaterial, incorruptible soul.

Since Aristotle's metaphysics in seeking the first cause of all being, necessarily proceeds inductively from the data afforded by the material world, he is proceeding in the area of today's physical science as it seeks successful hypotheses, namely, those which, because of their reliability, such as the first law of motion, indicate that they are tapped into the order of the universe. Although the holding of the order of the universe as objective is a prerequisite to science—no order, no possibility of reliable hypotheses—nevertheless it is held as something believed in, not proved. It is, however, the same objective order whether held as believed in or proved.

Modern science, in viewing the same data as Aristotle, nevertheless deliberately confines itself to the hypothetical or dialectical, excluding the demonstrative. Aristotelian physics and metaphysics, while including the same domain is more encompassing by admitting, along with the Catholic faith, the possibility of demonstration or proof—in particular, the proof for the existence of God by proceeding inductively, for example, from antecedent proof of the order of the universe (believed in by science) to proof of the existence of God as the orderer. Meanwhile, for practical purposes, the hypothetical mode suffices. In this vein the same admitted order of the universe admits of differing successful hypotheses. Thus it is the same ordered universe which on the one hand allows for a Ptolemaic or geocentric hypothesis (causing it still to be used today for celestial navigation) and, on the other, a Copernican or heliocentric hypothesis.

Failure to perceive this, namely, that the same order in the universe, the same appearances, may be interpreted in different ways, yielding equally predictable results, can lead to one interpretation's being taken as fact, thereby excluding other interpretations as possibly objective. What is the condition for such an exclusion? It would be that the interpretation in question, e.g., that of the Ptolemaic theory, with the sun daily circling around an immobile earth, would have to be perceived as the *only possible* explanation. This would be the case, for example, should the earth be conceived as embodying the heaviest element, the center of gravity of the universe, a notion dispelled by Newton's positing of universal gravitation deriving from mass, subsequently experimentally confirmed. (The success of differing explanations of the order of the universe indicates, first, that they must be somehow tapped into that order, and second, that they do not actually mirror that objective order since they differ from one another.)

Aristotle himself, in his logical work, the *Posterior Analytics*, laid down the conditions for accepting a given interpretation of appearances as factual rather than simply as explaining the appearances in a way allowing for reliable predictions while not excluding other possible and practically utilizable explanations. The latter is the case with the Ptolemaic theory as matched with the Copernican theory.

One way of avoiding having subsequently to cancel out a supposedly factual explanation as nondefinitive for lack of apodictical proof, is simply to consider all explanations as dialectical, held, not as proved true and factual, but because they produce predictable, reliable results. Such is the case of the first law of motion. The latter supposes that all motion is basically rectilinear. Its holding is not based upon a proof, but on the fact that, this supposition once made, reliable practical predictions can be made from it, as in the launching of space shuttles.

In effect, the holding of *any* explanation as proved and factual is now eschewed by science. (Today, when the word *proof* is used, e.g., in mathematics, it indicates simply that in a given proof, the conclusion follows from the premises, the latter not being claimed in advance as true and factual.)

Aristotelian insight is indispensable in the domain of modern science as drawing attention to the fact that all of it functions in the dialectical realm by virtue of being acceptable solely on the reliability of prediction, which does not require that the basic premises, i.e., hypotheses, be factual. Presupposed, of course, is the compulsory and undisappointed act of faith in the objective and utilizable order of the universe.

The founders of modern science such as Newton are not exempt from mistakenly accepting as true and factual suppositions which, while productive of desired results, are not true. Thus Newton's supposition in the *Principia* that, given a rectilinear area greater than a curved area and a rectilinear area less, there must be a rectilinear area equal to the curved area, while a fruitful supposition leading to integral calculus, is nevertheless false—since it presupposes the squaring of the circle, admittedly impossible.

How can this phenomenon of hypotheses that, while not proven true, are able to produce desired reliable, predictable results be explained? They can only be so on the basis that the order of the universe, whose uniformity they reflect in their results, must be such as to allow such adaptations—for example, the reduction of the curved to the rectilinear, as above—for practical purposes, while nevertheless not being themselves objectively true.

This calls, therefore, for a twofold intellectual outlook. First, the acceptance of *any* hypotheses, as such, that have proved themselves workable in the practical realm, such as Galileo's mathematical formula, the reward of constant experimenting, to the effect that the distance covered by an accelerating body in free fall is proportionate to the square of the time. (It is this formula, combined with the pure supposition of the first law of motion, originating from him, that allows for today's reliable orbiting of space shuttles and satellites.)

Secondly, the success of such hypotheses implies two things: first, that actual proved fact is not required for successful supposition; secondly that successful reliability in predictable results indicates that the hypothesis is somehow tied in with the order of the universe, even though it itself may not be true. Thus both the hypothesis that the earth does not rotate daily on its axis (Ptolemaic theory) and the hypothesis that it does (Copernican theory) yield reliable predictions in navigation. Both work but cannot both be true. Each, however, is part of a cosmic concept of the order of the universe which, because of its reliable workability, must be somehow tapped into the objective order of the universe.

Aristotle in his *Metaphysics* arrives inductively from the physical world and its motion at the existence of an immobile and immaterial First Cause, God, who is Pure Act. In this induction the final physical motion is seen as a daily circular motion of the heavens such as daily appears. (This motion is intermediately attributed to immaterial separated substances, subordinated to God, corresponding to the concept of angels.) By the time of Aquinas the precession of the equinoxes had been detected. In the Ptolemaic theory it was explained as a shift of the whole heavens of one degree every hundred years. This motion would underlie the daily motion.

Since the Ptolemaic or geocentric theory upon which Aristotle based his induction, with Aquinas in agreement, is not proved as factual (the Copernican or heliocentric theory being even more plausible), Aristotle's proof of the existence of a First Mover utilizing the apparent daily motion of the heavens is not realized. (This would not exclude another proof, independent of both the Ptolemaic and Copernican systems, based on the analysis of motion itself, undertaken by Aristotle and Aquinas.)

In the process, Aristotle clearly presumes with today's science the objective order of the universe. His supposing of the various motions of the sun, moon, planets, and stars, later incorporated into the Ptolemaic theory, which continues to hold good today for practical purposes, is clearly tapped into that objective order along with its companion Copernican theory. Even should one be prepared to accept the Copernican theory, clearly an expression of the objective existing order of the universe, as proved and factual, the methodical doubt of modern science—nothing may be considered certain—forbids this. Consequently both Aristotle's and modern science's perception of the objective order of the universe are to be considered dialectical: saving the appearances and usable, while not proved as factual.

Meanwhile, both Aristotle's physics and metaphysics, adopted by Aquinas, and modern science are at one in holding the objective order of the universe, by the former as proved, by the latter as an object of faith. They both represent a grasping of the order in varying degrees which, if not perfectly representative, nevertheless serves in the making of reliable predictions, utilizable for practical purposes. Both are at one in deducing practical results from dialectical hypotheses acceptable, not because proved, but because they work. Thus the basic law of modern science, the first law of motion, presumed in all physical formulations, and first enunciated by Galileo, while subsequently set by Newton at the head of his *Principia*, is fully in line with Aristotle's delineating of dialectical reasoning in the *Posterior Analytics* and *Topics*. So too is Galileo's experimentally discovered and numerically expressed law for the distances covered by accelerating bodies in free fall. Both of these are intrinsic to the successful and predictable orbitings, for example, of space shuttles and satellites, and both are perfectly in line with Aristotle's provision for successful dialectical deductions from hypotheses.

Within this mutual and congenial domain of dialectical physics, Aristotle renders the precious insight deriving from his consciousness of the dialectical as not to be confused with the proved and factual. Hence he points out and demonstrates in *Physics* VI that, because of the continuity of motion and the material in general, extension is not numerically divisible in reality, nor is a moving body at a point.

Thus after real curves are reduced to unreal straight lines, starting with the calculation of π, the straight lines themselves, as in the calculation of the acceleration of free falling bodies, are stated in artificially introduced numbers, the same numbers that artificially measure time. Aristotle renders a service to science by demonstrating the dialectical nature of such procedures which otherwise might be taken as realistic.

As has been noted, the outlook of today's cosmologists, while holding with Aristotle to the order of the universe as an objective reality, perceivable and utilizable, however dialectically, varies as to positing a cause of that order, pursuing a spectrum from God to chance. While some few posit God, the greater number would appear to maintain uncertainty, making no commitment. At the other end of the spectrum are those who come down squarely, and unprovedly, for chance. For the origin and differentiation of the living, this unprovable belief is encapsulated in the notion or doctrine of natural selection

This doctrine holds that the status of the universe, including the objective order of the universe upon which science is based for its operation, is the result of chance or randomness, specifically excluding any ultimate and first orderer. The arbiters of today's theoretical physics, even if uncommitted in this respect, do not appear to feel any need to question the doctrine, affirmed and accepted as an ultimate explanation in the media and textbooks.

Where is chance positioned in Aristotle's physics and metaphysics endorsed by Aquinas? Clearly it is excluded as an ultimate explanation. In effect, the notion of intricate order, such as that manifested in the material universe, having arisen randomly, has no basis experientially or theoretically. It is simply something that its supporters choose to believe. It does not, however, dispense from holding an objective order of the universe, since all scientific predictions depend on holding this. How does chance, the operative chance of natural selection, deriving for the living from the random mutation of genes, enter in?

A frequently selected illustration of this chance-dictated natural selection is that of the selecting of dark-colored moths in England subsequent to the unpredictable, or at least unpredicted, industrial revolution. Originally the successful strain of moths was light-colored, making them less vulnerable to predators as they rested on the light-colored bark of trees. With the coming of the soot of the industrial revolution, however, the light-colored bark turned dark-colored, thereby favoring among light-colored moths certain dark-colored chance mutants which then developed into the naturally selected surviving strain.

Must such a surviving strain be excluded by Aristotle and Aquinas as being selected by chance? Only if their concept of a operative First Cause needed to exclude chance in the development of new species, which it does not.

It is plain that chance is involved in the general fulfillment of the laws of nature in the physical world, in keeping with the plastic nature of matter. Thus of ten planted tomato plants, while a person may have the well-founded expectation that most will survive, he will not be overcome if not all survive. Tomato plant resiliency is not such as successfully to resist all possible intrusions. One does not expect a punctured tire every time one takes off in a car. But neither is such an eventuality precluded. Since, if and when it does occur, the occasion will be unpredictable, the occasion will be a chance event. Thus chance events may be designated as those events which, in things that occur for the greater part (i.e., the greater number of tomato plants may be expected to survive, the greater number of auto trips may be expected to be punctureless), occur in the unpredictable, since unforeseeable, lesser part.

For some one who holds, with Aristotle and Aquinas, a first ordering cause, this presents no problem, since such a cause, the cause of all being, will be the cause of those events predictable by us (what occurs in the greater part) and those unpredictable by us—those occurring in the unforeseeable lesser part of those things which occur for the greater part. To what extent God, the First Cause of all being, will cause some new strain to arise from an unforeseeable (by us) chance mutation, or from a mutation predicted by and even engineered by the human being, will depend upon God's plans.

Meanwhile among those predictable events and processes occurring according to the perceivable order of nature is one permanent intrinsically unforeseeable one: the act of the human will, which is intrinsically free and unpredictable. This may be illustrated by the fact that someone at the end of a telephone line has no way of predicting when and from where someone, known or unknown, may freely pick up the phone and call—or not call. This is an event humanly unpredictable, but a being, an action, completely under the control of the cause and orderer of *all* being.

Consequently, one conceiving of God as the cause of the science-acknowledged order of the universe, while excluding chance as a plausible ultimate cause of that order, does not exclude chance as an unforeseeable cause, in the lesser part, within that order.

Bibliography

Anderson, James F. *Introduction to the Metaphysics of St. Thomas Aquinas*. Washington, DC: Regnery Publishing, Inc., 1969.

Aquinas, Thomas. *Commentary on Aristotle's Physics*. Translated by Richard J. Blackwell, Richard J. Spath, and W. Edmund Thirlkel. London: Routledge & Kegan Paul, 1963.

_____. *Commentary on the Metaphysics of Aristotle*. Translated by John P. Rowan. 2 vols. Chicago: Regnery Publishing, Inc., 1961.

_____. *Exposition of the Posterior Analytics of Aristotle*. Translated by R.F. Larcher. Albany, NY: Magi Books, 1969.

_____. *Summa Theologiae*. Edited By. T. Gilby. 60 vols. New York: McGraw Hill, 1964-74.

Aristotle. *The Basic Works of Aristotle*. Edited by Richard McKeon. New York: Random House, 1941.

Bobik, Joseph, trans. *Aquinas on Being and Essence*. Notre Dame, IN: University of Notre Dame Press, 1988.

Burrell, David B. *Analogy and Philosophical Language*. New Haven, CT: Yale University Press, 1973.

Catan, John R., ed. *St. Thomas Aquinas on the Existence of God: Collected Papers of Joseph Owens*. Albany, NY: State University of New York Press, 1980.

Chisholm, Roderick. *On Metaphysics*. Minneapolis, MN: University of Minnesota Press, 1989.

_____. *Person and Object: A Metaphysical Study*. Chicago: Open Court, 1979.

Diggs, Bernard J. *Love and Being: An Investigation into the Metaphysics of St. Thomas Aquinas*. New York: S.F. Vanni, 1947.

Doig, James C. *Aquinas on Metaphysics: A Historico-Doctrinal Study of the Commentary on the Metaphysics*. Hague: Nijhoff, 1972.

Elders, Leo J. *The Metaphysics of Being of St. Thomas Aquinas in a Historical Perspective.* Kinderhook, NY: E.J. Brill, 1992.

Gardeil, Henri D. *Metaphysics.* Vol.4 of *Introduction to the Philosophy of St. Thomas Aquinas.* Translated by John A. Otto. St. Louis: Herder, 1967.

Halper, Edward C. *One and Many in Aristotle's Metaphysics.* Vol.1 of *The Central Books.* Columbus, OH: Ohio State University Press, 1989.

Hart, Charles A. *Thomistic Metaphysics.* Englewood Cliffs, NJ: Prentice-Hall, 1959.

Henle, John Robert. *Method in Metaphysics.* Milwaukee, WI: Marquette University Press, 1980.

Ingardia, Richard. *Thomas Aquinas: International Bibliography, 1977-1990.* Bowling Green, OH: The Philosophy Documentation Center, 1993.

Kreyche, Robert J. *First Philosophy: An Introductory Text in Metaphysics.* New York: Holt, 1959.

Maritain, Jacques. *A Preface to Metaphysics: Seven Lectures on Being.* New York: Sheed and Ward, 1940.

McInerny, Ralph. *The Logic of Analogy: An Interpretation of St. Thomas.* Hague: Nijhoff, 1961.

Miethe, Terry L. and Bourke, Vernon J., eds. *Thomistic Bibliography, 1940-1978.* Westport, CT: Greenwood Press, 1980.

Owens, Joseph. *An Elementary Christian Metaphysics.* 1963. Houston, TX: The Center for Thomistic Studies, 1990.

_____. *An Interpretation of Existence.* Milwaukee, WI: Marquette University Press, 1968.

Reith, Herman. *The Metaphysics of St. Thomas Aquinas.* Milwaukee, WI: The Bruce Publishing Comparny, 1958.

Smith, Gerard, and Lottie H. Kendzierski. *The Philosophy of Being, Metaphysics I.* Milwaukee, WI: Marquette University Press, 1983.

Smith, Vincent E. *The General Science of Nature.* Milwaukee, WI: The Bruce Publishing Company, 1958.

_____. *Philosophical Physics.* New York: Harpers, 1950.

Smith, Vincent E., ed. *The Logic of Science.* New York: St. John's University Press, 1964.

Tresmontant, Claude. *Christian Metaphysics.* New York: Sheed and Ward, 1965.

Wippel, John F. *Metaphysical Themes in Thomas Aquinas.* Vol.2 of *Studies in Philosophy and the History of Philosophy.* Washington, DC: The Catholic University of America Press, 1984.

Witt, Charlotte. *Substance and Essence in Aristotle.* Ithaca, NY: Cornell University Press, 1989.

Woznicki, Andrew Nicholas. *Being and Order: The Metaphysics of Thomas Aquinas in Historical Perspective.* Catholic Thought from Lublin. New York: Peter Lang, 1990.

Index

abstraction, 14-17, 44-45, 61-62, 235, 258-59

accident

as being, 74-75, 190-91, 195-96, 274

in lesser part, 166, 176-77, 267, 296-97

not substance, 166

as prior, 140

way to define, 154-55, 190-91, 194, 195-96, 204

accidental being

cause/effect as, 115-16, 267

cause of, 175-77, 180-81, 296-97

determinism denies, 177-78

existence/nature of, 177-83, 267, 296-97

no science of, 175, 177, 185-86, 194-95, 267

not generated/corrupted, 175, 202

in predication, 123, 129-30, 131-32, 134-35, 175

and providence, 178-83

reducible to per se, 186

sameness as, 134-35

act

definition of, 217-18, 219-20, 282

and happiness, 222-23, 284

named from motion, 215, 217, 222, 269

and operation, 218, 222-23

prior in notion/time/substance, 219-23, 280-81, 282

substance of first being, 3, 203-4, 223, 226-27, 268, 279, 281, 282-84, 294

universal has less in, 26-27

See also potency; potency/act

action (predicament), 130-31, 269-70

action and false theories, 89, 96, 178, 180-81

active (moral) science, 171-72, 265

alteration (quality), 147, 156-57

analogy, 72-75, 107-8, 128, 195, 259-60

Anaxagoras, 36, 37, 43, 44, 47, 48, 54, 90, 92, 98, 191, 263-64, 280

Anaximines, 37

animals' knowledge, 13-15

appearances only, 91-95, 114-15, 263-64

aptitude and privation, 157-58

Aristotle on caused heavens, 63, 173, 283-84

Aristotle on immortal soul, 172, 277

arithmetic, 26-27, 261

art(s)

can teach, 17-19

from experience to, 14-20, 86, 216, 220-21

factive (mechanical), 171-72, 265

grows through many, 60

hierarchy of causes in, 17-18

DATE DUE

Printed
in USA

DATE DUE

JAN 2 9 2002			
MAY 2 4 2004			
			Printed in USA

HIGHSMITH #45230